Of Thorns, Roses and a Devil's Lie

Of Thorns, Roses and a Devil's Lie

Jana Meador

A Novel

ISBN-13: 978-0692553183
ISBN-10: 0692553185

Copyright © 2015 by Jana Meador
All Rights Reserved.

Printed in the United States of America.
Pine House Publishing.
"Of Thorns, Roses and a Devil's Lie" is a work of fiction.
www.janameador.com
Front cover design and interior illustrations by Ian Welsh, www.behance.net/vicariouspress

Table of Contents

Prologue ix
Chapter 1 1
Chapter 2 12
Chapter 3 24
Chapter 4 43
Chapter 5 68
Chapter 6 82
Chapter 7 96
Chapter 8 110
Chapter 9 127
Chapter 10 138
Chapter 11 155
Chapter 12 174
Chapter 13 188
Chapter 14 205
Chapter 15 221
Chapter 16 236
Chapter 17 251
Chapter 18 267
Chapter 19 281

Chapter 20 · 297
Chapter 21 · 315
Epilogue · 333

Dedication

To you with your soulful soul,
A beautiful spirit,
You hear the tones and variations first-
To you, who willed and lived the music,
By sharing this gift of wonderful melodies with the world.

Prologue

"Sometimes when I walk, I look closely at people I pass. And I noticed that whenever a couple held hands, their faces soften and their eyes gleam with a gentler light in them. I've passed a crowd of thousands random faces, voices, heights and weights, I've passed different colors and ages and rhythms of healthy and disabled, criers and complainers. I've passed thousands and they all spoke their language with various tones of dialects and foreign accents. But laughter was sparse. Whenever I heard someone laugh I smiled and my mind and my heart filled with joy. Music entered my body, mind and my heart, and I thought why don't people laugh more often?

It's free, easy to do and it unites and brings us all together and closer. Human laughter is a powerful thing. Just like love and a hug, so whenever I passed a couple holding their hands I thought the world is still a nice place to be."

Jana Meador

CHAPTER 1

Alaska, 1990

THE OCEAN WAVES BRUSHED SOFTLY over the sandy shore, and the laughter of people enjoying the sunny afternoon mixed in the air with the seagulls that flew above the salty waters. Little sea shells scattered alongside the beach, many of different colors and shapes and irregular edges. The wind blew in the hair of those, who read their books and magazines, lying down on their beach towels, sipping on drinks or eating citrus fruits. The Sunday afternoon carried over with a causal and warm presence of happy, smiling faces, tan bodies and souls of those, who lived in the small, country seaside town Lingit. A short distance by plane from Washington state, many came in for the three-day weekend to escape the city noise, enjoy a corn dog or a snow cone, and dip their feet in the cooling ocean before the summer ended and the autumn entered with its typical morning fog and rain.

Margot Smith watched through her binoculars as two seagulls fought over a piece of bread a child had dropped in the sand. The stubborn white feathered fowls pulled on the sweet doughy pie, each from one side, until the bread broke in half, and the foolish birds flew a different direction, but each with a proud possession in their beaks. A wet stream of drops fell on Margot's back. She put the binoculars down and turned around. A soaked, happy dog, pushed its body onto hers tan thigh and rolled upside down and onto Margot's towel.

"I'm sorry."

Margot looked up and her eyes cringed against the midday, bright sun. She immediately placed her right hand over her forehead.

"I hope he is no trouble for you," the man answered as he hooked a fabric black leash onto the dog's collar.

"Kurt."

"Excuse me?"

"Kurt. That's my name," he said and smiled at her.

"Margot Smith."

Kurt extended his arm and shook Margot's hand. Her firm grip surprised him as he stared into her green colored eyes. The dog sat down next to Margot's feet. She smiled and scratched him behind his wet ears.

"That's Holton."

"Holton? What an unusual name for a dog."

"Nothing's casual in Lingit. Are you from here?" Kurt sat down on the sand next to his dog.

"Alaska? No… No, I'm not. I am here on business."

Kurt curiously looked at her.

"Business? I've heard people come here on a vacation but never a business. It's a very small town; what kind of business that may be, Margot?"

"I'm a photographer. I work for a wildlife magazine."

"Then you are here on business and pleasure." Kurt stood, letting his dog off the leash. He threw a ball in the air and Holton chased after it. "If you need anything, you can find me downtown. I run the grocery store."

Margot wrapped a towel around her wet, freshly shampooed hair, making two twists into a turban shaped head cover. Streams of water slid on her tanned shoulders as she walked to her desk and sat down. Her red painted nails typed fast on the laptop keyboard. She paused and looked at her handwritten notes in the diary next to the computer. She retyped the name of the bird species then pressed save and shut the laptop screen. Her pretty eyes looked at the three seagulls out the window; the two large males fought over the last piece, while the third, smaller bird watched, standing on the side as if a referee, amused over the quarrel of doughy substance, as it was being ripped apart from one seagull's beak and quickly grabbed by another. The strongest, largest one of them proudly flew in the air with his main prize. The show was over, and the two white-feathered fools each raised its wings up high toward the sky, and disappeared from Margot's view. She got up and went to her bedroom. She dressed herself, and let the wet turban fall on the floor. Her long, thin fingers softly brushed through her damp red hair.

She grabbed a tea kettle and poured cold water in it, and then she turned on the gas stove and set the kettle on the range. As she placed a green tea bag into a large, wide-mouthed mug, a telephone rang.

"Hello?" she said softly. "Hello?" she repeated as she heard no answer on the other side. Then a sharp static noise entered through the receiver and into her ear. She shrugged and put the receiver father from her ear. A man's voice greeted her. She immediately recognized the all familiar grasped, deep, slow speech as her mind projected an image of John Ford, the owner of the Natural Bird magazine in Seattle.

"How is my girl?"

"John, it's good to hear your voice."

"Is everything all right? I haven't had any email from you since you left two days ago."

"Yeah, everything's fine. It just took longer to set things in here."

"How's the log house?"

Margot turned her body and looked around. The living room was spacious but not too large. There was a wood fireplace, framed with heavy, square stones. A three-seat sofa made out of brown leather and two side tables on each side. There was no television.

"I like it. Feels like home."

"Good, I'm glad to hear that. You're going to be there for many months. It better be a great place."

"It is, John."

"But you are all alone there. Don't you feel lonely?"

There was a pause, before Margot replied to the receiver. "No. There's nothing wrong with being alone. I think it can be a beautiful thing, because it also creates liberations." And there's so much to do for me, John. I think I'll be just fine!"

The whistling sound came from the kitchen and spread throughout the house and to the living room, where Margot stood.

"I have to go now."

"Wait...don't forget to send me some photographs and notes."

"You got it. Bye, John."

"Bye, kiddo."

Margot rushed to the kitchen and turned off the flame from underneath the boiling water in the kettle. The whistling noise slowly died in the air as she poured the hot water over the tea bag and into her handpainted mug. Her thumb and forefinger wrapped around the large, thick handle as she carried the hot, steaming liquid to the living room. She sat the flowery-smelling tea mug on the coaster and sat down in the brown-leathered sofa. The wise words of her father Adam came to her mind: *Always be grateful for people that you have in your heart.* Margot reached over for a book that lay on the side table and next to the lamp. The light from the dark orange shaded lamp made the room cozy. She brought her knees from the floor up on the sofa, making herself comfortable by placing an oversized pillow behind her back. She extended her arm and brought the mug with green tea to her rosy, full lips. She took a sip and immediately felt the hot liquid fill in her mouth and throat, sliding down her causing a tingling warm sensation down in her stomach. She licked her bottom lip as she returned the mug on its coaster. Margot opened her book. Her lips curled into a smile and her green eyes softened as she looked at the black and white photograph placed in between the pages. Her right palm with her perfectly red-painted nails brushed over the face of a woman in her early twenties. The woman's brown curly hair were cut just under her chin and parted to the sides. Her left side showed a small ear that bared no earring. Her lips were full and parted, the corners slightly curled into a shy smile. Her large, frightened eyes were haunted. But deep down underneath, the woman's eyes carried a lot of pain. She wore a light colored blouse with a simple V opening that uncovered a part of her flawless completion on her neck and chest. Margot's eyes stopped at the woman's neckline, where the golden chain carried a pendant with a single rose. A feeling of loneliness suddenly washed over Margot's heart. She shivered. The dimmed light in the living room lifted with a beam of sunshine that protruded through the closed window stripped off the curtain. The moment felt as if the ghost of the woman on the black and white photograph entered the room.

"Edith," Margot whispered as she looked at the woman's face. She slowly turned the page and covered Edith's photograph. Margot read, her lips mumbling in the rhythm of the words imprinted in front of her. The inside house was quiet and even the birds outside left now and flew into the early spring, evening sky.

Margot woke up on the sofa, the book still open and set over her stomach, the blanket partly on her legs and partly on the hardwood floor. She reached behind her head and let her hand tap the side table until her finger's finally reached for the watch. She checked the time, 2:21 in the morning. She stood up and walked across the room. Out of the window she watched the scattered clouds move fast in the wind. She regretted not having any windowsills. It was too early to go shopping and still pretty early to call John in Seattle. John never got up before ten. He liked to get a late start in his day and work and until the late night. But there was one person, she wanted to speak to. The four-hour time difference between her and Adam made if perfect. She reached for the phone and dialed the number.

"Hello?" a bright, pleasant voice answered on the other side of the receiver.

"Dad!"

"Margot! What time is it over there at the end of the world?"

"It's going to be two thirty in the morning here." She turned her face toward the large window. "There is nearly a twenty four-hour light outside. It woke me up."

"It must be nice. It's pretty cloudy here, and if it continues raining like this, we're gonna be flooded soon. The goddam rain will ruin everything in the garden. Edith worked so hard on it."

"Is she asleep?"

"Yes, thank God. But the nightmares always wake her up. They'll never leave her alone, until the day she dies."

"Dad?"

"What is it, baby?"

"I think Edith will finally find peace soon."

"You take care, and send us some pictures of the birds. You know how much we like to read and see your work in the magazine."

She walked to her desk and turned on her computer. The screen lit with a colorful front cover of *Natural Bird* with a trumpeter swan staring straight at Margot.

Adam Smith was a child of Irish descent; both of his parents came from Northern Ireland. He had red hair, green eyes and freckled skin. He grew up a smart man, with a sharp mind and unusual wit. Adam began his early working life as a newspaper boy for *The Coastal News* when he was just eleven years old. Riding his bicycle from house to house each morning before school started, he knew every person in the neighborhood. When World War II started, he wanted to join the army, but was not accepted because of his weakened heart condition. A doctor wrote in his medical papers, "Adam is not to be stressed out," and the recruiting officer gladly put a red ink stamp that said, DENIED. And so the young, Irish boy had decided to heal his weakened heart by properly exercising its muscle by the oldest remedy in the world. Laughter soon entered Adam's daily life as he created various cartoon illustrations for the very same newspaper he used to throw in the driveways of his old childhood neighborhood. Adam inherited his sense of humor from his own father, Eamon. The Smiths on the masculine side had always thrived on being goofy. After the years of very important daily contributions Adam Smith, became a newspaper's manager. The year the war ended, Adam's heart physician proclaimed a miracle, by announcing his patient's heart to be healed. Later in life, Adam learned the physician was paid a lot of money by old Eamon Smith, thus excluding young, eager and naive Adam from joining the war.

He married Grace Lee, a soft-spoken daughter of a local florist. Together, they welcomed a baby girl and named her Margot. When Grace became ill and died of leukemia, Margot was just five years old. Scarred by the family tragedy, Margot never liked to think about the past. The only time was, when her father found his new love and married again. Edith Altman became the love of Adam's life and stepmother to Margot, whom she admired and loved as her own. When his only daughter

Margot Smith told him, she was leaving the East Coast and going to Seattle to work as an intern for a wildlife magazine. She told him about John who didn't make a good impression on Adam who had only one thing to say about him: "John can fall down and miss the floor."

Margot opened her laptop and started writing. Soon the white page became filled with her notes about a flock of shore birds that wheeled over the Lingit's beach the day before. Western Sandpipers fed along the surf line, the migratory birds descended to Alaska in early May; some of them flew thousands of miles to get to their summer grounds to breed. The aviation commuters often weighing only an ounce or two were able to make their annual trip all the way from the coasts of New Zealand or Australia, making it the longest seven-thousand-mile nonstop migration above the Pacific Ocean. If the Western Sandpiper could no longer fly, and become weak, unable to make his migration, then he would let his body fall down and into the unsettling, endless salty waters of cold Pacific. He would become a source of food for others in the waves. Margot paused and looked out the window. She hit save button and closed her draft. She lay down on the sofa and shut her eyes hoping to catch on her sleep.

§

A loud snore echoed through the store, as Margot knocked on the open door. The midday sun shined on the sky, and sunbeams entered together with Margot when she opened the glass door. No reply came back, so she stepped inside the fabric store, and the snore became louder, as she followed it across the room. There, in the corner, sat a man on a chair, a loose fabric lavishly thrown over his lap, his chest deeply moving in the rhythm of his own breath. The man's thick, ungroomed grey moustache seemed alive, and its knotted ends pointed sharply toward the ceiling. Both of his hands rested on his large stomach. The man snored through his half opened mouth. Then the loud gong of the clock in the corner rang four times, announcing it was eight in the morning. The man woke up and got startled by the presence of his spectator. He sat up quickly, picking up the fabric from the floor.

"I'm sorry, I didn't mean to startle you," Margot said apologetically.

"How may I help you, young lady?" The man's heavy body slowly stood up, with his large, thick fingers holding onto the wooden-hand-carved cane in his left hand.

"I'd like some dark drapes for my windows."

"The light's botherin' you?"

She replied shyly, "Yes, yes it is."

"You are not from here, are you?"

"No." She followed the man to the front of the store. He walked slowly, his right foot limping, struggling to keep up with the left foot.

"What's your name, young lady?"

"Margot."

"I'm Wallace Walla." The man stopped and closely looked at Margot's eyes. "But everybody calls me Walla Walla." Margot's corners of her lips curled into a warm smile.

"Nice to meet you, Walla Walla."

His lips parted and uncovered a mouth of missing teeth.

Walla showed her several thick, dark fabrics, assuring Margot, no light gets through them, not even in the land of the midnight sun. She picked the purple drapes, thanked the crippled man and as she was leaving his store, he yelled after her, "Where are staying at?"

"I'm at the log cabin by the shore, where it forks into two dust roads."

"Ahh, the Moose cabin. All the windows point south, the sun rises over the Pacific Ocean and reflects on the house."

Margot joked, "I thought the sun never goes down here."

Walla's face broke into a wide smile, two front teeth on the bottom stared at Margot, while the top was bare as a baby's butt. "How long are you staying?"

"Just until the fall," she said and waved at Walla. The fresh salty air brushed over her face as she walked through Lingit, a town so small yet very charming.

CHAPTER 2

KURT AND HIS BROTHER ALFRED have lived in this town their whole lives. One strong, with toned muscles and wide arms, the other quiet, and tucked in his own world. Alfred was the younger brother and spoke with a stutter. Some said he had a mind of a child. Kurt was his older brother, much stronger and wiser. The two lived together in a house, they inherited from their parents. The place was spacious and built from three stories. Downstairs was the small, convenient grocery store. Kurt ran the local grocery store and Alfred helped him. The two men kept for themselves. Kurt knew well, the curious eyes of others had always had many questions. He grew tired of the inquisitive people and what was there to tell anyway? Alfred had an accident when he was two years old, and the fall from the stairs decided his fate. He was slower, and quieter, but he had a good, kind soul. Locals knew about the Groenewegs and they left the brothers alone.

Alfred sat on a bench outside the store, a sharp knife in one hand and a piece of untreated wood in the other. He observed the wooden piece for a moment. Then he firmly made a sharp cut in the upper part. The birch slit in half and he let the loose piece fall on the ground.

He pressed his finger against the light-colored wood and closed his eyes. His right thumb was scarred with several lines that turned into dark lines from overusing the knife against the finger. His nails had dirt behind them, and the large, square palms seemed like they didn't belong to his short, slim figure. Alfred's hair was dark brown and hadn't been cut in several months. The back was tied into a ponytail and the sides had loose strands, curled into multiple rings that rested on his collar bones.

He had a plaid black and grey checkers shirt on, the top button half way through the hole, followed by the next button completely torn and missing. The shirt's sleeves were cuffed and stretched; the rims carried old dried dirt. Alfred's jeans were too big for him, secured by a brown leather belt. His boots were equally brown color to match his belt. The above ankle boots were well worn out, and his shoelaces remained carelessly untied. Alfred's face carried the expression of a child, stripped of wrinkles, but his skin hidden under the ungroomed dark beard. The light around Alfred sitting on the outside bench suddenly darkened, a shadow crept in front of him, and made him stopped carving the birch wood. Then shadow grew longer when it touched Alfred's boots, and finally spoke to him.

"What's up scruffy face?"

Alfred lifted his head.

"Whatcha doin'?"

Alfred opened his mouth, but no words came out. He tilted his head to the right and stared at the man in front of him.

Sharp steps clapped on the concrete floor and behind Alfred's back. The sound swished through the open door, and for a brief moment the sound disappeared, and then returned in a more intense, uptight tone.

"Alfred, come on inside."

Alfred stood up fast, and with his head low to the ground he entered the store.

"Get lost!"

"Kurt, I was kidding with your brother. You know me, I wouldn't hurt a fly." His foot stumbled as he backed up, his ice-cold pale blue eyes and ash colored sunken face with high, protruding cheekbones stared at Kurt.

Just like his father, Bob drank every penny he made on a fishing boat. Soon, no fisherman could trust him to employ him on their boats. He liked to pick on Alfred. "Get out of here," and for emphases added, "Get lost!" Bob took quick steps back and his shadow shrunk, until it no longer existed.

Kurt returned to the store and shut the door behind him. He walked over to the counter register where Alfred sat down. "You are safe here." He touched his brother's shoulder.

"T...thanks," he said shyly.

Without a further word, Kurt stood and watched him as he skillfully carved a rose out of the birch piece. Alfred brought the rose closer to his face and smiled. He lifted it and pointed toward Kurt.

"It's very nice, Alfred. Now you have to bring it to life. What color will you choose?"

Alfred frowned and paused. Then his bearded face and brown eyes lit with cheer. He looked up at Kurt.

"Yell...yellow. Like the s..sun."

A door bell rang, and a customer entered the grocery store. A local carpenter, an older guy with a feathered face and heavy, thick fingers, he grabbed a bag of sugar and brought it up on the counter together with the rest of the groceries. Alfred got up and eagerly placed the coffee, the sugar and the milk in the paper bag.

"Thank you, Alfred. You always put on a good day of work." The carpenter paused and then muttered, "Saw Bob on the way to the store. Hope he didn't cause any trouble for you, boy."

Alfred shrugged and kept quiet, never making an eye contact with the current customer.

"Kurt." The carpenter lifted his hat and walked out of the store, passing the older brother.

"You wait here. I'll be right back with your colors," Kurt said. Alfred nodded and Kurt walked out the door when he heard the door bell again. He knew Alfred could not handle it himself, and so he quickly grabbed brushes and colors and palettes and returned to the register.

"Here you go." He set the color supplies on a small table father away from the register. Alfred moved over and like a hungry child started sorting through the various shades of yellow.

Kurt glanced at the customer with a straw hat and a light pink blouse, with sleeves rolled up, the left one higher above the elbow, the right sleeve rolled just in mid forearm. The woman had on light colored jeans with bare, slim ankles and a pair of blue sneakers. He could smell her mandarin perfume all the way to the register. The lightly scented smell made him suddenly crave the citrus fruit. She came closer with a basket in her right hand. She wore large, dark sunglasses, but Kurt recognized her face from the other day on the beach.

"Margot. Margot Smith. Nice to see you, again."

"Hey." She smiled at Kurt and placed her grocery basket onto the counter. She kept her sunglasses on. Alfred, oblivious to his surroundings, painted his carved rose. Margot stared at him and Kurt said, "That's Alfred. He's my younger brother."

"Hi, Alfred."

Alfred gave Margot a two-second glance.

"I'm sorry, he's not much of a talker," Kurt said apologetically.

"I can see that. What's he working on?"

"Roses. Albert likes to carve roses out of wood, and then he paints them. This one will be yellow like a sun." Kurt and Margot both looked at Alfred at the same time.

"Oh, how nice. What else can he carve?"

"Just…roses. He's always been carving roses." Kurt shrugged.

A distant dog bark came from the outside and grew louder as it entered the store. Holton, Kurt's large, furry mutt, came in charging from behind his master's back.

"Holton. Where'd you come from? Don't you know you you're not supposed to be in the store?" Kurt bent down, but Holton was faster and ran around the counter and from the side he stopped at Margot's feet.

Her face instantly broke into a great smile. "Hi dog! Do you remember me?" she reached down scratching Holton on the top of his head. The mutt made two loud barks and quickly ran to the end of the counter, where he disappeared into Alfred's lap.

Margot caught herself staring at every move Kurt made, she watched him as he slowly reached for a mozzarella cheese, tomatoes and fresh basil. He took out two bottles of blood orange Italian pop soda and placed them in the bottom of the paper back. He stacked the rest of the groceries in and gave Margot a wide, warm smile.

"It's on the house."

Margot looked at him and then she said jokingly, "What? No. Please, I have money."

"It's my treat, then." Kurt reached under the register and took out a bottle of Italian white wine.

"I think you may enjoy this with your mozzarella, and tomato." He paused before adding with a soft voice, "I'm sorry it's not chilled."

Margot's red lips parted, she took a deep breath, but before she could reply, Kurt moved the paper back across the counter to her.

"Hope you have a nice day."

"Thank, you. Bye Alfred."

Alfred took his colors and brushes and newly carved rose outside. He sat on a bench in front of the store; an image very familiar with the locals. What would the Groeneweg store be without the simpleton sitting outside? His hands worked fast as he dipped the tip of the brush in the liquid golden color and painted over the top portion of the rose. He repeated it several times, until he was happy with the final result. The color slowly dried and faded a bit. When it was dry enough to touch it, Alfred took another brush in his hand and dipped the tip into a darker green water color.

The long stem, accompanied by sharp thorns transformed from a light brown to a vivid green.

"T...thorn," he whispered and pressed a forefinger pressed against the needle-sharp end. He saw a tiny drop of bright, red blood coming out of his finger. He quickly wiped his hand over his pants.

Two lines of mixed yellow and green stained his jeans. He carefully placed the rose on a sheet of paper, lying on the tray. He let the colors dry in the warm, sunny midday. The younger brother sat on the bench, with his hands folded and rested in his lap, and without a movement Alfred stared at the calm Pacific Ocean waters ahead of him. A bee landed on his flannel shirt, and he looked down his chest, quietly observing the curious insect that walked over his black button. When the bee climbed higher on his shirt and closer to his bare neck, Alfred blinked several times with his chin pressed against the collarbone. He frowned and bit his lower lip, while raising his left hand. At last the bee opened its wings and lifted up in the air and flew away in the calm breeze. Several customers passed Alfred, each gave him a smile some greeted him aloud, as they entered the grocery store, and greeted him again as they exited. After a while, Kurt brought over Holton, and the dog sat by Alfred's feet keeping him a company. The sound of the ocean, with its whitecaps hitting the sandy shore mixed in the air with the various birds that flew above it. Some walked in the wet sand, feeding, their sharp pointed beaks cleaning the shore, while their quick feet danced around, escaping the salty waves. Some fought over the food, others loudly expressed their opinions through the open beaks and their necks stretched against one another.

Kurt checked out the last customer of the day and walked to the front door. He turned the sign to *Closed* and stepped on the fresh, early evening air. He locked the door and headed to the bench to see Alfred. His large knuckled hand carried a plastic cup with a lid with a blue straw pierced through the top. He passed the drink to his brother.

"Here, it's your favorite, root beer." Alfred took the drink and took and sucked onto the straw.

"You've been sitting here all afternoon. Come on, let's get some dinner." Kurt said softly. Alfred grabbed the yellow rose and Kurt took the art supplies. Holton, the furry four-legged friend also got up and followed in the footsteps of his master. Alfred had a slight limp, his torso bend forward and his head down mapping the ground. His arms moved in the rhythm of his slow steps. There was a reason why Alfred always kept looking at the ground in front of him. He meticulously avoided anything alive that crawled on the ground, in the dirt and between the rocks, or on a paved sidewalk or the black surfaced road. Kurt admired his calmness and sensibility. In a way Alfred made Kurt a better person. Thanks to Alfred, younger Kurt had noticed things that would otherwise go totally unnoticed. Like the lady bug, that needed help when it flew onto a table and got stuck in a sticky substance of spilled honey. When Kurt approached the table with a damp cloth in his hand Alfred could not get the warning words out of his mouth fast enough. Instead he pushed Kurt with a full force.

"Be c…careful!" Alfred said angrily and pointed his finger toward the lady bug. He brought his hand closer and stuck his pinky into the sticky substance. He got some of the honey under his fingernail, but the lady bug managed to climb onto Alfred's finger. He brought it outside and gently placed it into a bloom of one of the red rose bushes outside the house. He turned around and shouted, "I'm h..happy now." Kurt smiled at him and Alfred smiled back.

§

Kurt thought of the newcomer with green-colored eyes, red hair, full lips and pale, flawless skin. A mystery surrounded Margot Smith. Was she really a journalist, a photographer? Did she really come to Lingit to do a study about migrating birds? There have been outsiders in the past coming to town, many of them curious, more and less experienced, skilled and troubled. Some couldn't handle the nearly twenty four hour day light, complaining of headaches and sleep deprivation. Some loved the day and night light. Some left early and some stayed beyond they call of duty. They all had a mutual thing. They were all men. Very rarely the locals would meet an outsider who was a woman and was not accompanied by a man. Lingit was surrounded by wilderness. A small, oceanside town on a peninsula, best reached by a plane. There was one grocery store that belonged to Kurt Groeneweg, one doctor that was universal, and also treated animals, domesticated and farmed. Yet the wealthier found their way in on their private Cessna's and Beavers and other two engine planes, and made the secluded town their weekend and seasonal home destination.

   He wondered if Margot flew on one of those private flights from the lower forty eight. Where's she staying, and for how long; would someone join her? What magazine does she work for? Why this town? So many random questions flooded his mind. He shook his head and sat down in the iron chair in the back yard. He looked up at the beautiful scene of various smattering of vibrant, embossed lanterns that he had hung up on the tall, strong and old cotton wood tree with the help of Alfred. The lanterns glowed in shades of green, blue, red and orange, ocean and gray, light brown, white and dark brown. Kurt's hand pressed on the cold, canned beer in his hand. He cracked the aluminum open and watched the foam rise from the can. He liked moments like these, where the breeze calmed down, the town quieted, the night never got dark, but the sky changed into a dimmed color. Kurt looked at his watch. Ten minutes past one in the morning, and the sun and the light will soon rise above his head. Alfred slept in the house, in the upstairs bedroom. If Kurt had ever envy anything, it would be the ability to fall asleep fast, like a baby, without rushing thoughts and worries what the next day may bring. Alfred was just like a child, stripped of any responsibilities that adults tackle on daily basis, which gave him his true personality and likeability. Many spoke to his brother as if there was no problem and he was mentally equal. Kurt appreciated it very much, and he knew although Alfred couldn't tell or understand the difference, it made him happier. He joined conversations of town folks who came to get their groceries; he would help carry paper bags of produce for the elderly to their houses. The feeling of usefulness was more important to Kurt than Alfred, but together they have always made it work. Kurt took another sip of beer. He tilted his head and glanced over to the red rose wild bushes on the left side and in front of the kitchen window. The bushes had already budded and some had juvenile blooms of bright red colors. The roses have been a part of the house as long as Kurt could remember. They filled most of the back yard and some bushes decorated the front of the building, mainly around the bottom part of the house, and the grocery store. But in the backyard, the roses dominated by far and had grown tall and strong with sharp pointed thorns and beautifully deceitful flagrant red, white, pink and orange-yellow blooms. Kurt and Alfred grew up taking care of the plants, trimming, cutting, fertilizing, watering and whispering to the petals as if the roses were just another sibling to them.

The older Kurt grew, the more he realized that their mother Charlotte Groeneweg didn't have a passion for the flowers. It was more of a *duty*, more of a chore, more of a must do and work, than anything else. He saw no love when Charlotte fertilized the ground around the roots. He never saw her smile or pause and smell the roses. He never saw her talk to the petals, or cut a few and place them in a vase in the house. Alfred cut the stems and filled in the crystal vases at her mother's house. What he saw in his mother's eyes was grief, pain and almost diabolic nature to keep the roses alive, to bring them to bloom every spring of every year and bring them to rest of every autumn of every year. The cycle repeated for four decades. The brothers had no choice but to keep the roses around the house, for their mother's sake, and for their own sake.

When he tried to ask their mother what the sick fascination with roses is all about, she fidgeted in fury and gave Kurt an angry look. He remembered one year when a section of the roots frozen over the winter, and he did everything possible to bring the stems to life as soon as the snow melted and the outdoor temperature warmed up. But it was too late, and nothing could be done to fix the dying bushes. The winter was exceptionally harsh and produced little snow. There was little insulation for the roots in the ground for so many months, the freeze killed them.

Charlotte's furious face turned red and her voice deepened. Her pale grey watery eyes sparkled with little red, bloody veins around in the corners. Charlotte's skinny arms swung in front of her face like a conductor setting a tempo in front of a big live chamber orchestra and into the rhythm of melancholy music.

Kurt never understood what the roses meant to his mother. Certainly it wasn't a joy. Whatever it was that drove Charlotte Groeneweg crazy was utilized in her past. And she was not telling or sharing it with anyone. A flicking light in a green lantern above Kurt's head brought him back from his deep thoughts. He finished his beer and walked to his house. At the end of the road, on the outskirts of town, lived their sixty seven year old mother, Charlotte Groeneweg, a woman of a secret past, and a slight German accent.

CHAPTER 3

§

A WOMAN SCORNED RESTED IN a deep, old-fashioned armchair, her back against the gold and white and black fabric. Across the living room in the far corner, an old-fashioned gramophone spun a vinyl record. She listened to the voice of a solo opera singer, performing a beautiful aria in soprano in the German language. Eyes closed, Charlotte's lips barely moved as she hummed the song. Long, thick curtains of dark green color with golden edges covered the windows, making the room nearly dark. The hands folded in her lap had a slight tremor, and her large forefinger knuckles carried signs of painful arthritis. Her hair, neatly twisted into a bun at the top of her head, with just few loose strands around her temples, perfectly framing her face. Never fond of someone else touching her hair, Charlotte Groeneweg kept the same hairstyle for decades. She dressed simply, never keen on getting noticed by others or looking for an attention from town folks; keeping mostly to herself, often spending most of the time in the house or on the porch. She surrounded herself with her thoughts and pictures of her two sons, Kurt and Alfred.

Charlotte had Alfred's wooden carved roses everywhere – some were laid out carelessly on the fireplace mantel, or decorated the walls of living room and bedrooms, some were placed into pots with real flowers and plants inside her house. The place became full of roses and thorns, of various colors and shapes and sizes. All of Alfred's were made out of birch wood, were painted and very beautiful. Charlotte never threw any of them away.

One day, her older son Kurt visited her and asked, "What's all about this obsession about roses, mother?"

"Obsession?!" Charlotte repeated bitterly.

"Yes. Let's call it for what it is. You made us plant wild rose bushes all around the house, front and back, and every day you want us to work around them, to make sure, the dead branches and blooms are clipped and thrown away, and new ones come to life. It's a plant, Mother, not a human being. I don't remember you spending so much time on me and Alfred when we were little. I remember father used to do most of the work!" Kurt looked over at Albert. The younger brother sat quietly on a far end of the bench, his head low, his fingers working and carving through the thorns, the wood chippings falling on his knees, or the ground, and finally on his boots. Alfred was oblivious to his surroundings, to his mother and his brother's argument. "Look what you've done to Alfred. Just look at him." Kurt desperately pointed his hand toward his brother.

The high, angelic opera voice filled Charlotte's dimmed living room. She reached for a cigarette and lit it. The opera singer sang about a young woman, who just gave birth to her first child. The spirit of the child wanted to live, but the human hand prevailed and killed the newborn, crushing his neck, cutting the air and letting the spirit out of the newborn's body.

Those, who did not speak the language could easily imagine, the opera singer sings about something powerful, beautiful, and full of vibrant color as her voice changes though the notes from deep to high and the highest, angelic, exquisite voice. Then it quiets down and the words slow and almost as if she whispered for a moment before the orchestra strengthens like a hurricane and the singer battles the ocean waves the strong wind caused, can't but keep up against the inevitable force before her defeat comes and silences her forever. The music gave Charlotte goose bumps every time she listened to it. Yet, she could not resist and replayed the ode several times in a row and listened tensely. She suffered through and through as if she was a masochist and the music was her master, doing it willingly and for a purpose only known to Charlotte Groeneweg herself.

She finished her cigarette and wiped the tears away from her eyes. The living room once again became silent. The opera singer finished her aria and Charlotte got up from the armchair and walked to the gramophone. She dusted the wood and brass that decorated old-fashioned gramophone daily with a soft fabric cloth; gently swiping over the brass trumpet inside and out, polishing it and then again over the wooden bottom portion that held black vinyl record. She allowed no one else to touch it. Charlotte played music every day, sitting in the very same armchair, with the green and golden curtains semi shut on the large windows that led to her garden. This was her daily routine and her solitude. Yet, there was nothing cheerful about the older woman. Her face carried scars of pain and sorrow; her hands had brown spots, the signs of aging. She reached to a side table on her right and grabbed a black and white photograph. She felt the cold, iron frame her fingers touched as she brought the picture closer to her she pressed her chin against her chest. Her breath intensified, and became louder as she studied the smiling baby on the photograph. The boy had his chubby arms to the sides and slightly lifted from his body; both of his palms were curled into fists. He sat on an overlarge pillow and his back supported a cushioned sofa. The kid's wide smile uncovered bare gums and his large, round eyes, oozed with innocent joy. He was dressed in an overall, with an image of a rabbit sown on the front of his outfit. Charlotte's lips parted and the corners of her mouth curled into a slight smile. With her right hand index finger she brushed over the pendant the baby wore around his neck. The half-rose was attached to a short golden chain. Charlotte firmly pressed her lips together and returned the picture back on the side table, mumbling to herself, "Past. Everybody has one." Charlotte walked up to the phone that was nailed on the living room wall. She paused and suddenly felt weak in her legs. Her hand touched the wallpaper, as she closed her eyes. Her mind took her to a darker place, to her own past, when she was young and when she lived in Europe. She saw herself in the hospital, over forty years ago. The sound of screams and hysteria entered her room, intensifying in a split moment. She didn't see the face that produced the human cries, but she could feel the tremendous pain in her own body, in her heart and bones. She didn't know what happened on the other side of the hospital wall, but whatever caused the other woman to scream, had to be orchestrated by the devil itself.

Young Charlotte pressed her palms against her ears and yelled aloud from her lungs. The flash of the past dissolved and went away and now, the old Charlotte with her back pressed against the living room wall opened her eyes and exhaustedly lifted the phone receiver.

"Hel...hello?"

"Alfred, it's your mother."

"M...mom!"

"Is Kurt there? I need to speak to him. Can you put him on the phone?"

Charlotte listened to footsteps slowly fading away from the receiver. There was an absolute silence for a brief moment, before Kurt got on the phone. "I need more fertilizer."

"Mama, there's enough in the dirt in your garden."

"The roses need more nutrients!" she ordered sharply and hung up.

Charlotte walked outside and her face shrieked under the bright sun. She quickly moved into a shade and her feet buried into a soft, dark brown potting soil then lowered her back and brought her face close to the bright, red petals. They opened had just a week ago, providing a brief moment of joy in Charlotte's life. She placed a rubber glove on her right hand and smelled the flowers, as wrapping her palm underneath and squeezing against the stem. She held on tight, like she wanted to choke the beautiful, red bloom. Finally, she let go and looked at her hand. The thorns pierced through the rubber gloved and bloodied her palm.

Kurt slowly, quietly approached his mother. "Let me see that," he said softly, and Charlotte took of the gardening glove and opened her palm and he looked at her wound. "Oh, mama, we have to get this cleaned. You can get an infection in it."

He took Charlotte back to the house. Music from the he old fashioned gramophone let the music echo through the walls from room to room. Kurt stopped it and opened the heavy curtains to the sides. The room came alive with the sun, but Charlotte didn't like it. She placed her arm in front of her eyes.

"No, it's too bright in here."

"It's too bright outside, and look what you did yourself over there." He took her to the bathroom and cleaned her wounds. Charlotte watched the snow white clean cotton ball changing into a bright red color, and then Kurt's hand throwing the discarded piece into a trash can.

"You need to be more careful," he said.

"Did you bring the fertilizer?" she asked, as watching him to place a bandage over her palm. "I think I lost it for a while…"

"You need to stop thinking about the past. You know you can't bring father back."

"This wasn't about your father."

Kurt looked at her, and then he replied, "Whatever it was about, I can assure you it's better left alone. Look at your hand. How are you going to use it now?"

"What would I do without you, Kurt? My precious son… How is Alfred today? Is he still carving roses out of wood?"

"Yes, Mama, just like he did yesterday and today. Tomorrow won't be any different."

Minutes later, Kurt warmed up a tomato bisque soup. He placed the hot cup on a plate and cut a fresh slice of sourdough bread. The large deep, silver spoon lightly bounced off the side, clinking off the china plate. He brought the plate over to Charlotte in the living room. "Eat some. It'll make you feel better. You need some liquids in your body."

Kurt sat in the other armchair and watched his mother in a complete silence. An occasional sound of the spoon against the plate entered the air.

"Do you need anything, except the rose fertilizer?" he said at last.

"No."

"I know you miss dad. But you can't change the past and you can't bring him back."

Charlotte didn't reply nor did she lift her eyes off of her plate. Kurt quietly stood up and walked on the decorative carpet across the room. "Close the curtains, please."

Charlotte has always wanted to tell him about his dad. Who he was, and how much Kurt resembled him. But today wasn't the right time to do that, she decided; today, Charlotte Groeneweg decided she's going to leave the past alone.

§

Kurt decided to make a stop by the beach. He leaned his bicycle on the street lamp, kicking his shoes off and barefooted he walked on the sand that led down to the water. The wind picked up and blew across his face. He was the only person there, besides and occasional bird. Kurt walked in parallel with the salty waters, letting his skin soak into the Pacific Ocean. White caps lined the shore with their brief existence before being forever washed and soaked into the wet, Alaskan sand.

Kurt's only human footprints reflected against the sun, slowly fading away with every new wave that came over them. The beach stripped of the bodies, voices, laughter, thoughts, past and future, cries, and whispers and souls existed purely and entirely on its own, undisturbed, but not innocent. This part of the shore had dark secrets, knowing Kurt's pains and gains and losses and small and big victories since he was a child. He first went to Devil's Cove with his father.

"Promise you won't tell mom where we flew the kite today," Jack said quickly.

"I promise, Dad."

Later that night, Kurt woke up to an argument between his mother and his father. As the little boy promised, he didn't tell his mom but did confide in his younger brother. Kurt looked at the other bed on the opposite side of the small bedroom. Alfred was sound asleep. Little Kurt took quiet foot steps to the door and firmly pressed his ear against the wood.

"Why? Why would you take him to the Devil's Cove?" his mother cried helplessly.

"I took him there, because it's the best place to fly a kite. The wind from the ocean hits against the rocks and Chetan Mountain and the beach between is the only place you can walk and really fly a kite." Kurt heard nothing for a moment, which seemed like an eternity to him. He imagined his mother in a blank stare, standing close face to face to his father.

"People have drowned there," she said coldly. "It's a forsaken place. Don't ever take my son there, ever again."

Kurt tiptoed back to his bed. He covered his entire body under the blanket, as if he was some kind of an animal, a sea turtle perhaps, and needed to hide where it felt the most secure. "People have *drowned* there," echoed through his ears.

"I won't ever share anything with you, anymore," Kurt mumbled under his breath to Albert before the kid fell asleep.

A screaming seagull brought Kurt back to reality. He lifted his head and immediately saw the reason for the outburst – an adult eagle circling low above the hill, ready to get his next meal. Soon there was another seagull and then a third and a fourth, chasing after the big black and white bird. Kurt watched in amusement as one of the white feathered seagulls flew higher and above the eagle and then lowered its body, parachuting itself and clawing into the eagle's tail, then his head, and back at his tail again. The seagulls were like bodyguards for every other aviator in the wide open skyline, on water or on the ground or in a tree. The majestic eagle finally gave up and lifted up high and disappeared in the distance and across the nearest hill.

Kurt has seen a single magpie fighting an eagle in the sky, when the big bird flew over a Wahya Lagoon. Many times seagulls, magpies or crows protected the sky against the sharp, yellow beak and eagle's claws in order to save the newborn lives of mallard ducks, loons or Canadian geese and other sweet waterfowl. But now, Kurt walked through the place that locals religiously avoided. His feet suddenly came to an abrupt stop buried in the wet sand. He stared at a figure in far distance from him. His curious eyes mapped the small almost like a statue sitting silhouette down facing the Pacific Ocean. His mind brought on various people, but he knew of none so brave to come over here to battle the myth of a sad legend this cove was forever imbedded in. He felt a strange sensation for the first time seeing someone else in this place of complete solitude. To have another human to share this sand, this water, this piece of sky and the high, rocky cliffs behind almost felt as if he was robbed, and stripped of the place for this very moment. Kurt shrugged, and his mind brought on a more positive outlook. His face softened, his arms moved into the rhythm of his feet, as he walked to the now very familiar stranger on the beach. "Margot."

She turned her and smiled, "Hi."

"I wouldn't expect to see you here."

"No? Why?"

"Umm, did no one tell you?"

"Tell me what?" she asked curiously and watched him as he sat down on the sand next to her.

Kurt paused. If Margot had no idea about the legend of the Devil's Cove, he didn't want to be the one to tell her. "Oh, it's nothing, I've always thought of the Devil's Cove as a nice place to be. But locals see this piece of land differently. They believe the myth."

"What myth is that?"

"That a little native boy drowned here, and when the Pacific Ocean finally released his body, he became a chetan, a hawk. The locals named these high, rocky peaks that surround Lingit, *Chetan Mountains*. When the water rises and a tide comes in, the beach is a trap." He twisted his torso and looked and pointed at the high cliffs that dominated in the background. "This whole area where we're sitting now, is under water at a high tide."

"Jesus!" Margot gasped and panicked. But Kurt placed her arms around her, and said calmly, "It's a low tide, and we're safe here, for a few hours now."

Margot looked at him surprised and let out a nervous laugh. Kurt looked at her and shrugged. "So, this is where you go," she said, "when you don't work at the grocery store, or take care of your brother…"

"Yeah. I guess, I like the emptiness of the place here."

"I'm sorry to be the one to interrupt the serenity for you…"

"No, of course not. I'm sorry, I didn't mean anything by that. I don't mind you're here…I'm glad you are here." He looked toward the Pacific Ocean, spoke softly and calmly. "There is the ocean and the fish in it, the life on the beach with the grabs and sea turtles. There's life in the air, the birds, the dragonflies and the bees…This place is not empty. It's full of life!" Kurt's energy projected into every gesture and word he said. "May I ask you something?"

She nodded.

"How did you know about the Devil's Cove? It's not exactly a tourist attraction."

"I saw it on the map in your store. There was a red circle, and it got my attention. I asked Alfred, but he shied away and didn't say anything. It only got me more curious, so I decided to check it out."

Kurt raised his eyebrows and smiled at her, before he replied, "We should get out of here. The high tide is coming up. No one should stay here while the tide is up."

"What? But you said, we're safe for a few hours…"

"I didn't want you to freak out." He got up and extended his arms toward her.

They walked side by side back to the road.

"Where's your dog?"

"Holton stayed with Alfred. I don't like to leave my brother completely alone."

§

Later that night, Margot worked on her laptop, rewriting her findings, notes and comments onto the pages of the screen in front of her. Her fingers pushing quickly on the keyboard, creating a word by word and into a sentence and into a paragraph until the white page in front of her filled with black letters. She read the piece about the Red Neck Grebes out loud and her quiet room arose with various colors and melodies and rhythms with Margot's voice. She attached many beautiful photos, pressed SEND, leaned back onto the chair, folding her arms behind her head. A feeling of accomplishment washed over her, when almost on a cue she turned her head and looked at the phone on the wall across the room. The corners of her lips curled up in a smile when she heard it ringing. She quickly got up from her seat and took quick steps to the kitchen. Margot spoke softly and laughed often, as she spoke to Edith, her stepmother. She placed the phone back on the receiver, Margot walked over to a sofa, kicking her shoes off, and reaching for a dark green soft, suede pillow that she placed under her head. She lie down on the leather sofa and shut her eyes. Her arms relaxed by her side, and her long, skinny legs stretched and supported by another suede pillow.

Her living room invited in beautiful tones of a musician, playing a cello. The only sound in the house penetrated deep through the objects and walls and inhabited the space for the next few minutes. Margot listened to the dramatic music that brought strong emotions to her inner self every time she listened to it. She imagined a woman scorned, all alone in darkness, her cries unheard. There was no one who cared about the woman, and she knew it. Yet, she hoped for a miracle to come to her, to pull her out and bring her light and let her eyes show the beauty the world can offer. That's why she never gave up on herself. To Margot the woman existed in her mind and re-emerged with the sad, nostalgic tones of the cello. When she was having a bad day, she would turn on music to help her deal with whatever bothered her mind. She used the various tones, as a remedy to her mood, to her soul and well being. Music was always there when she needed it. When the last sounds of cello swished through the air, Margot kept her eyes closed and enjoyed the complete silence that followed. Something she had not been able to do for many years by living in a city. All of the sudden she had this luxury and she couldn't get enough of it.

"What? You're leaving for three and a half months into a wilderness? Are you serious?" John Ford asked angrily.

"I'm not going into a wilderness. The town I'm going to be living at is called Lingit. It has people in it. Who knows, maybe I like it and I'll stay until the fall."

"What's the population? How many people live in *Lingit*? Margot, you are a city girl! Come on, you have so many places to pick from, migratory birds are anywhere, you can do reports and images from Vancouver, or travel to the Oregon coast. Why go to the middle of nowhere? Why would you do this to yourself? I don't think it's safe." Margot frowned and two small, and thin wrinkles showed up between her eyebrows, she said crossly, "That's why. That's exactly why I want to go. I've read about Lingit in the past. I've always wanted to visit. And now I am finally doing it!"

John said, as though to himself and in lowered voice, "All right. Okay. Whatever makes you happy. Then he added with emphases, "You'd better be sending me great stills on all those birds you'll see there."

Margot finally smiled, yes, John was right, she was a city girl, but now she didn't miss any city noise. At night, the Alaskan Lingit had no ambulances to interrupt people's sleep with their loud rushing wheels through the dark streets. There were drunks shouting or attempting to sing in the early morning hours. No traffic, no roaring engines, iron cage elevators, or slammed doors behind neighbor's late returns. Margot liked the city for its unique atmosphere, and for that very same reason, she was slowly falling in for the Southeastern part of this peninsula's land of the midnight sun. Margot opened her eyes. Lingit at night was dead quiet, and the spring night lit with the sun still shining on the wide open sky made a spectacular view. The birds ruled the air and sang various songs, a little piece of paradise.

She put her running shoes on and got up from the sofa. On the way to the exit door, Margot grabbed a light wind jacket and walked out of the house. She looked at the watch on her wrist. Fourteen minutes after eleven at night. The sun was just about to go down on the sky. Margot ran toward the beach, deliberately leaving behind her camera at the house on her work desk. She wanted to make her own memories of the first sunset on the far west coast. She stopped in the middle and gazed over the red sky that spilled just above the edges of the Pacific Ocean, as far as she could see with her eyes. Her existence suddenly felt small against the beauty in front of her that took over the skyline, for a brief, unforgettable moment. The pink, orange and red colors collided and blended into each other and then joined the salty water, as the sun slowly exited horizon and fell down and behind; sinking deeper and deeper into the ocean waves. What a magnificent sight! Was Margo ever a city girl? If so, it was a different girl, at a different time with a different person. Suddenly, that Margot stayed behind in a distance, like a shadow and felt more like a stranger to the present girl that watched the sunset on the beach at a nearing midnight hour. She proudly seized this moment and made it into her own lifetime memory.

When she returned back to her log house on the hill, before she opened the double glass door on the front, wooden deck, she paused for a minute and shut her eyes, and listened to sound of the ocean, the sound of the waves so peaceful, and soothing. Her face broke into a wonderful smile. But reminder of the Alaskan air soon set and she shrugged, and felt the lower outdoor temperature through her wind breaker jacket. The temperatures during early spring at night dropped down to mid forties, not just quite the time to sleep with the windows or doors opened. Margot looked forward to warmer nights and she had all summer until the early fall to enjoy the sound of the Pacific Ocean. Her palm pushed on the double glass sliding door that led to the open living room area. She stepped in, thinking about her next adventure. Kurt had promised her to take her to Wahya Lagoon.

He said the place is filled with sweet water fowls and of all sorts of bird varieties.

§

Alfred stood in the yard, his black leather boots buried in the soft soil, shoelaces untied, blue jeans cuffed to his ankles, with two dirty stains on each knee, and splatters of white, green and red paint staining his thighs and sides of his pants. His right hand nervously trembled, with his fingers tapping his leg, his shoulders sunk and his back bend forward. His red and black checkers flannel shirt had misbuttoned buttons as he watched his mother Charlotte as she was furiously digging in the dirt, ripping some rosebushes and throwing them on the side. She mumbled under her lips, but Alfred could not make anything out it. He tilted his head the same direction every time she threw more dirt on the side. This repeated almost mechanically, back and forth, several times. Then Charlotte stopped and Alfred stopped and the younger son just watched his mother in silence. Charlotte turned and her eyes sparkled with fury.

"Where is it?" she raised her voice angrily.

"D...don't know what y...you talking about," Alfred replied quietly.

"Where's the damn box?" she shouted and with her hands, and gloves she dug lower in the dirt like a rodent. Charlotte wiped her sweaty forehead and a black smudge stayed on her fair colored skin.

Alfred suddenly turned around and ran away from her, from the dirt, roses, rocks and the house itself. He kept on running, passing the neighbor's residences that appeared to be empty and deserted to him, with their doors shut, windowsills down and no cars up front. Alfred crossed from one sidewalk and onto the paved road, and back on the opposite pedestrian side. A passerby yelled after him, "Your shoe laces are untied!"

But Alfred didn't slow down, didn't stop. He ran beside a kid on a bicycle, and passed an old lady and her aging small dog, and then he turned on his street, where his brother worked in the store a place where they both lived, in the three story house, Alfred's home. He was out of breath, when he appeared in front of Kurt, and couldn't manage to get his stammer under control. His shaking large hands moving in fast motion in the air and in front of his face, while his restless legs from the run burned inside, the younger crippled brother stood there as Kurt read the horror in Alfred's face. And without throwing out questions, the older one said, "You stay here. Okay? You wait here!" Kurt ordered and Alfred quietly nodded. Kurt grabbed his bike in front of the store and paddled fast. He knew where to go. He knew what was happening and he knew he has to try to fix it.

He passed an old lady and her small, old dog, and then he passed a kid on a bike. A passerby yelled at him, "Hey, I saw Alfred a minute ago. He ran for his life. His shoelaces were undone."

Kurt waived at the man and then he crossed the street and looked up at Charlotte's house. He let the bike fall on the grass and took few sharp steps toward his mother. "Mama!" Kurt yelled quickly and with concern.

Charlotte didn't even twitch. She continued in her fast pace down on her knees, buried in the dirt, digging with her hands. Her pants, blouse, arms even face were covered in dirt.

"Mama, what are you doing? Stop it!" Kurt approached her from behind, lowering his body and gently taking his mother's arm into his as he lifted her up from the dirt, thorns and her rosebushes. "Look at you; you're a mess, Mama. Come on inside. Let's get you cleaned up."

Charlotte twisted her arm from Kurt's grip. "I'm not finished yet," she said with a wry smile.

"What's the matter with you?! Let me guess. You can't find the box you buried yourself last fall right before the snow had fallen on the ground." Kurt looked at all the destroyed roses. They just started budding, after winter and their life got cut short. He picked up those stems that weren't broken. "I'll clean these and put them in the water for you. He paused and then he said, "They'll look pretty in your crystal vases."

"Wait," Charlotte said quickly without raising her face from the ground. "I found it."

Kurt looked at the dirt and her hands where she clutched a simple wooden box.

"Yes, you did," he said and with the roses in his hand entered the house.

He turned the faucet on in the kitchen and washed the stems, and then he reached into a drawer and cut the bottom, damaged parts. He placed the red roses in the crystal vase and carried it to the living room and set them aside on a side table, right next to the old fashioned gramophone.

As he turned his body, his hand accidentally touched the handle, and the old black vinyl started spinning. An opera's German voice filled in the space, with her angelic voice coming from the singer's heart, and through her tones and the song's melody let the opera's inner emotions through her mind and body. Kurt turned the record off. He walked to the kitchen and there, through the window he quietly watched his mother as she knelt down, a small wooden box still firmly in her hands. He saw her slowly open the box, but the lid didn't come all the way up. She paused for a brief second and then she abruptly shut the lid, letting it drop from her hands into the dirt she frantically started grabbing the soil between her fingers and pouring it onto the box. Then with the open palms she flattened the surface several times. When she was done, she stood up and her eyes met with Kurt's. He instinctively looked away, and when he looked out again, he no longer saw Charlotte outside. She came into the kitchen and her loud voice sharply ordered.

"We'll need some fresh rose bushes, with live roots."

"Yes, mama. I'll go get them for you." Kurt passed his mother, carrying his head down, with his chin close to his chest. He sat on his bike and paddled away, the tones of the angelic voice still throbbing in his ears. The local nursery had many fresh flowers to pick from. He immediately followed back to his mother's house, and planted the bright red roses in the ground. Charlotte stood in the kitchen and watched him, until he was done.

"Good. It'll do until the next time," she muttered under her lips.

"Until next time," Kurt whispered to the flowers.

Suddenly raindrops fell from the midday sky.

"You can't wash it all away – there isn't enough rain to wash all of her *past* away!" he yelled at the clouds that hung over his head.

CHAPTER 4

The Pain In Her Belly intensified until she felt like her body was on fire. A nurse in a white uniform and a white cap pinned down to her dark brown hair rushed to the bedside. The young aide wiped the sweat from her forehead and reached for another cotton cloth. She damped the clean fabric in the water and twisted the ends, until no drops fell from the small sheet.

Charlotte estimated the German nurse could be about three or four years younger from her. "How old are you?"

She replied shyly, "I'm seventeen." And then she added with emphasis, "But I've been working as a midwife for two full years."

Charlotte's body screeched as her contractions grew more frequent and a lot more painful. The young nurse twisted the ends of the cloth again, making sure all the access water is gone and back in the metal bowl. Then she placed the cloth on Charlotte's forehead.

"You have a temperature. The doctor's on its way."

Charlotte screamed from the depth of her lungs. She placed her hands over her belly, as an awful, sharp-bladed pain entered her insides. Then she let her arms fall besides her body as she stretched her fingers on the white sheets before grabbing the bedding inside her palms and twisting her hands into firm fists. She screamed again and her head came up from the pillow and then she let it fall back onto the soft down pillow.

Charlotte tossed and turned in her bed. The dark silhouette of a man grew bigger as his image crept closer to her bed, a light shining around the man with two horns on the top of his head, the blinding light giving him more power; his long coat buttoned with a single large black button under his chin, the rest of the coat moving to the sides as the wind blew into his dark face. His laughter, deep and strong and overwhelming, scared Charlotte to death. Then the creature came to a stop, and its image didn't expand any further. The wind quieted and the dark, faceless image leaned over Charlotte's head and whispered into ear, "You are the devil."

Charlotte woke up. At first she didn't recognize the room she was in. She focused her eyes around the bedroom and realized she had a nightmare. With the foreman of her right hand she wiped the sweaty forehead. A few strands of hair stuck and wet and glued to her skin alongside the temples, her mouth dry longing for a glass of water. She covered her eyes with her stone cold palm and let out a deep sigh. "Leave me alone," she said angrily. But there was no one there with her in the room.

She got up and walked to the bathroom, running cold water through the pipes and the faucet as she lowered her head and brought her lips to the clear pouring liquid. Charlotte shut her eyes, as she let her lips receive the ice cold water, then she let her head under the stream and wetted her hair, splashing her cheeks before turning off the faucet. Charlotte dried her hair and face into a soft golden towel and looked at herself in the mirror.

"Forgive me," she whispered at the image in front of her eyes. Who was the other woman staring back at her?

A sharp, loud cuckoo sound startled Charlotte. She let the towel fall carelessly on the bathroom counter and quickly exited the room. She walked over to the living room, where the wooden bird on the wall came out of its house with a long shingled roof and a single window in the middle of the house in the loft. The bird came out of the house on every even hour, announcing loudly the time passage and surely getting its attention. The clock on the wall was old; Charlotte couldn't remember how old exactly. Her husband Jack got it for her birthday. Charlotte was delighted as it reminded her of her European background. The antique, mechanical cuckoo clock was a work of precision, passion and art. Made in Germany and hand-carved, beautifully decorated with forest motives of pine cones, and small birds attached to the top part of the cuckoo's house, the cuckoo had two weights in the shape of long, realistically looking pine cones and the weights were accompanied by two gongs, once each half hour and the number of hours on the hour. The clock relied on an old-world time keeping mechanism and didn't require any batteries. She was only in the new land for a very short time, a month or so, when she met with Jack. Charlotte didn't speak the language, the precious thing she had on the entire world was her one year old baby boy. She traveled a long distance, far away from her homeland. Her body was lean from starvation and her face was sunk with a protruding cheekbones.

She was exhausted from the travels, leaving her past behind, but she hoped that one day, she would return to the place where she was born, where she went to school, the place she grew up and made some friends. But the world circumstances and the war had different plans and so she adjusted and left her hometown in exchange for a better life if not for her, then she definitely did it for her baby boy. Wanting to go as far as possible, when she met with John, who traveled to New York city on business, and told her, his home is on the other side of the coast in a land of the last frontier, she felt that's the place, where she can raise her son and start her new life. She didn't expect to fall in love with the American. Jack took Kurt as his own son.

Charlotte adjusted more quickly to her new life than she thought she would, and she learned the language day by day and made some friends between the neighbors and her husband's friends. Charlotte insisted on having her last name hyphenated. And if there should ever be another child, she wanted the child to carry the same last name as her and the first born. She set the cuckoo clock manually, something she did daily, in order to keep the little loud cuckoo on. Charlotte placed a light coat around her arms and walked outside the house. She drove herself to the outskirts of Lingit, a short distance from her house a quiet, lonely place, surrounded by large, tall spruces. Charlotte's feet stumbled upon a rock that probably had fallen from a hill on the right side and as it rolled it stopped in the middle of the forest path. She smiled and wondered how long the rock laid there, and how many people came upon it, just like her and hitting their toes in their shoes against the hard surface of the stone.

"Ouch." She stopped and lifted her left foot. She brought her knee to her chest and with her right hand instinctively wrapped her fingers over the top of her shoe. She was glad she didn't break any bones in her toes. And then she saw two perfect cones, attached to one another on the end of the spruce branch, someone had torn and probably carried in hand when that person stumbled upon this very same rock, and let go of the branch and its twin cones. Charlotte picked up the branch and smelled it. The fresh, intense scent indicated the branch was not abandoned for a long time. The two cones reminded her of her cuckoo clock. They were the nearly same size in length and in width. She carried the branch home and placed it in a crystal vase and set it next to her cuckoo clock. At first she was hungry for everything new, the air outside smelled different, better than what she remembered back at home in Bavaria. The sky seemed higher and more open, for the first time she saw clouds having different colors, not only white, but she discovered there were shades of gray, yellow and blue. The young German was delighted to see the nature had familiar trees, such as birch trees, spruces and pines, and rocks and grass, and hills and ponds that reminded her of her life in Europe. And then she liked and welcomed the new, exciting things and animals she's never seen before. She remembered the very first time she saw moose; a giant beauty with long legs, and oddly shaped skull that in a statue was three times the size of a horse. Her husband Jack warned her before the close encounters with the Alaskan wildlife; the grizzlies and the moose and told her what to do if she ever encountered one of the majestic creatures. She's seen many moose that wondered from the forest and into town walking on the paved roads of Lingit, curiously observing its human companions and cars and loose dogs that roamed through the streets. Charlotte has seen brown bears, from a safe distance, but once she came really close to a black bear. She remembered she felt no fear. Returning from her walk, the young, naïve woman entered a small tunnel under a bridge, a short cut, that she had taken many times, when her legs got tired and the air was hot, and she didn't want to walk around the usual bypass that turned and curved back to town. She saw a shadow, low to the ground walking slowly toward her. The bright day light blinded her eyes for a brief moment as she entered the dark tunnel. Although neon lights lit the narrow space, she had to take down her sunglasses to have a better vision. At first, it seemed there is a large loose dog, perhaps a black German shepherd, merging toward her. As the animal came closer and its head lifted, Charlotte's feet came to an instant stop. Unlike her, the overly large black bear continued in his slow pace, his four chubby furry feet coming closer to her. The bear mastered the paved sidewalk, looking directly into Charlotte's eyes. She realized the animal had to see her first, knowing it is approaching human, yet didn't hesitate, didn't slow down and didn't come to a stop, like her. Her husband's words echoed in her mind, as if he stood right behind her, whispering into her ear. With the highest calmness possible, Charlotte took slow, small steps back, without ever turning her eyes off of the bear. Since the animal was alone, and it most likely was a male, looking at its massive size, she felt she had a high chance of getting out of the narrow tunnel without an injury.

The path outside the tunnel split in a three-way fork. She quickly counted, that the bear would most likely enter straight into the bushes, rather than choosing between two paved paths and one dirt road. Charlotte turned and rushed away from the bushes, choosing one of the dirt roads that lead into a large meadow hoping there would be people there. The voice in the back of her head came louder, reminding her importance of staying calm and not to run. When she got to the meadow, she turned around and saw the black bear sprinting on all of his feet, his huge shoulder blades dancing in the rhythm of his paws as he maneuvered himself out of the tunnel, across the forest path. Over the grass, his head swayed from side to side he looked at his human companion with his small eyes, his nozzle sniffing the air and mouth opened. Her heart pumped faster, and her face stiffened. Charlotte's eyes shifted to the ground, frantically looking for a large stick she could snap and hopefully scare off the black bear. The animal ran out of the hot sun and into a shade, and finally headed into the thick and green brush, attracted to the low bush red berries. Charlotte heard the branches and twigs crack under the heavy feet of the animal. A huge relieve came when the running bear entered the bushes and quickly disappeared into the forest. Charlotte thought about the bear later that day. He was probably scared of her, a human, as much as she was scared of the animal. When the bear walked out of the tunnel and his paws no longer touched concrete but a nice, natural forest path, he rushed into his habitat and out of the civilized danger.

Charlotte knew she got lucky that early spring day. Had she met with a sow and her cubs, things would not necessarily go this way. She hadn't seen anyone, not on the meadow, where she usually ran to various people, small and big, walking, jogging, playing Frisbee or people just walking their dogs. On that day, she came across with a black bear, the very young immigrant, Charlotte Groeneweg, was truly and entirely alone, but had luck on her side. Her life could had been decided for her right on that day and the hour, but fate had its own plans. Kurt, her firstborn son, was one of them, together with the secret that she brought over the pond from the old continent.

The cuckoo came out loudly, breaking the silence in Charlotte's living room, taking her out of her thoughts, pulling her out of her past and delivering her into the present. Charlotte caught a reflection of her face in the glass of the curio that held her china and crystal. She brought her hands to her face and lightly touched her cheeks. Time has changed her appearance, on the outside, three deep wrinkles imprinted into Charlotte's forehead and another two, deep and long framed her face each on one side and around her lips, a constant reminder of the older age, her silent companions, waking up with her each and every day and going to bed to be only deeper, longer and more visible as time went by. Her lips used to be plump and full and red in color, like ripen raspberries, but now, even the lips shrunk, thinned, and the color once so vibrant and kissable, faded into the past.

§

Margot got up from her sofa; her hand grabbed the opened book and shut it, moving it onto the side table, when a black and white photograph from her book fell on the floor. She left it unattended and walked to the ringing telephone.

"Hello?" said Margot, and her face softened as soon as she recognized the voice on the other side of the receiver.

"Margot, it's so good to hear your voice. How are you?" An older voice spoke to her through the phone receiver. Margot has always found Edith's voice soft and calm and very soothing.

"I'm fine. How are you, Mom? Is everything all right?" Margot twisted the long cord around the finger of her free hand. She pushed the receiver closer to her ear, as if this would make Edith closer to her. The phone connection was clear, and out of static, creating an illusion Edith is right around the corner from her, and not across the coasts, a full four-hour difference between the women. They spoke like best friends, chatting and laughing and time went by quickly as it always does, when people share some quality time together. Edith asked about Lingit, and Margot talked about the locals, the ocean, the beach, trees and mountains. And then she went onto the birds, and her written projects, and how much more there is to see in such a small, yet very beautiful Alaskan town.

"I'm so glad you've found what you like to do," she said. "There aren't many people that are blessed to find their niche."

Margot spoke about her adventures, what she has seen, and what she plans to see and visit and take pictures of, and Edith told her how things went on the East coast, and how her father Adam Smith worked on new cartoons for the upcoming Sunday's papers. When Margot said good-bye and hung up, her mind kept on, and Edith's image and voice persisted in her thoughts. She opened the refrigerator and took out a bottle of white wine. She poured herself a generous amount and took a sip of the chilled, golden liquid as she strolled back to her living room sofa. She picked up the black and white photograph of a young woman, smiling shyly at her and made herself comfortable, bringing her feet up from the floor and on the sofa; Margot placed two pillows behind her back and pushed against them.

When Edith Altman married Margot's father Adam, a widower of about two years, Margot was only seven years old. The little girl, who lost her mother when she was five, fought her feelings toward Edith. Little Margot saw the new woman in her father's life as someone who wanted to take her father away from her. She threw tantrums on purpose, she would not eat food Edith had cooked for her, just like a child, she stubbornly shut herself off, perhaps hoping, this would bring her mother back. Except she grew closer to Edith, and deep inside as a child she liked the woman who spoke with a foreign accent. Edith had a lot of patience with the seven-year-old girl, still saddened by the unexpected death of her own mother. Some years later, on a very windy, and rainy afternoon, a freak accident changed Margot's mind and the bond between the girl and her stepmother became even tighter. The bad weather and a hard pouring rain forced the two girls inside. Margot and her best friend Laura rushed in the kitchen, soaked and shivering. They dropped their coats and shoes on the floor and then the eleven-year-old Margot told Laura she was going make hot chocolate. Without any particular reason, Margot placed her right arm onto the iron wired electric stove top. She immediately screamed with pain that entered her entire body like a lightning bolt. Laura panicked and screamed even louder looking at her best friend.

Margot pulled her hand from the stove and with her left hand held her right wrist staring in horror and shock at her bright red palm. Edith rushed to the kitchen, seeing Margot's hand blistered, tears rolling down her cheeks; Edith immediately turned on the cold faucet valve and grabbed the girl. Crying for her life, Margot watched the clear cold stream pouring over and over her burned hand, her fingers stretched and her body shaking from the intense pain. Margot's vision narrowed as if she entered a narrow tunnel. She no longer saw her best friend in the same room, even though she still could hear her voice; Laura felt very distant and Edith's body felt far away, but her soothing voice was right by Margot and the voice calmed her down internally, and a warm breeze washed over her and when she looked at her burnt palm the pain lessened. The skin blistered quickly under her middle finger and close to her thumb. She felt her whole arm being lifted and away from the cold water. She followed Edith's voice, but her vision still very narrow made her head spin. She tilted her head to the left and saw the kitchen's wall. Daisies rose up from the wallpaper one after another, as if they wanted to greet her and when she passed them, they disappeared into the wall. Soon, Margot entered the tunnel completely and saw nothing, but darkness. The tremendous thirst and dry mouth woke her up. Her tongue glued to the top of her mouth. Margot's lips parted and she licked them with her dry tongue. The eleven year old child lifted her head and saw a white bandage over her right hand.

"I got burned," she whispered.

"You blistered your palm."

Edith sat at the edge of Margot's bed. "You're going to be all right. There shouldn't be any permanent scars on your hand. I poured flour over your wound and greased it with lard." Edith ran her fingers through Margot's hair.

"Thank you...*Mom*."

The blisters slowly went away, the old skin peeled, and new skin grew after they were gone. Margot's hand healed, leaving no permanent scars, just as Edith told her. The thirty-six year old city girl opened her hand and stared at her smooth skin on her left hand. She let out a loud sigh, before taking another sip of chardonnay. The two women became best friends, as Margot turned into her teenage years, and then their relationship strengthened, making Edith not only her true mother, but someone Margot could trust and confined in.

A repetitive knocking sound came from the outside and got Margot's attention. Even though she felt tired from the fresh air, and a walk earlier at the Devil's Cove, and now the wine made her muscles pleasantly relaxed, she got up and walked to the window. There, a Steller's jay looked at her curiously on the other side of the glass. She paused and stared at the black and blue bird with a funny dark black Mohawk on the top of his small head and beautifully deep blue feathers on his wings. The bird wasn't shy, nor was he scared of her human presence. She slowly raised her arms and carefully opened the window. The Steller's jay tilted his head to the side back and forth several times, checking out her new companion.

"I think I've got something you may like," said Margot.

"Don't go anywhere," she said teasingly.

Margot opened a food pantry and reached up high on the shelf for the natural unsalted whole peanuts in shell. She took two between her fingers and returned to the window. The little bird moved closer to her and stretched his neck, lowering the high black Mohawk toward Margot's hand.

"Here you go," she said and extended her arm toward his sharp pointed dark beak. The bird quickly snatched one shelled peanut from her fingers. Margot's face broke into a wide smile. She watched the Steller's jay as he lifted up high and away from the window and flew toward a nearby pine tree. He landed on a branch, where he sat the nut close to his feet and with his beak skillfully opened the shell, eating the peanut inside. Margot placed the second treat on the windowsill and shut the window.

"I made a friend," she said to herself as she finished the glass of chardonnay and crashed her body on the sofa.

The next day, Kurt waited for her in front of her log house. He stepped out of his car, shut the driver's door and leaned his back onto the vehicle. He liked the house Margot stayed in. Built up high on the hill, the only property around on a private beach, surrounded by tall wild grass and sand, the house had two stories, and the kitchen and living room faced the ocean, while the main bedroom overlooked the other side, where the Chetan Mountain peaks hovered up high toward the sky. The wooden house had oversized windows all around, and glass French door that opened on the front deck, overlooking the wide beach. But it was a very windy place, making the winter stay uncomfortable. Kurt knew Margot rented the house from spring to fall, and that her main reason was to come here to do a bird study. Or did she have another, only to her known reason, to visit Lingit? He admitted to himself, he was suspicious if the Seattle-based magazine photographer had come to his town just to write some articles about birds. And then he questioned himself, if that really matters. He just couldn't get her off of his mind. She represented something he couldn't just yet figure out and it drove him crazy. Holton brought a big stick and dropped it by Kurt's feet. His jaw opened, and the long tongue danced in the open air. The dog lifted his front left paw moving it several times back and forth in a swift motion. Kurt picked it up and threw it to the dog on the sandy beach. Margot finally stepped out of the house. He watched her from the short road distance, the wind immediately messed up her red long locks. She asked, "What's the best place to go to watch sweet water birds?" He offered he would take her to a Wahya Lagoon. Kurt thought that the city girl sure made herself look all fancy for such a trip; bare legs in mid calf high cowboy boots, oversized straw hat that has already nearly blown out in the wind, summer dress with short sleeves. She carried a bag over her shoulder. Most likely for her journal so she can put down notes, Kurt thought. Margot looked like she put a lot of effort into her morning's looks. He watched her to come down to his car. Her long, lean arm held the top of her straw hat, with the strands of hair blowing around her shoulders and slim neck and into her face. Holton noticed her and recognized her and instantly ran to her carrying his stick in his mouth.

"Hi Holton, you're always so happy." Holton dropped his stick by her boots. She picked it up and threw it across the street where Kurt stood. "Fetch!"

Kurt drove slowly so Margot could see the surroundings, local houses scattered across the hillside, most of them having two or three acres just to themselves, in the wooded areas, where birch trees met with spruces and pines, and mixed with tall cotton trees. She saw an eagle flying low above their car, carefully scattering the ground to spot voles, chipmunks and other rodents. Kurt looked over at her from his driver seat and said, "You know, we have no snakes here. It's too cold for them."

The road behind town became dirt. Someone decided that's where the end of town ends, and the wilderness begins. Kurt's Land Rover Defender station wagon bounced off the smaller and bigger holes, and uneven surface, and rocks flew to the sides as he downshifted for the steep hill ahead of them.

"This is fun." Margot cheered as she held onto her seat. The dog's head looked out the window in the back of the truck.

"Holton seems to be enjoying himself," she added.

"Yeah, he's actually kind of upset."

"Upset? Why?"

"You're sitting on his seat."

"Oh." Margot turned her back to the dog, "Sorry, Holton."

Margot stared in silence at the view in front of her. She felt she reached the top of the world. Once they got up on the hill, the scenery opened wide on both sides, from left to right; her eyes mapped nothing but spectacular nature. The dog now sat down between her and Kurt, but his furry body leaned onto Margot's bare legs. She smiled and took a deep breath and closed her eyes. When she exhaled she opened them and let all the beauty in front of her enter her body. Margot felt the rush that electrified, there were so many emotions going through her; everything around her blossomed in various shades of green color. Until then, Margot had no idea green can have so many variations, tones and shades. She definitely could not see this in the city.

The valley below spread for miles, and filled the air with oxygen by strong forest. There were ponds here and there, smaller and bigger, deep and shallow, of irregular round shapes and water color. Boulders mixed with rocks and moss covered them on the north side of the stones.

Kurt looked at her asked, "Ready?"

"Ready," she replied with a smile on her face. They walked a short distance from the Defender around the curve heading south. Holton ran to the front and showed them the way to the Wahya Lagoon.

"Looks like your dog knows his way around here."

"Yeah, pretty much so."

"How often do you come here?"

Kurt shrugged, his arms moved in the rhythm of his steps. He kept his eyes down on the rocky road, replied casually, "I come here whenever I need to seek serenity."

"I see, this is your place of solitude."

"Yeah, I guess it is." He lifted his head and Margot noticed his smile. Kurt had a great wide smile that lit his entire face. Few wrinkles showed up around his eyes, deep, and long. When they reached the top of the hill large deep sweet water Wahya Lagoon opened in front of their eyes.

"Come down here." He waved at her and she followed him on a narrow path.

Margot took deep steps down the hill, thinking her cowboy boots are not the most comfortable attire at the moment.

"Be careful. You don't want to scratch your fancy boots," Kurt joked warmly.

He stretched his arm and helped her down the steep rocks. Some rolled down in the mixture of grass and dirt. "Here, come sit down over here." He pointed at the large logs that lay down on the ground. Holton surprisingly didn't run for the water. Instead, he sat down right next to Margot and leaned his furry, warm body onto her legs.

"Holton doesn't like to swim here?"

"He does. He's just waiting for my approval. I want you to see as many birds as possible, before he dives in."

The edges of Wahya Lagoon on the side and ahead of them were framed by many green water lilies, the foliage just awakening after winter, waiting to open their white flowers. The blue sky had an occasional cloud here and there, and the air was still, with no wind, making the surface of the water smooth, creating a beautiful reflection of the oval island in the middle of the Lagoon. The island had several birch trees, and tall bushy grass, and was surrounded by small rocks of white, gray and black color, that lifted from the water. New plants of fireweed pushed proudly up high, against the open skyline, ready to bring their purple colored flora to the world. Mid May and the fireweed has grown a foot tall and spread around the lake; the future light and dark purple kings and queens of the summer were there to delight the spectator's eye and soul.

Margot, Kurt and even the dog watched various kinds of birds, inhabiting the area. Caspians glided above the water and interfered with gulled billed terns. Black capped chicks walked on the rocky sides of the small island, seagulls loudly announced their presence while various breeds of loons cruised on the surface of the sweet water Wahya Lagoon.

All the birds coexisted one next to another, with each carefully taking care of their loved one, occasionally a Canadian goose hissed at another, a little territorial vocal exchange.

From a high bushy grass, full of cat tail stems, emerged a female mallard duck and behind her emerged nine, recently-born hatchlings. Margot estimated that they came to world probably about two weeks ago, maybe less. They all walked behind their mother, chatting aloud, with their little beaks, and tiny feathered bodies, bravely stepping through the grass and various obstacles, such holes and loose, fallen branches. Their will at life – to be alive, to stay alive, to get through the grass, and enter the water – was admirably the strongest. When their bird mom stopped all of her babies came to stop, too creating a small, tight irregular circle, within themselves, loudly chatting to one another. The reason the mother stopped soon became obvious to Margot who couldn't take her eyes off of the little chipper creatures. There was a tenth duckling, which stayed behind and as soon as it popped its head from the tall grass, and with its tiny feet rushed to its siblings, the mother mallard continued her way and proceeded to the water. One after another, her babies plunged into water, and started paddling with their bright orange feet following her. They felt more confident and soon spread around. The mother bird seems not to worry where everyone is. What a delight to watch them dive under water and quickly pop up on the surface. Margot without saying a word got up, and took steps to the shore. She snapped some pictures, and then she focused on the wooded hill behind the Wahya Lagoon.

She brought the lens closer to her eye and zoomed at the top of the flat spruce tree. There, a large nest stood up at the tree's crown, and was occupied by two eagles. One adult, with its black feathers, and white colored head, and one small, and grey, another baby. Except this young fella was most likely born a year ago. And for the next four years it will keep its grey color, until it becomes an adult, like its parent, to blossom into what's a well-known eagle's appearance. She took more photos and then switched her cameras and took some in black and white. Margot returned back on the log and reached into her bag, taking out her diary, she put down her notes and observations. She was so deeply absorbed by the surrounded beauty, that she didn't even noticed Kurt and Holton being gone. She lifted her head from her handwritten notes and looked around. Standing up she yelled aloud, "Kurt? Holton? Where'd you guys go?" And then with the tremendous speed a soaked dog ran toward her and didn't stop. She quickly moved to the side, but the mutt was faster and greeted her by standing on his hind legs, and with its large, wet front paws he pushed onto Margot's shoulders and gave her a giant slobbery kiss.

"Holton! Down! Get down, dog!" Kurt yelled after his dog from a far distance.

Kurt came running, apologizing to Margot. "I'm sorry." And then he turned and spoke to his dog, "Are you crazy? What are you doing?" Holton hung his head and shook it sharply, splashing more water over Kurt's pants.

Margot laughed. "It's all good. He's just being a dog."

Kurt looked at her and saw two large muddy prints on her fancy dress. He pointed his finger. "I'm really sorry, I guess he's just not use to company." He paused and then he added softly, "He likes you." And then he lowered his head and looked at his dog.

"Come with me. There's something you'll like to see." Kurt said.

A narrow path, with recent signs of footsteps led Margot to a place, where a loon sat on her nest. The nest floated on the top of the water, close by the shore, yet far away for a human to reach it.

There was one loon that sat on the nest while another paddled nearby diving its head under water, several times, finally disappearing from Margot's sight, only to reappear farther away in the Wahya Lagoon's water. Margot stood there, a camera in her right hand ready to capture the bird emerging on the air. She counted 33 seconds for the bird being under water, and feeding on various plants from the Wahya Lagoon's bottom. After that the loon headed to the nest, and without making any loud noise, the two birds quietly, and carefully exchanged their position on the nest they built. The female was first; she got up and stretched her neck, uncovering four snow-white eggs underneath her feathers. She plunged herself quickly into the water, while her male companion got up and very carefully maneuvered his feet between the four eggs. He lowered his back first, slightly rocking his body left and right before slowly and very gently covering the precious eggs underneath him, before proudly letting the rest of his body down, bringing his chest to the nest and never letting too much warmth out of the eggs. The exchange of the birds over their future offspring had to be done fast and with a precision. Margot captured these very beautiful moments in her many stills.

"Funny, you know how much people in the city pay for fern? And here, it grows everywhere," she said moments later, looking at the green plants growing in a shade. Kurt smiled, but kept quiet. He watched her, as she tore a green stem of another forest plant.

"What's this?"

He looked over and finally replied, "That's fiddlehead."

"*Fiddlehead*? Is it a real name?" she asked amusingly.

"I don't know. I've always known it as fiddlehead," he said, and then he continued, casually, "People eat it."

"What?" Margot looked closely at the green, thin stem, that slightly resembled dill, before she said reluctantly," No way." She stared at the flowerless plant in her hand, bringing it closer to her face and smelling it like a dog.

"Before it grows taller and opens its sides, people come and harvest them and then boil them in the water, or steam them. It tastes like a broccoli."

The light outside darkened with grey clouds that covered the sun above them.

"We should head back to the car. It's going to rain," Kurt said and called Holton to his feet.

Margot looked at the sky; nearly two thirds remained blue. "No, it'll clear," she said confidentially.

Kurt glanced at her and wondered if this city girl is for real. He wanted to answer impulsively but decided to hold his breath instead and look at the blue part of the sky. Margot gave him a quick look, and her mind wondered, if his arrogance is for real, or if he's just testing her. As if on cue, drops of rain started falling from the sky.

Margot shrugged and laughed. She spread her arms to the sides and asked, "I give up. How'd you know?"

"Whenever the sky gets like this, with clouds on one side but bright blue sky on the other, you have to look for signs… When you see clouds above the mountains, it means it won't rain in the city. All the rain usually falls down on the Chetan Mountains before it can get to the city. But if there are dark clouds above the Pacific Ocean, then it almost always means it's going to rain in the city." She looked at him and her lips parted, but he spoke first. "Let's get out of here."

The same evening, Margot went through the digital images she took several hours ago, and then she retyped her notes into laptop. This time, she didn't send it to John Ford at Natural Bird Magazine. Instead, she decided to wait. She wanted to return to Wahya Lagoon when the baby loons are born and document them. A hunger made its way to her stomach and announced its presence with a loud, complaining sound. Margot walked to the kitchen and opened the fridge; eggs, yogurt, cheese and butter lay on the top shelve. A carton of milk and a few cans of Cola-cola stared at her from the middle shelve. Some veggies and fruit occupied the bottom. She didn't even bother to check her freezer. There were only two items there – a bottle of vodka and some ice. She shut the fridge door and walked over to the pantry. Her chest lifted up and down as she let out a loud sigh. Should she call for a pizza? She wasn't even sure whether Lingit had a delivery service. Margot caught a reflection of her face in the mirror above the kitchen sink. The mirror was small, round and had sunbeams around it. She saw a city girl looking back at her. Margot made an ironic smile, lifting only one corner of her lips. Life in the city had its advantages, such as there were always places to go and eat, even late at night, seven days a week. Although she liked cooking, she never just cooked for herself. On days like these, she would grab a coat and run downstairs and onto the streets of Seattle. There were so many various places to pick from; all in her downtown neighborhood. Italian, Chinese, Korean, European and all-American; she would get to go order and brought it home and eat it on her sofa, relaxing and listening to music, while her TV screen muted in the background, with just the changing colored pictures jumping from a shot to a shot.

She turned her way away from the sun-beamed mirror. Out the window, the ocean waves intensified, powered by the rain, wind and dark clouds. Looking at the deep, endless water, Margot's thoughts returned to her life in the city. The view outside her apartment was entirely taken by the building across the street. At first, she let the windows stripped of any treatments. When the light outside darkened and people turned on lights and lamps, she would lie down on her sofa and watch the windows in front of her eyes. There would be bright yellow lights, orange and red, neon purple, or the windows would reflect in fast paced multi-shaded colors, powered by the television screens. Margot lay in her living room, her ears open up to music that entered her space from the CD she put on, but her eyes saw something different. There were windows of happiness, and windows of sadness, glass and frame that held the window to ambition and another to ignorance. She saw a row of three windows, right under the building's roof, one belonged to life, while the second window was consumed by vanity and the third one visited by death. Margot brought her feet up and pushed herself up from the sofa. She slowly and quietly walked to the glass, watching an old man, who sat behind his table, his head deep buried in his large hands, rubbing his forehead, and eyes, muttering to himself and placing his right hand over his face, reaching down and bringing a large handkerchief and wiping his eyes. Then the man suddenly looked out his window. Margot shrieked and stepped back. Could he see her, could he notice her watching him? She has lived in the same place for several years, looking at the same windows, and seeing the very same old man, eating Sunday morning breakfasts with his wife. That morning, the man sat there alone, just like this very same evening the man still sat behind his table, *alone*. Margot wanted to run out her place and give the man a hug, tell him, he's going to be all right. Just like her own father held her, telling her everything's going to be all right after her own mother died and she was just five years old. The next morning, Margot got up and shopped for the nicest, thickest curtains she could find. She never wanted to watch the windows across the street ever again.

Margot looked at the sticker on her refrigerator, *"Longnose Sucker,"* and underneath in italics *the only sucker in Alaska*, with a drawing of a fish. She checked her watch. If she hurries she may still get an order of catfish and chips there. She slipped into her cowboy boots and reached for a rain jacket on the hanger next to the door and ran out on the fresh air. The windshield wipers furiously moved in front of her eyes, back and forth, fighting the heavy rain drops. She parked on the handicapped spot; the closest distance from a car to a restaurant's door and with few, quick steps entered the Longnose Sucker, the only sucker in Alaska.

"Hello? Are you still open?" she asked loudly and looked around.

A heavy man, short of statue, with thick hands and fingers and thick, grayish hair came from behind the register. "Are you lost?" he asked.

"Lost? No, I…I live here…I'm staying at the log cabin on the hill."

The man studied her face as raindrops fell from the cap of her raincoat and drizzled on the wooden floor of his restaurant. "I see. Well, what can I get you?"

"Catfish and chips…to go, please. I wasn't sure whether you're still open."

"We have a customer, we are open." The man gave Margot the warmest, fattest smile she's ever seen. His face expanded, his lips parted and his eyes sunk under the chipmunks chubby cheeks.

CHAPTER 5

§

Edith Altman Sat On A Bench of Fenwick suburbs of her house. She watched in a silence a large tree in front of her; its green leaves moved into the gusts of wind and at times only a few branches swayed, and then more leaves joined them, like a part of an orchestra. Edith shut her eyes for a brief moment and slowly rocked her head into the rhythm of clarinets, basses, trumpets and drums. She opened her eyes and looked at the tree. Only the crown moved gently in the summer breeze, and Edith heard somber violin music, while the rest of the orchestra quieted down. The music entered Edith's mind electrifying her entire body. She lifted her hands and as a conductor she moved them into the rhythm and colors of the leaves, she closed her eyes and let her body be absorbed by the strong, rhythmical vibe, the wind picked up and the tree obeyed, branches bending leaves flying and drums beat loudly trying to shut the wind. And then, everything muted, and the only sound through the air was the beautiful violin. The energy released up high and out into the universe. Goose bumps appeared on her naked arms, and Edith shrugged. The outdoor temperature lowered. She got up and entered the house.

Adam Smith sat behind his desk with his forearms leaning onto the paper, his left elbow touching several multicolored pencils, finally pushing them on the other side of the desk. His back hunch over and his eyes close to the drawing he was working on. A single overlapping lamp shining its light on the project, he's been working on for three days now.

Whenever he got an idea, he would start working on it fast, the more he drew, the more his idea grew and gained shapes, names and voices. Soon, Adam was able to transform a piece of blank paper into a black and white cartoon inhabited by new figures and animals. After that, each character would gain color and finally a voice. He very rarely changed things, if anything at all. This way Margot's father came up with a brand new cartoon for the newspaper he's been working for many years. The Fenwick Press has been publishing his cartoons in Sunday's papers for more than thirty years. This week belonged to a reindeer, saved by a good Samaritan as a baby and brought up in the Samaritan's house as a pet. He named him Star. When the reindeer grew to his adulthood, the owner built him a special enclosure in his backyard. Star could predict the future by listening to people and then rubbing his feet on the ground. Many came from far away to seek Star's services. One day a little girl came up to him and asked him to make her dog stop peeing on other people's back, because when she visits a local park, her dog runs around peeing on people. Star leaned forward and through the fence she whispered into the girl's ear, "Some people deserve to be poo on." The little girl cheered and thanked the reindeer. She rushed home and told her dog exactly what Star advised her. The next day, when the girl and her dog went to the park, her dog pooped right on a man's foot. The man was furious, besides himself. The little girl stopped and her bright blue eyes looked at the man's furious dark pupils.

She said, "Funny shit happens, and it can happen to you."

Edith stood quietly in the doorway. Her eyes curiously watching Adam work. She didn't want to disturb him. His work was important to him, and she respected that. Besides, she was his biggest fan, having the privilege to read every new cartoon as his first admirer.

"You need to bring humor to your life otherwise life is not worth living. Life without humor is only half-way lived," he told her.

"Writing is a solitary thing. You are always alone."

Adam's eyes softened, "No. You're never alone. You are surrounded by thoughts, and those become words and words take on sentences, as they create places and people." He looked at her, and said softly, "You like music." Edith sat on his lap, and he walked his fingers around her slim waist, and continued, "It's kind of like composing. You surround yourself with music – thus you're never alone. Your mind transfers to another world, to another place that you create and whatever you do with it is entirely up to you." He paused and then he added with emphasis, "Whether that's what loneliness is, than I say, I long for it. I wouldn't create half of my work, without somewhat feeling lonely."

Edith smiled at this memory, her index and thumb finger of her left hand pressing onto her golden pendant. She felt the rose petals underneath the tips of her fingers, and the cut edge, an incomplete rose. Her smile instantly disappeared from her face. She brought her hand down and let the pendant fall back on her chest.

"Rolf," she whispered breathlessly under her lips.

She clapped her heels on the wooden floor, echoing between the house's walls, furniture and occasionally disappearing, when Edith walked on the small carpets that connected two rooms together. When she got to her bedroom, she shut the door behind her. Her body became motionless for a split second when her eyes landed on the chestnut six drawer dresser. Edith took a deep breath and with a firm step she walked to the dresser and opened the second drawer from the top, sliding her arm inside until her fingers touched a wooden box. She brought it over to her bed, leaving the drawer open. She stared at the box, the corners of her lips slowly turning into a slight smile, as she slowly opened the lid.

"My sweet Rolf, I miss you so much." She brought the photograph close to her face and with her lips she gently kissed the firm paper. The baby boy stared at her with his huge round eyes, his teeth less mouth opened as it lay naked on a snow white blanket. "I miss you so much!" with her trembling hand, she brushed her index finger over the baby's rose pendant necklace. He wore the second half, the other half of the golden rose. "Until we meet again." She returned the photograph back to its wooden box. A feeling of exhaustion entered her mind and body. She kicked her shoes off and brought her feet up on the blanket. She lay down on her side and drew her knees to her chest, sliding both of her palms between her thighs and feeling the warmth of her own flesh. A single tear came out of her eye. She pressed her eyelid against it and let it slid down from her cheek onto her chin, felt it on her neck before the tear forever disappeared into the cotton fabric of her pillow.

Edith spent many years fighting her urge every day not to go back to her past. Usually she succeeded by simple daily tricks, such as occupying her mind by various tasks. Cleaning the house, doing laundry, cooking. But this was tiresome after a while, so she brought on long reading, long walks, talking to neighbors, gardening, volunteering at the pet shelter, until finally her soul found a refugee in music. First, she started listening to opera, and even though she didn't understand Italian, she used her imagination to translate what the beautiful voices sang about. Then she went on to the compositions that were entirely written for the orchestra and its instruments. She loved the freedom that music gave her. She felt secure, unbeatable; her soul long for the harmony and this was a way to achieve the serenity. The only time she felt she lost control and was in her sleep. The helplessness of the night could drive her crazy. That's when the soft touch of Adam came to rescue her, when her own body twitched and turned and screamed, tormented by nightmares of her own mind, of her own past that was an inevitable part of her younger life.

But today was different, not because she gave up, but because the feeling of the past prevailed and demanded to be heard, crawling into her mind, and bones and spreading through her blood and into her veins, pumping faster and with a greater force than ever before, until it reached her heart and locked it with truth of her past.

A tall, broad-shouldered man nervously paced back and forth, around the room, his face covered with a white mask, his hair hidden under a white cap, his eyes large, intensely blue and round. Edith tried to look for answers in them, but all she could feel was a tremendous pain in her lower abdomen. The man suddenly leaned closely above her bed and she heard his fast paced breath, before he dissolved into a blur and doubled in her vision. Where there two men with her? She tried to say something, but she could not pronounce the words that had left her mouth.

"Oxygen," one of the two blurred men said.

"Quick, I'm losing her," the other replied.

A devilish insane laughter came through the door. She woke up. Her heart pumping blood fast she gasped for air. Edith being a strong woman didn't like moments where she could not control her thoughts, as if in the sleep her own mind betrayed her and showed her who has the power over her and over her life. She started going to bed later and later and sleeping fewer hours than ever before, as soon as she realized her nightmares will most likely stay with her until the day she takes her last breath. Sometimes she had dreams of slowly suffocating, with an oxygen cutting her airways, leaving her, leading her and letting her to a slow agonizing death. After that she would wake up, eagerly taking as much air into her lungs as she could. The way out of this misery was her music, her husband, and Margot. She loved that girl since the first day Adam introduced the two of them. Years later, Edith told Margot, "I long for the music. It makes my days brighter, richer and happier. It makes everything around me more vibrant and alive, the colors I see are brighter and they exist in whole, not just as a color, but as an entity, that tells its own story. Music helps me heal, whenever

I feel down, it never betrays me. It doesn't talk back; it's not deceitful or greedy."

Margot had inner scars when she met Edith. Although two years had passed since her mother died, the little seven year old girl still grieved and Edith had her own pain, deep inside, and so it was nearly effortless the two women found a common ground, a language that bond them together, like mother and her child, a friend to a friend, they trusted one another, they confined into each other. Edith helped Margot to get through the puberty with a dignity and confidence, she never bashed Margot's boyfriends, nor she told her the world will have enemies, and once she grows up, she'll have to face her nemesis. Edith lived in a moment and the same she thought Margot. She let her to learn how to forgive, but not forget. That was the hardest thing Margot had to overcome as a child let behind, when her own birth mother died of cancer. Margot was mad, furious, angry at her, and could not understand how her mother could leave her to live without her. Edith told her from the beginning, she is not going to replace Grace, but she would do the best and she would always protect her. Margot's dad couldn't be happier and he truly believed he's got the best women in his world. He felt blessed by meeting and having Edith enter into his life. But the woman had secrets.

"Secrets? Everyone has one." Edith replied confidently.

"Yes, but they eventually come out, sooner or later... I told you all of mine!" Adam spread his hands on his hips and shrugged.

"I'm not ready to share mine, though. Not just with you, but with anyone," Edith replied, and her stare spoke million words to Adam's eyes. He never asked her about her secrets ever again.

§

Breathing, something we all living beings and animals do… breath in and out – one can't be without the other – since the moment we were born to the very last moment of our lives, and then the breathing stops and never repeats, our heart never beats again. Not in the same body, not for the same life. And maybe, the soul reincarnates and inhabits another body, in another time, circumstance, and for the purpose to take a first breath again, until the process repeats until the very last lift of the chest of a human being on this earth. It's so simple, and we all do it, without really thinking about it, we take deep breaths, we inhale and exhale. We should be grateful and humble, while we can.

§

When Margot finished high school and was accepted to Seattle College, Edith supported her in everything even though she felt sad Margot won't be living with them anymore. The only way Edith got over the fact that Margot was leaving, was the hope that she would come back after her graduation and work for The Fenwick Press, the same newspaper her father Adam has worked for. That way Edith and Adam would have their Margot close, in the same town, she was born and grew up.

Fenwick spread on the East Coast, alongside the ocean, the big water, that separated Edith's past and connected her to her future in America. But when Margot told her parents she met a guy and she was staying in Seattle, Edith had to overcome yet another of the life's many hurdles. She spent even more time listening to music and taking long walks through the town she liked so much. She liked walking in the rain. Edith maneuvered her rubber boots on the sidewalk, trying not step on earthworms. There were so many of them, their underground holes flooded with the heavy rain, now crawling on the pavement, some very long, stretched out, vertically, some curled up in circles.

The next day, the rain was gone, and the sky lit with the sun, Edith went on a walk, and decided to take the same path, as yesterday. Except today, all those earthworms laid there, scattered across the pavement, dead, their lifeless corpses dried in the sun, being stomped on by people, eaten by birds. A voice from the outside called her name and brought Edith out of her thoughts. She got up from her bed and exited the bedroom. She walked to the front door and saw Adam standing there, flowers in his hand.

"Sorry, I forgot my keys, again," he said apologetically, as Edith looked at the flowers. "These are for you."

She looked at the colorful bouquet of various blooms of roses, gardenias, lilies and carnations. "They are beautiful." She brought the petals to her face. The sweet smell made the corners of her lips turn into a smile. Later at the dinner the vase was the centerpiece of the oval table.

"I miss having Margot around."

"I know. But she is a grown up girl now, and she is doing some important stuff up there in Alaska."

"I wonder," Edith replied in whisper.

§

Margot returned to Wahya Lagoon, just this time she was by herself. She got up early and parked the car at the same spot where Kurt did the last time she visited the lake. She walked through the grass, still covered with morning dew. The loon sat on her nest, the green leaves of water lilies surrounded her floating kingdom, some of them opened with a beautiful single white flower pointing sharply against the broad sky. This was the loons' private island, their oasis, their very own endless serenity. Margot kept quiet, fascinated by the beautiful birds and their piece of precision work, art that stood out on the Wahya Lagoon. She hoped to find their offspring on the water, but the loon still only sat on her eggs.

Margot took a few snapshots then decided to leave the birds to themselves. She wanted to explore the area more, and so she walked around the water's edges. The path had been walked on before, the stables of the grass broken, and interrupted, lay to the sides. She wondered if it was from Kurt and his dog Holton, or perhaps the wildlife. Moose liked to come here and drink from the clear lake, bears did too. With that thought, she shrugged and the fingers of her right hand instinctively touched the bottle of pepper spray in the side pocket of her backpack. Her eyes couldn't get enough of all the colors around her, keeping her a company on her hike adventure through the wilderness ahead of her. The late spring welcomed the various shades of pink, white, blue, purple and red, yellow and green and orange. The nature put on a feast for human eyes.

An ironic thought made its way to her mind. She was grateful she didn't suffer from a pollen allergy, otherwise this place could quickly as beautiful as it is, transform into hell. The beauty can be deceiving, as she leaned her back down and over a full bloom of wild daisies and smelled their centerpiece. The fragrance tickled her nose and made her sneeze. A grey mountain hare with its long, spiked ears popped his head from the grassy field in front of her. Margot with a fast reflex snapped multiple photos of the shy beauty, before it disappeared into its safe habitat.

Happiness stepped into her heart, and released through a cheerful whistle that bounced off the water, trees, flowers, and fields around her. She kept her head up high as she hiked to the cliff.

The wide view opened in front of her and she gazed at the horizon in the far away to the deep salty waters as far as her eye sight reached from left to right she saw nothing, but the ocean. The waves were calm, under the slight spring breeze, the air so clean she spread her arms to the sides like wings and closed her eyes, and inhaled as much as her lungs could absorb at once. She indulged in that very moment, seizing every second of it just for herself, wishing such relentless freedom would last forever.

Margot experienced the happy sensation throughout her body, as it pumped through her blood, into her heart into the very tips of her fingers; she suddenly felt a part of the nature, away from daily hassle, traffic, ringing phones, people's bother. Where she stood, there was no misery, no human tragedy, no crimes or hate. She just existed for in that very moment, in a serenity and harmony with herself and with her own soul. The sunlight glowed over the waters and softly touched the surface, the color reflected and danced into the rhythm of the majestic wide waves, moving them closure to the shore and finally meeting with the white caps that washed over the sandy beach and under the cliff where Margot's bare feet rooted in the grass. A sniffling and snorting sound came from behind and interrupted her. She opened her eyes and slowly turned around. Her feet could not move, frozen with fear she clutched her camera firmly in her right hand. She's never until now came into such a close encounter with the wildlife.

"Think," she reminded herself in her mind, "stay focused."

The male adult moose stood three times taller than a stallion, his head proudly carried a wide set of antlers. If she extended her arm, she could touch the tip of moose's nose; that's how close the male walked behind her back. It seemed as if her vision became absorbed by certain details of the animal ahead of her, and nothing else existed. The moose's eye grew bigger and soon filled the entire space Margot was staring at. She noticed the animal's long, thick eyelashes framing his upper eyelid and curling up toward the sky. The eyes dark and calm and Margot sensed something very beautiful looking in them. She blinked and moved her vision to the moose's long and somewhat oddly shaped skull and his mouth. The jaw, vigorously chewing on twigs, and one, thin branch stuck out of his mouth to the sides, his lips moving, top against the bottom, sideways, uncovering his large teeth for brief moments, Margot's ears listened to the chewing sound, the rhythmic tempo repeated until the moose ate the rest of the twig in his mouth. His brown lips seemed soft and his oval nostrils deeply and loudly inhaled and exhaled, as the moose stood motionless in the staring contest with its new encounter. Margot moved her eyes higher toward his ears. Both of them stood straight up against the sky, she saw tiny hair that grew inside, probably the softest part of the moose's coat. Then one of the ears moved quickly back and forth, trying to get rid of the annoying mosquito that flew too close to moose's head.

The reality set in again, and Margot's vision widened to the sides and she was well aware of the fact, she couldn't take any steps back, because she stood too close to the cliff's edge. The only way for her was to move forward, and she had no idea how long the male moose would stand there. She knew these animals could be stubborn and could stay in one spot for good thirty minutes if they desired.

"Great," she whispered, never taking her eyes off of her companion. And then the mosquito started bothering her, buzzing around her head and ear. She quickly waved her hand in the air. She hit the mosquito with the bridge of her palm and for a second thought the moose laughed at her funny gestures. He sure had the right to do so. She wondered why she no longer felt any fear. Was it normal? Has the spring in Alaska changed her so much already?

"The danger is not the animal; the real danger comes from humans," Kurt said softly, as he approached from the left side.

She turned her head and asked surprisingly, "What are you doing here?"

Instead of answering her, Kurt extended his arm, "Come on. It's time to get out of here."

She walked ahead of him, navigating her feet through the narrow path at the edge of the cliff. Kurt followed behind her until the path widened and they were far away enough from the animal. On the dirt road, right next to Kurt's truck, Holton awaited them, wiggling his tail into circles, dancing with his rear and finally rewarding Margot with one big slobbery kiss on her rosy cheek.

CHAPTER 6

Margot Kept Quiet In The Car; her bare knees slightly bumping into one another as the Land Rover Defender's tires rolled over the rocky surface and down the winding road, until she no longer desired to keep her lips shut.

"Did you follow me to Wahya Lagoon?"

"No," Kurt replied softly, never leaving his eyes off the road ahead of him. Margot tilted her head and looked at him. He had a good looking profile, with high cheekbones, strong and determined chin, and a nose that just fit his face. Kurt nose was quite perfect, Margot immediately thought it wasn't fair, because her nose was slightly cricket to the right, after she fell on a bike and broke it, when she was about seven years old. Two stitches on the bridge of her nose, close to her eyes left a constant reminder of her accident from the youth.

"Then how come you knew, where I was?"

"I didn't."

Margot waited for more, for a longer answer, watching Kurt's lips part then shut again. She estimated he hasn't shaved his face for about a week. His right hand reached down and very close to Margot's knee. She instinctively shied away. She watched him as he moved his leg higher and with a press of his right knee he steered for a brief moment, while his wide hand wrapped around the shift stick and then back on the steering wheel. His left arm and elbow rested casually on the open window. His briefness drove her crazy. Random thoughts filled her mind. She sensed a hint of cute arrogance in his behavior. Was he just playing with her? Did he take her as a city girl who knows nothing about wilderness? Who does Kurt Groeneweg think, he is?!

"I carry a bear spray," she said firmly.

"What?"

"I said, I have a bear spray in my backpack."

"Good for you." He replied and for the first time his blue eyes looked at her.

"Are you making fun of me?" she asked.

"No. I'd never make fun of you. Why would you think that?"

Margot shrugged. "It's very smart of you to carry a spray," he added. They kept quiet for the rest of the bumpy ride. Holton stood up on the back seat, leaving more than half of his body out of the window, his ears flopping into the moving wind and his snout opened with a long, pink, tongue and his jaw jittering under the potholes, smaller and bigger. The dust clouds that lifted under the car's screeching wheels slowly settled back on the road as Margot watched the yellow-grayish dust in the rear view mirror.

When they got to the lower portion of the mountain and onto the paved surface, the Defender suddenly quieted down, and Margot felt her ears pop.

"I can't believe you walked in those cowboy boots all the way up this hill." Kurt said finally, as he stopped the car right next to Margot's parked Jeep.

"I felt like walking. Just wanted to stretch my legs... feel the terrain." Kurt smiled and looked at her shiny, new cowboy boots.

"Sure," he replied, and the corners of his lips curled into a wonderful smile.

Margot stepped out and Holton followed by plunging himself from the back seat and through the open window and onto the dusty road.

"Holton! Get back!" Kurt yelled at his dog, but Holton ran to Margot's Jeep and jumped through the open door onto the driver's seat and then moved over to the passenger's.

Margot laughed. "I've got a new co-pilot."

"Holton!" Kurt yelled again and then he whistled. Margot stood in the open door, curiously looking at her new furry friend, who made himself at home on her Jeep's seat.

"I guess he wants to ride with me," she said finally. She jumped in and shut the door behind her. Kurt waved at her from his car. He started his engine and drove off first, leaving lines of dust in the air behind him.

Margot waited for the air to clear. This time the dust, mostly from Kurt's Defender, didn't settle down on the paved road. Instead, it slowly dissolved in the air in the midday breeze. She stepped on the gas and with her new passenger by her side, drove down to Lingit. She followed Kurt's truck, but once they got where the railroad tracks divided the small seaside town, he drove through the tracks, when the light started flashing and the poles went down right after he got on the other side of the tracks. A long freight train beat loudly against the metal and honked several times. Margot didn't care, she knew where to drop Holton off, and the dog would most likely found his way around the town himself, if he needed to. The large mutt pushed his front paws up and stood up on his back feet and howled at the oncoming train. The conductor blew his whistle twice, as if greeting the dog himself, the loud noise from the whistle echoed and overwhelmed the sound of beating metal wheels of the wagons against the railroad tracks. Sometimes moose kept dangerously to tracks and to avoid any collisions, the conductors always let the whistle blow several times, before entering tunnels, or crossing the roads. The whistle was important not only for people, and their cars, but for the wildlife, that ruled the Alaskan hills, meadows, valleys and prairies. The dog wiggled his tail, and the bushy, long hair brushed over Margot's right shoulder, and even touched her cheek. The train was long; Margot lost her count, just gazing at one fast passing wagon after another. And finally, the last one in the row showed up, and behind it pushed another engine, that's how long and heavy the train was; needing two engines, one up front and one in the very back. The train's wheels passed on tracks and the sound of grinding metal slowly faded into distance, pulling the last wagons of the long freight.

    Margot looked for Kurt's Land Rover, but didn't see it parked in front of his house. She stopped in his driveway and before she could open the passenger door, Holton had already jumped out of the car and ran to the entrance. She knocked on the door and waited. The dog sat behind her feet and waited with her, all the sudden polite and trained. Her fingers pushed the bell and then her knuckles knocked on the door again. There was no sound of Kurt anywhere in or around the house. Margot walked by the wooden gate and opened it.

"Stay here. Okay?" she ordered, and the dog ran inside the closure and sat down.

Margot made sure she shut the wooden gate well and walked back to the entrance. She rang the bell one last time and waited for an answer, lowering her head close to her chin, when something caught her attention. Margot lifted her foot and noticed a bumblebee stuck between the wooden poles.

She bent down and laid her hand next to the bumblebee's wings. "I almost stepped on you." The insect pushed itself and onto the Margot's finger. She felt the slight tingle and smiled. After she got up she placed the bumble onto a bloom of a white rosebush.

"Here go you," she said and watched as the insect happily sniffed inside the rose's yellow pollen beads. As she retrieved her hand, a sleeve of her polo shirt caught onto the thorns. She pushed the sleeve from the bushes, with her left hand, but another thorn slit the top of her skin on her palm. Sharp, piercing pain entered the top of her hand.

"Ouch." Margot looked at her right hand and saw a drop of bright red blood coming out of the tiny wound. "Damnit." She wiped it with her left thumb, but a new bloody drop reappeared on her skin. She looked at all the red, pink and white rose bushes, planted thickly one next to another on both sides of the entrance of Kurt's house. As she was about to leave the door opened.

"W...wait!" the voice behind her ordered.

Margot turned and surprisingly looked at Alfred. "Alfred? I thought that no one was home. I knocked and I rang the bell...I just came to drop off the dog."

"I...I know," Alfred replied, standing motionless in the frame of the entrance door. "Your hand." His eyes looked down at Margot's bloody line that leaked down to her middle finger.

"Oh. That's nothing. I just scratched it on the thorns." She tilted her head to the rose bush next to her shoulder. Alfred took a step back inside and waved at her.

"C...come in!"

Margot hesitated for a second, she looked at her hand and slowly entered the house, quietly closing the door behind her back. She bent her elbow and with the support of her right hand held, so the blood would not drip on the floor. The inside opened into a large living room with high vaulted ceilings. The hard wooden floor was made out of firm, one piece thick logs, and stained into a light brown color. The top of the ceiling had the same logs, long and heavy, that matched the floor. The walls were painted with white color and made a beautiful contrast to the mahogany wood. It was a work of art. Whoever created the beautiful wood floors and beamed ceiling knew he had an eye for an exquisite taste. She followed behind Alfred, but could not help herself and curiously observed the room around her. The place had crystal vases on several mahoganies, round shaped side tables by each of the three large windows. In the clear, hand-cut European vases was placed a single rose. Margot stop as she passed the last vase. She stared at the rose and realized, it was carved out of wood. She suddenly remembered the first time she saw Alfred sitting in front of the grocery store, hands and pants stained by watercolors, wood carvings spread around his feet and on his lap, a knife in his hand and a rose in the other.

"You carved these roses?" she asked breathlessly, and then she added with emphasis, "You carved all of them!" With a quick look she mapped all the vases and all the wooden roses colored in red, yellow, white and orange and purple. Alfred didn't smile at her. He impatiently stood between the living room and the hallway that led to the downstairs bathroom.

"They are all very pretty," she said, but Alfred already disappeared in the hallway. She bent her elbow and with the support of her right hand held, so the blood would not drip on the floor.

"Sit." Alfred pointed at the rim of the bathtub. He opened the first drawer under the sink and took out an antiseptic cleanser, followed by cotton balls and a Neosporin antibiotic cream. He frowned and muttered something under his lips that Margot could not understand. Then he victoriously and with a smile showed her a package full of bandages, followed by scissors. He placed all the items meticulously spaced and lined and looked at them again before he started with the antiseptic liquid and a single cotton ball. Margot kept quiet and let him do his work. He hummed a song that sounded very familiar, but she just couldn't remember the name. She joined and hummed with him, but was off the note or two behind. She broke into a brief loud laughter. Margot finally asked, "What song is that? It's so familiar; I just can't remember the name of it."

Alfred started singing, and his words no longer stammered, he pronounced them clearly and wholly and in German language. Margot was stunned. Her face froze and her eyes glued to Alfred's lips. Her arms got covered with goose pumps and her smile disappeared from her face. She opened her mouth and with a grasp voice, let the lyrics come out, she sang along with Alfred, in German, a lullaby she heard only as a little girl, after her mom died and Edith became her new mother. Edith would sing to her at night, when she awoke from a nightmare, her body covered with sweat and her face wetted from tears.

"Schlaf, Kindche, Schlaf, Im Garten Sind die Schaf. Sei all dei willen Meine Kindche beissen!"

Despite his physical size, height and weight, Alfred had gentle hands. His skin touched hers as he wiped off the blood and applied the antibiotic cream. She watched him as he cut a piece of bandage, a thick piece, that was not necessary, but Alfred wanted it to be like that. He peeled the paper from both side and firmly pressed the bandage onto Margot's hand.

"Thank you," She whispered.

Alfred turned and placed the items in the trash and without looking at her or saying a word he walked out of the bathroom. Margot jumped on her feet and quickly asked, "Alfred. Wait. Who thought you the lullaby?" Alfred didn't stop, nor turned. Margot ran after him and with her left hand she touched his shoulder. He stopped and his big eyes looked into hers.

"M...my mother."

Margot gasped, "Of course, your mother did."

The words echoed in her mind as she left Kurt's house, driving herself to Devil's Cove. Margot needed to seek a place where she would be alone. The ocean's calm waves and subsided wind allowed her to walk on the beach without sensing any danger. Unlike the locals, she didn't believe in the devil, that supposedly occupied the cove and obviously nor did Kurt, since he was the one, the only person, she bumped at when she first discovered this place. But now, he had to return to run his grocery store, no chance of seeing him here. And that was just what she desired at the moment, to be alone, outdoors, on a beach, with an endless Pacific Ocean ahead of her. Even though her eyes stared at the water and her ears heard the waves crashing tirelessly over the shore, her mind prevailed and pushed the German lullaby into her brain. The lyrics reemerged on her tongue as she stared humming the soothing song herself. She pushed her knees to her chin and crossed her ankles. Her arms firmly wrapped around her shins, she rocked her body back and forth in the rhythm of the lullaby, still remembering all the words in the song. The first time she heard it was when she awoken from a terrible nightmare. Her body twisted violently into the mattress and her feet fought the sheet that suffocated her with its heaviness, so that she thought, until she woke up and felt soft hands on her sweaty forehead.

"Mom?" Little Margot whispered through her chapped, dried lips.

"No, dear, it's just me, Edith."

Margot looked at her and pushed her torso up and hugged Edith firmly, wrapping her skinny long arms around Edith's chest.

"Mom," she said again.

Edith started singing a lullaby to her. Her voice soft, and soothing relaxed the little girl, who no longer felt frightened. Margot placed her head into Edith's lap. She closed her eyes and listened to the lullaby. Over the upcoming years Margot learned the words herself. As she grew older, the curious girl had always had one thing on her mind; did Edith have a child of her own? Did she used to sing this lullaby to her own daughter or son? She wanted to ask her stepmother many times, yet Margot never found the guts to do that. Edith Altman, a woman with a past and a secret.

As Margot grew older, she started noticing Edith would write letters, alone in her bedroom, while Adam was at work at The Fenwick Press newspaper. One day, Margot followed her to the post office and overheard the postmaster reading out loud the destination address. Her curious young mind got hungry for more information. Margot knew Edith came from Germany close to the end of World War II, but when asked, Edith always kept her story short, never really wanted to talk about her past. She always said she is not a person of the past, because she is the person of today and of the near future. And that's what appealed to Margot, having the same opinion, feeling the same way. Margot lived every day for that day, never really thinking about her future, *where, when, what ifs*. More than forty years had passed since Edith lived in the States and Margot knew, she herself now had her own secret that she was not ready to share with anyone. Not just yet, until she finds the last puzzle of the human past, that never went away from Edith's and now Margot's lives.

"Alfred knows the same lullaby," she whispered to the Pacific Ocean. She quickly got up and walked back to her Jeep, leaving the Devil's Cove behind and alone, at least for the night.

"*Beauty is in the eye of the beholder,*" Margot typed the first words on to the laptop screen. The cursor impatiently beat behind the quotation mark. She looked at her notes in the diary; her nice, easy to read, handwriting had only a few scratched words on the paper. She meticulously used a fountain black pen for writing, and when she reread her bird observations, she would add notes in blue ink. Usually she didn't need to do rewrites, which saved her a lot of time. Her mind was sharp and once Margot started writing, she set her tone and direction firmly and rarely had to do drastic alterations to her original texts. She looked at her most recent photos she took in color for John's magazine Natural Bird, and continued writing about a pair of trumpeter swans that landed on the sweet water lake. She mentioned the other varieties, such as common loons, mergansers, golden-eye ducks, grebes and scoters.

The seagulls sensed the danger long before it entered the sky above the Wahya Lagoon. What was a seemingly quiet site, transformed into a wild dance in the sky, with seagulls flying low above the island on the water that was occupied by mallard ducks and Canadian geese and their newborns. The seagull's loud screams made other birds aware a much larger predator is coming toward them. Soon, an adult eagle entered the air and flew across and when it got above the island, the seagulls lifted higher and chased after the eagle. Some got very close behind the black feathered tail nearly clawing into it, while others decided the fly above and attack the eagle's head in flight. The big bird seemed not disturbed and kept on its course, never changing speed or height. This didn't fool the white birds of the Alaskan sky as they persistently kept going after the eagle until he flew above the spruce trees and away from the water. Then, the birds returned and landed on the island, some on the water, some flew away and the life for the moment, returned back to the young ones until next time.

The loon that has been nesting on her private island surrounded by water lilies finally succeeded and her time, when she patiently sat on the four eggs produced four cute babies. Mama and her few days old newborns swam in the water and Margot realized their mom was teaching her babies to follow. Swimming up front, she would go straight forward for a few feet. Then she would stop and turn her body and swim back, cautiously watching if every one of her babies follows close behind. Even the littlest one of them all paddled for its life and kept close behind the third, much larger sibling. It was a spectacular site and Margot was grateful for the opportunity to be there at that very moment and capture it on her camera and in her writings.

Later, when she chose to walk around the water, Margot spotted a dead bird on the trail. It lay on the right side, with its eye shut. The black legs stiffed, its left wing partly feathered in orange and black tiny feathers. The belly still bare, with a pink exposed skin, the bird could had been probably a month old. A life unlived. The beauty is in the eye of the beholder, she thought. The newborn looked so beautiful, a perfect head, body and legs. It had it all, until it got either pushed away from the nest, or fell off on its own, or a predator, such as eagle or magpie snatched it and then dropped it to the ground and left it there unattended, for Margot to find. She bent down and picked it up. She looked up and there, above her head saw a nest on a V branch of the cotton ball tree. To her surprise there was a bird in it. An adult, probably the mom of the dead one, now in Margot's palm. The adult bird looked at her and Margot's emotions brought tears to her eyes. Her mind got overwhelmed by the despair and helplessness the mother bird had to experience upon noticing her young one lying dead down below the nest. Margot walked away with fast steps and didn't stop until she got a meadow. Using her bare hands, she dug into the soft ground and made a shallow grave for the bird. Surrounded by clusters of mountain avens that grew recently and opened with yellow centers and white petals proudly pointing toward the sky, Margot dug a small hole and placed the lifeless bird in it. She paused and her right hand fingers brushed over the camera that hanged around her neck. She grabbed it in her hand and focused it on the bird, now resting in his grave. Margot paused again before she snapped quick shots in black and white.

Beauty is in the eye of the beholder, no matter whether it's alive or dead. Sometimes the beauty is immortal, when captured the time stops and keeps it the same way for eternity. She finished the article and attached some photos to it. She kept the one with the dead bird away. An immortal beauty, now quietly resting in piece looked back at her from the digital screen. A repetitive knocking sound got Margot's attention. She stood up and pressed her hands on the desk, leaning her torso forward. The Steller's jay returned and made its presence known by clawing his beak onto the wooden bottom part of the window. Margot went to the kitchen and from the food pantry grabbed two peanut shells. She slowly opened the window and the bird took few steps back, his eyes curiously watching her hand as she expanded it toward his beak. With a quick snatched the blue jay took his reward and flew on a nearby tree branch.

"Welcome back, beauty."

She placed the second shelled peanut on the window panel. Margot was about to call it a day and draw herself a bath when she passed a night stand and with her hip bumped into a book that laid there. A black and white picture of a young woman in her mid twenties, the very same picture she studied few nights ago, fallen down on the floor. Margot grabbed it and slowly whispered to the woman with the golden half-rose pendant around her neck, "I think I found what I was looking for." She placed the photo back between the pages of her book and returned it on the night stand. While the water poured through the antique long faucet in the deep bathtub, Margot stripped her cloths on the floor and peeled off the bandage from her left hand. She stepped in the vanilla-scented bubble bath. The steam built up the room from the hot pouring water.

Then with both of her palm she wiped the water and white foam out of her eyes and leaned back onto the bathtub.

"Secrets. Everyone has one," she muttered under her lips and smiled. "Now I've got two." She added, looking out the window by her side and onto the sandy beach and the restless waters in the near distance.

CHAPTER 7

THE FULL MOON AROSE ON the night sky and moved above the Pacific Ocean, reflecting its image onto the waves, and into the rhythm of the wind that blew over them. Occasional scattered dark clouds of various shapes covered the round pale moon, but never for too long, leaving the upper atmosphere alone. There was enough natural light that the distant satellite provided as Charlotte decided not to turn on her lanterns as she sat in the wooden rocking chair on her front porch. She wrapped herself in an oversized, long, Bohemian silk gypsy scarf, that covered her back and across her breast. The black, red and gold patterns of square shape had decorative fringe on the edges in deep black color. She made a knot up front in the middle of her chest and then reached on a side table for a cigarette and a lighter. She has been an avid tobacco smoker ever since she was a teenage girl. Charlotte deeply inhaled and then exhaled and watched the smoke slowly rise into the open air. She liked to sit alone, and as she got older, she much preferred darkness to the light. But in Alaska, summer meant long days and nights with the midnight sun on the sky. The only time the upper atmosphere would get darker before the summer solstice in the second half of June, were the hours after one to two in the morning. The unobstructed view of the beach and the ocean allowed her a freedom she longed for. Charlotte carelessly let the ash from the burning cigarette fall on the bottom of the porch and next to her shoes. The night was quiet, and the street her house sat on, had no public lights. Her rose bushes were her only company and she indulged in their fragrant blooms as if she took the energy of the plants and used it as her own. They were her friend, but also her enemy, a reminder of the past she could never erased, a past that will be a part of her until her body descends to grave, and six feet under the ground. The roses were her curse and Charlotte Groeneweg knew it better, than anyone else in this world. The beautiful, deceitful flowers and their sharp, long, frequent thorns were her master, while she was just their servant. Charlotte persuaded herself that her younger son Alfred would never leave her, but she had doubts about his older sibling Kurt. The Groeneweg brothers grew up together in this house, and have lived their entire lives in Lingit. Kurt's only reason for staying there to take care of Alfred. Charlotte realized that very early on, but never mentioned it to him. She no longer feared death. Her sixty seven year old mind accepted the inevitable, that one day death will come no matter what. She believed in here and now, and if Heaven and Hell existed, she was only sure of one thing. Her beloved Jack husband waited in Heaven, but may wait for eternity, since Charlotte could enter Hell instead.

And if *here* and *now* is the only thing there is to life, than Charlotte didn't feel scared anymore.

"Death will come no matter what," she said out load to the darkness of the universe that surrounded her. The cuckoo on her living room wall came out and announced it was two o'clock in the morning. Charlotte looked up toward the sky.

"Shall there be light, again," she said ironically and with a hint of a disappointment in her voice. She finished her cigarette and threw the butt in the ashtray on the side table. Her back leaned against the rocking chair, she brought the gypsy scarf closer to her chin and slowly pushed her legs against the porch as she closed her eyes and rocked her body into the slight breeze that picked up through the quiet Alaskan night as she drifted into her sleep.

Young Charlotte nervously paced around her small hospital room, pulling on the strings of the dark purple satin gown. She was alone, surrounded by one iron chair, white sheets, and one simple iron side table that had a lamp with an orange shade on it. The new mother looked out the window and down in the courtyard where doctors with white long coats marched firmly across the concrete path that connected the two buildings. Finally, she walked to her bed and sat down high on her pillow, and covered her bare legs with a blanket. A very young nurse, with slim waist, long skeleton arms and pale skin and shy eyes, brought her a baby wrapped in a white cotton cloth. She placed the baby boy in Charlotte's arms and without a word, quietly left the room. The tiny, pink in color, newborn's face stared at her, a baby boy with big eyes and wide opened mouth demanded her attention, hungry to be fed. She unbuttoned her top and brought her baby's face to her breast. The infant's lips sucked hungrily on the mother's milk, except none came out.

After a repeated struggle Charlotte called the young nurse. She was distress and very upset and her emotions reflected in the infants hysterical, loud cries. The teenage nurse rushed to get the doctor and when he came in to Charlotte's room, he shut the door behind him and left the nurse standing alone in the hospital's hallway. He told her that her baby boy would starve to death if he didn't receive milk soon, and then he continued with harsh news, that Charlotte was unable to breast-feed her offspring. The German Dr. Siegfried Mueller assured her, he would get milk for her boy, even though the world struggled and caved under the pressure of the world war. She didn't ask for details. All the young nurses referred to the mid-age doctor as their *"Doctor Sigi."* She didn't want to know where or how the doctor will manage to feed her baby boy. All she wanted at that very moment was for her boy to live. She became a predator in her mind, a coward in her heart and a determined to step over hurdles in her character. No one was to stop her from having her child to live. She listened as the mid-aged, gray hair Bavarian doctor Mueller leaned closer to her and spoke in whisper, carefully choosing his words. Although she was frightened, she nodded to everything the doctor said on that early morning. In her mind, she imagined another young mother, *a savior,* that would help her newborn. Whether that was the truth, she had no idea.

The doctor took the baby out of her arms, and she instinctively reached back for a brief second before resting her arms and hands crashed in her empty lap. Shattering thunder echoed through the violent sky, crashing in distance and strong lightings with its smaller and bigger sisters by side reflected over the clouds. The moon got a company of angry visitors and hid behind the curtains of darkness that overtook the sky.

Charlotte woke up on her rocking chair, and the reality sunk in with the heavy rain beating hard on the ground, the petals of the roses bending under the pressure of the drops and wind.

"Is this the devil itself? I wonder..." she said bitterly as she got up and walked inside the house. As she passed the living room the cuckoo came out and screamed it was three o'clock in the morning.

"Oh, Halt dein Mund!"

Charlotte lay down in her bed, but couldn't get her mind to calm down. She rolled from side to side, unable to fall asleep, frequently checking her watch on the night stand. The storm outside came fast and unexpected; she didn't remember the forecast calling for it earlier. Used to various weather, that could change quickly; she wasn't surprised the meteorologist didn't foresee it. The ocean roared with high, dangerous waves that beat on the shore. She's seen it many times over the forty years she's lived in Lingit. Always an avid swimmer and runner, never afraid of any sports challenge she welcomed the open land of Alaska the first time she arrived and instantly fell in love with its sparse populations, eventually leading her to this small seaside town.

When she was young, she used to spend all day on the beach with her two boys by her side, building sand castles, digging small pools and constantly fighting the wind when her towels and clothes lifted and were taken by the ever present breeze. Kurt picked up swimming quickly, and didn't mind when the water got cold or if the waves were taller than him. But Alfred was a challenge. Alfred cried a lot, then he would twitch his little hands and form fists and beat into Charlotte's thighs until the flesh of her skin turned bright red. When she placed two inflammable floating sleeves around his arms, he didn't like the pressure that wrapped around his arms and refused to move. When she placed a tube around his waist, he didn't know what to do with it. He would throw it back at her and start a new tantrum. And then she realized, that it wasn't about the water, it wasn't about swimming lessons. It was all about being in the bright hot sun. Her older son Alfred didn't like the heat and didn't like the sun. Charlotte brought over a large umbrella and stuck it in the sand, and Alfred made his happy face, tolerated his tube around his small waist and finally walked down to the water. With the help of his older brother Kurt, Charlotte watched happily as the boy screamed with joy until he tasted the salty water in his mouth and spat it out quickly. When their little bodies shivered from cold and covered in goose bumps, Charlotte called them out of water. Kurt lay in the sun on his towel, while Alfred his from the rays under the umbrella. Those were one of the happiest times at her life; a private beach, a house near the beach and two, free-spirited children.

    A very loud thunder hit nearby her home, and the ground underneath her shook. She got up from her bed and went to the bathroom to drink a glass of water. She walked to her bedroom window and with her free hand moved the curtain. The clouds made the outdoor light dimmed, there were already large paddles in the dirt road and some of her rosebuds lost their pretty petals. The evil unleashed and expanded on the loose, without boundaries taking everything into its possession. Charlotte took a sip of water and set her glass on the coffee table. Her eyes brushed over the picture of her beloved husband Jack.

"Oh, Jack," she sighed. "You knew all about storms, lightning and thunders like this." She opened the curtains fully, freeing the window of the heavy, dark fabric. Charlotte sat down in a deep, old-fashioned armchair, it almost looked as if the armchair hugged her body or she got lost inside, as she stared at the window and out at the rain and listened to the storm. Her mind took her twelve years back, to 1978 a year of the biggest stormy night, except it wasn't in the summer, but in the fall, and the freezing rain and wind and the waves on the unsettled ocean surface where the highest of the season. Since that morning, Charlotte had a bad feeling in her stomach and her guts. She felt uneasy and pleaded with her husband not to go on a fishing boat since the early morning. The sun was out, and the air had a mild, warm wind, a seemingly nice autumn weather, especially for Alaskan coast. She prepared breakfast sandwiches and placed them into a paperback, as usual. He took it, gave her a kiss on a cheek and told her not to worry. Jack was out of the house, and that was the last time she had ever seen him and heard from him. Just like that, her husband vanished into the ocean several hours later. Charlotte walked over to her gramophone and turned on the vinyl record. Soon, the room filled with a chamber orchestra, and she no longer felt alone. After she sat in the armchair, she reached for a box of cigarette and pulled one out. Looking out of the window, Charlotte felt as she was watching a performance of all the evil that unleashed outside. She said crossly, "I'm not afraid anymore." The glass window screeched under the gust of strong wind and pressure, as the music got louder, and drums beat for their life, cellos joined in and trumpets screamed, and then, nothing but a solo piano with slow, deep tones entered the air and every other instrument obeyed and quieted down. The rain outside subsided as if listening to the music of the symphonic orchestra. There was no more competition. No winners and no losers. She felt she was being trapped by life itself that a twisted humor paid her a visit knowing, she wanted something so much for someone, that the only way to get it was to destroy someone else. Charlotte chose to be blind and deaf and not allow the thoughts of the haunted past to bother her. But she hardly prevailed. Oftentimes the moments of her youth, when she lived in Bavaria came back, alive in her mind, except, she knew better, she wasn't imagining anything. No one can erase past. Not even Charlotte Groeneweg. She took the last, long drag out of her cigarette as the black vinyl record finished playing. Charlotte got up; with a swift arm she closed the dark curtains across the window and lay down in her bed. The cuckoo on the living room wall loudly announced four o'clock in the morning. Charlotte finally fell into a deep sleep.

The long and wide hospital hallway was lined with black and white tiles, and its walls were painted with different shades of white and beige and yellow colors, and at times the paint peeled off and underneath was just a red brick that would show through the old paintings.

Young Charlotte thought this was perhaps in her dream, but she wasn't sure. Still in pain, and on drugs, her bare feet walked on the black and white hospital tile. The hallway was wide, and spaces, to fit whatever hospital beds on wheels, wheelchairs, portable tables in it, together with the loud talking doctors and nurses who accompanied them. But now, at night, the hallway was empty and Charlotte was the only patient walking, passing large windows, holding herself onto the scraped painted walls. She stopped and the fingers of her left palm pressed against the uncovered red brick, the prime skeleton of the building that she had occupied for the past week.

She heard a distant voice at the end of the hall. Now, she heard two voices, his and hers, and being drawn to the sound she walked toward the sound. Quietly, almost like a ghost, she stood in the open doorway, staring in amusement at the mid-aged doctor whose back leaned on the wall and whose eyes faced Charlotte's. She remembered when he introduced himself to her, "I'm Dr. Siegfried Mueller. But you can call me doctor Sigi." Dressed in a white, unbuttoned coat, the doctor rolled up his sleeves as the very young, teenage nurse closely whispered into his ear. The doctor laughed, and his thick dark brows scowled. Then his arms wrapped around the nurse's waist as they kissed. Charlotte shied away, not knowing whether the doctor saw her. She rushed back through the cold hospital corridor, holding and leaning onto the wall. And as she was about to enter her room, another nurse, with short black hair, and olive skin, walked out from around the corner, where the hospital wing split into a fork. And just like with the voices before, now she was drawn to see, what another nurse was doing, where did she come from, who did she just take care of, who was that person, how old and in what shape, what was the name of the patient, was the patient alone, struggling or healing? Charlotte moved across the hall and leaned onto the opposite wall as her steps brought her closer to the room, with a cracked door. Slowly and carefully she pushed the door a little bit more so she could see inside. She lifted her heels from the floor and leaned forward with her chest, stretched her neck, and her rosy lips parted as she looked at the young mother on her hospital bed, a newborn in her arms, wrapped in a white cotton blanket, his mother's eyes watching, as the baby boy fed on its mother's milk. His lips so small and pink and very hungry moved into a rhythm. And then the mother lifted her forefinger and the little one instinctively wrapped his two fingers around as he continued feeding. Charlotte, fascinated by the quiet beauty, couldn't but stare at the unknown woman and her child. The mother could have been her age, perhaps two or three years older than her. She had brown, wavy hair that parted on the side, pale, almost perfect complexion, as if her skin was never touched by sun. Charlotte didn't see the baby's face, only the light blue hat, and thought of her own baby boy, perhaps both women delivered on the same day in this hospital. What was his name? His mother didn't know Charlotte's standing and watching them. It seemed as if the two were in their own world, much safer place, than the reality that surrounded them. The war happening around them, yet the mother and the child got spared as if they were inside a magical circle, and the evil was unable to reach and touch them. Charlotte suddenly missed her newborn son and wondered whether he was asleep in the nursery with the rest of the babies and under the nurses' supervision. She missed her gramophone and music and wished she could already go and take her son home with her. But Dr. Sigi told her that the baby needed more time, needed to eat and to gain some strength, and since she couldn't provide milk for her newborn child, they both had to stay in the hospital longer. Suddenly, Charlotte envied the woman in front of her and the feeling of feeding her child, something Charlotte herself would never experience. She shrugged her shoulders and tightened the belt around her silk gown. The dark sky through the hallway window glittered with the North Star. When Charlotte returned to her room, she wide opened the window and for a brief moment her eyes glared at the sky and the moon. Then she shut her eyelids and let her mind play the instruments from her favorite opera, imaging the symphony orchestra in the background, musicians playing their first part opulently and then going into the second, interpreting it quietly, letting the music flow. Charlotte hummed the melody to herself and the alluring, quiet, dark night was a pretense to the reality the world lived in. Charlotte shifted on wooden chair that had with uneven legs, her elbow carelessly leaned out of the window. She lifted her head slowly up toward the sky and her eyes came to life once again glaring up high at the universe. Charlotte's passionate soul still frightened by the new status of motherhood fought an inner battle of the future yet unrevealed and stained by the uncertainty of war. The world caved and rushed under the pressure of guns, bombs, planes and the ever-present smell of death and fear. She whispered with a coarse voice out the window and into the wide open space, "What lies ahead of us?" Her face stiffened as she arose from the chair and moved to her bed. She pressed her head against the pillow and one last time looked at the North Star, while folding her hands on her stomach, Charlotte then shut her eyes and her mind and dreamed and wished for a better, safer place for her and her newborn son.

The restless night and the loud thunders woke Charlotte up. At first she didn't know where she was. She looked at her hands, now covered with dark spots from aging and placed them on her face.

"Oh, God," she gasped, while another thunder echoed in the distance. She brought her blanket closer to her chin as if she wanted to hide, like a child. A deep sleep came fast, but didn't give her any break, her mind could not seek any piece, during a day or at night, and now, her memory took her once again into her past, into Europe, into her youth and into her deepest burden. Charlotte stood in the bedroom of her suburban house, her eyes darting from the four soldiers to her husband who sat on the bed in front of her.

"What are you doing, Klaus? They can't stay here!"

"They have nowhere to go. They can hide here, and wait until it's safe outside, then they'll leave." Kurt said with a lowered voice.

The four, skinny and frightened, young soldiers with big, hungry eyes and unshaven faces sat in the living room, not saying a word, their hands marked with scars, and dried blood, their muddy boots now staining the carpets at Charlotte's house. Klaus took Charlotte's hand pressed it between his hands. "Charlotte, please. Please, let them stay," he pleaded with his wife, while holding onto her soft palm. She paused, and looked at him, and then she raised her chin and glanced over the four new souls that entered her life, unexpectedly, and without a warning.

She took a deep breath, and then she replied firmly, "Okay. Okay they can stay."

Klaus brought her hand to his lips and kissed it, "Thank you," he said.

The same night Charlotte prepared dinner for five men, four of whom she saw for the first time and didn't even know what their names were. They offered to introduce themselves to her, but she refused. This way she felt in the instance of something happening, she never has to connect a name to a face, and perhaps the face will fade away, with less of a pain, after all, they all were living through hell already. A single lit white candle stood in the middle of the oval, dark wooden table, with a polished top, a handmade crochet decorated the center and the candle in its holder provided a dimmed light. Heavy curtains precisely shut against the windows. An occasional scrape of a fork or a knife against the china plate, a sound of glass being placed back on the table, the five men and one woman ate quietly, six hearts beating behind the table, in the farm house close to Holland in late September 1943. Klaus Groeneweg was first to break the silence. He spoke calmly, with soft tones in his voice, the words pronounced in Dutch, and then first smiles appeared on the weathered faces of the four soldiers, and even Charlotte's lips curled up in a smile and then more voices mixed in the air, as she looked around, happy for her husband, speaking in his native Dutch with the soldiers from Holland, a brief moment of normalcy and happiness. They opened the door, and kindness stepped in together with humanity and their souls intertwined, and even the hands of the youngest, the most terrified soldier stopped shaking, all they lived for this moment, even though the moment may not last forever.

And then the devil came in and told them a lie that they would live, under one condition; Klaus let all the soldiers go and they all would live and nothing would happen. The only thing Klaus had to do is to gather his horses and a carriage, and take the Dutch soldiers on the road, and into the woods. And Klaus refused, knowing it was a lie. And then the Satan pleaded one more time, and said he would spare his life for the lives of the soldiers, he would spare his wife's life, too, if he obeyed, he would let them go free. And Klaus refused again. The German troops took the men onto the Klaus's carriage, driven by Klaus's two horses he lead the way up the road, and into the woods, where death awaited all of them. The Germans first fired at the four Dutch men, and one by one fell down, the noise from the bullet roaring through the forest, birds flew in the air and away, because they could. And Kurt saw the birds and the sky for the last time in his life, before a bullet came for him and killed him, sending his body down on the soft, green moss, by the large tree. The devil spared Charlotte's life, and left her alive and with an unborn child. She moved from the western part of Germany to east and settled in Bavaria region, and stayed with her friend, until the time came for the baby to be delivered. And then her baby was hungry and she could not provide for him, and when the nice doctor came by and told her, he can help her baby, she was grateful to him and Charlotte agreed, not asking any questions. Little she knew, that the devil made himself reappear once again, and certainly not for the last time. Charlotte's face twitched in her sleep, as she turned on her bed, the sheet tangled between her legs. The dreams of her past paid her a visit again, and made her memories so fresh, deliberately wanting her to relive her past. Was this barbarian evil forever embedded in her life?

CHAPTER 8

THE CRASHING LIGHTNING FROM THE night storm caused fire on the hill behind Lingit, flames glaring high, the fireman engines honking and rushing to get it under control. The wind blew over the town and the smoke of burned wood spread across and people shut their windows and doors. Some had respiratory problems and called ambulances to their homes. Kurt ordered Alfred to stay inside and watch the dog, while he ran to his car and drove to the burning site. Four fire engines parked on the dirt road, hoses rolled down on the ground, and firemen working fast in effort to seize the fire and minimize the damage. One of the crew members spotted Kurt and yelled at him, "Get to work!" Kurt put on a protective gear and grabbed a hose and followed behind the fireman. The light from the flames was diabolic, the heat was enormous, the intensity of the fire scorching the spruce forest with such a force, simply astonishing. About thirty men and volunteers bravely fought the fire that sparked overnight by lightning storms. Although the wildfire didn't threatened their residences, the firemen worked timelessly to seize the dazzling flames, with hoses snaked across the ground tons of water splashing toward the hot, golden force One of the local onlookers unexpectedly ran too close to the fires, and a tall, burly fireman shouted loudly at him, "No, don't go in there! It's unsafe for you…it's unsafe for us!" While other two men jumped forward and grabbed the silly, old man and pulled him to the side and away from the burning hell. The horse-voiced, man shambled around, still showing his fearlessness until he was finally restrained by another two, burly men. Kurt looked at him and he could swear he saw the burning flames reflecting from the mad man's eyes. The fire he plunged against was already inside him. He had a huge head full of long curls, that fallen on his back, over his shoulder blades. He was short in statue, skinny and wild. His bare arms had colorful tattoos that at first sight didn't make any sense. Kurt smiled and thought for himself that the man's tattoos were probably like that on purpose. Kurt knew him; his real family name was William Clash, the wacky man lived an estranged life, alone, in the woods. William would never cause a fire, if that's what some people may think. His face red from the sun, marked by several deep, long wrinkles on his forehead, with crow-feet around his large eyes, and thick lips. He moved quickly on his feet, despite his limp in his left foot a self-inflicted injury with his own gun, when he was in a high haze of drunken oblivion a few years back; a jolly, dissolute maniac.

So what was so special about him? When he was younger, he made himself known as the first bore tide kite rider in and around Lingit. His home-made board was a work of perfection, and he spent many hours polishing it, constantly improving it, until he was satisfied and finally took it out on the ocean.

There, in the salty waters, he waited for the first tide of the evening, called Bore tide to come so he could ride it. Timing was everything, together with the right wind, William Clash mastered the wave and rode it for as long as one's eye could see. On that day, he got a nickname *Leaf*. Because just like a leaf, that falls into water, never really dives, never sinks under the water. Leaf glided with an ease to the evening sun. A local legend got also admirers from the tourists who came to see him, spectators gathered on the sandy beach, and waited for the water to slowly fill in, followed by the white cap of the first, and the most important wave, the Bore tide.

After a while, the firemen contained the fire, and the black smoke in the air slowly arose and mixed with the white smoke after the fire was finally gone. The men's faces covered in black ash, with bright, white smile cheered as they retrieved their hoses back and returned to the firemen's trucks. On-lookers turned headed back home, some in their cars, some on their bikes, mopeds and motorcycles.

Kurt wiped his sweaty forehead leaving a black smudge across his face. He walked over to Leaf, to make sure, the legendary Bore tide rider is okay.

"Leaf! Wait up, man!" Kurt yelled, but Leaf kept going through the smoky, burnt grass and brushes. Kurt ran to catch up with him.

"Hey!" he finally tapped his hand onto Leaf's shoulder. "Where are you going?"

"I gotta safe the wolves," Leaf replied and then he added with emphasis, "The mother left them in their den. I know it. I know, she did…"

Kurt tilted his head and glanced over the direction Leaf was looking at.

"Where...where is the den? Show me."

Fearing the worst, Kurt followed Leaf, lifting his legs over and across the wetted, burned area, the smoky smell tickling his nose and throat; he covered his mouth with his left hand for a moment as they passed the worst, and headed into to woods. He admired Leaf's persistence, his will not to give up, to keep going on, now he understood, why Leaf threw himself against the flames earlier. He had a reason. Leaf wasn't a maniac, as others thought of him. He had a goal to move to, to safe puppy wolves. Leaf simply had a plan, and he was stopped by the firemen.

At that moment he didn't see clearly, he could endanger himself. Leaf didn't think of himself, he thought of the animals hiding in their den. There weren't many people like the free-spirited, hippy bore tide legend. Kurt thought of how everyone he knows always wants something. One person demands something from another, people doing favors to others for another favor.

But Leaf was different. He had a pure soul, he didn't make demands on others, he didn't ask for favors, he just existed, in his own world, as if his inner spirit was untouched by human greed, vanity, violence...Leaf existed in his time, in his day and at his night, just for the purpose of inhaling air through his lungs, eating, looking at the flowers to bloom in the spring, chasing the waves during the short Alaskan summer, and picking mushrooms for the winter, he walked around and cut the grass, then let it dry in the sun and collect it later, just to walked in snowshoes and carry the hey in a large cotton blanket on his back through the woods, and place it in feeders he had built himself. Leaf did it for the animals, and he did it because he wanted, because his own heart blended with them, with the mountains, grass, lakes and the ocean. The hippie made his heart open and didn't want to be tight up by boundaries. Leaf didn't request or demand anything from the society, from others, to be like him. He made his conscious decision himself, and that was the life he chose. And then he signed up and fought in Vietnam War, and it broke his free spirit and when he returned, he no longer believed in humanity and kindness, he started drinking, and a bottle of liquor became his friend and his biggest enemy. Kurt was the one who came to help him Leaf at his weakest moments, and took care of his fragile body, his wounded leg.

One day when Leaf sobered up, he asked Kurt, "What do you want from me? What do you want me to do now?"

Kurt replied, "I want you to become Leaf again. That's all I want from you."

Leaf lifted his head, took Kurt's hand into his, and asked, "I don't have to do anything for you? No one I know does things because they don't want anything from you…"

"It was William Clash, it was Bob, who went to Vietnam, and whose spirit got broken. I want Leaf to come back to Lingit, I want to see Leaf surfing his kite and riding the Bore tide. I want Leaf to come back, because I believe, he's still here. Leaf never left you. And only you can bring him back."

And now the two men stood past the area, where they defeated the flames. Leaf went down on his knees, his hands buried in the soft, wetted moss; he stretched his torso and his neck and cautiously looked inside the den's opening. Kurt waited, quietly watching and listening for some noise, but he heard none. Finally Leaf stood up and his face broke into a victorious smile. His head nodded and his body turned toward the den, Leaf pointed his arm and his forefinger lifted in the air and then he suddenly hugged Kurt and let out a loud laugh. *"The puppies are alive!"*

"They are in the den?" Kurt asked.

"They sure are, sir!" Leaf let go off the hug.

Kurt instinctively bent down and wanted to reach and take the pups out, but Leaf abruptly stopped him.

"No!" He placed his hand on Kurt's shoulder. "Don't touch them."

"Why not?"

"The mother wolf would smell you on her puppies, and she could reject them."

"Oh, I guess, I just didn't think about that," Kurt said apologetically, and then he quickly added with emphasis, "But how do we know if the puppies are all right?"

And then a growl came from a close distance. The female grey wolf stood on her long legs, with her head lowered down. She showed her white sharp teeth, and her nose wrinkled, and her pink gums showed. The wolf's yellow eyes intensely watched Kurt and Leaf, and her hair on her back lifted in a mohawk. She very slowly placed her right front paw ahead, and growled again, this time, a spatter of saliva hanged down on the side of her lips.

"Don't let her know your fear," Leaf whispered. Both men slowly backed up away from the wolf's den, keeping their eyes on the wild predator.

Kurt saw the happiness in Leaf's eyes. His face lifted in brightness of the moment, that the pups didn't get harmed in the forest fire and that the mother returned back and her family reunited. That little made Leaf's life happy, and the concern washed away from his face in an instance. Kurt wished to be at least a bit like his friend, to have the ability to find the beauty and harmony in the simplest things, whether they are directly connected to him, or if they come from another source, the nature, or the animals around him. Kurt has yet, but not mastered this, and hoped that one day, he can see the world through Leaf's eyes, even though if it meant to be for a brief moment. It's easy to talk badly about someone. It's also more common to do so. To say something nice, to encourage, to believe and to have someone else say something positive about another person, that is a real courage. But to be whole, the courage needs to have a character. And this can't be thought, nor can it be forced. It needs to come out naturally and the person has to mean it.

"The pups are very lucky, to have you," Kurt said.

"Yeah, Leaf would never leave them. Ever." Leaf smiled.

Kurt offered to give Leaf a ride back to his log cabin, but Leaf politely refused, saying he'd rather walk. The men parted and Kurt undressed from the fire gear and headed back to his house, to take a shower. The burnt smell persisted as he drove with all of his windows down, back to Lingit. The open, empty road led alongside the seacoast. Kurt leaned back to seat and let the right foot down, pressing harder on the gas paddle, as his Defender sped up on the open road ahead of him.

Leaf was much stronger on the inside than anyone Kurt has ever known. It took a big man to do and decide to deliberately remove himself from the world that is now ruled by social status, job, what one has. That kind of liberation must come from within. It cannot be bought or thought or bargained. It's a one man's decision. Kurt had ties. And the ties bound to an angler that lay in the deepest waters, surrounded by bottom sea sand, and darkness. He couldn't leave Charlotte not now, perhaps never, after his father Jack died, Kurt had to step in. And he knew well, he certainly couldn't abandon Alfred.

Yet he yearned in his heart that there is more to life, there is more than just life in Lingit. Perhaps the biggest difference between him and Leaf was the fact that Leaf would not want to live anywhere else in the world. But Kurt, on the other hand, could see himself elsewhere, and for some reason, maybe the reason was as simple as his mother's European background, he felt his life could be on the old continent. A fresh start, he longed for. Yet there was so little he knew about Charlotte's life before she came to America. Never fond of talking about herself, Kurt didn't have many stories, to put together of his mother's youth. He knew she came from Germany, escaping war, she explained she wanted to go as far as possible and so the last frontier seemed the right place. She said there were no grandparents or brothers or sisters. Charlotte wanted to let her knew friends know, there was no one she left behind. She wanted to start a new life, and she got a chance and she took it. There was nothing no-one would question.

A yearling black bear that charged from the bushes and onto the road made Kurt suddenly step on his brakes. The tires screeched against the black tart as his torso moved forward. The black bear looked up and his yes met with the animals for a split second before the bear rushed across the street and disappeared between the green foliage. Kurt let out a deep sigh and with his left hand he pulled on the tight seatbelt that pinned him down back to the seat. He leaned his left elbow out the window and stepped on gas. His restless mind didn't want to let him relax, not even for the upcoming night. As he approached the house on the hill that Margot had rented for the summer his right hand sharply steered to the left and onto the dirt road that led up the hill. He drove up slowly, didn't want the engine to rumble, and he turned off the lights. Kurt sat in the car, staring at the log house in front of him. The fingers of his left hand hanged out casually out the window, as he tapped them into the rhythm on the door next to the handle outside. He looked at his face in the rear mirror. His skin still covered with black smudges from the fire, stared back at him, his cloths gave out a burnt odor. Kurt was about to start the engine, when the living room window opened and he saw Margot placing something onto the window panel. She didn't notice him, since she never raised her head, and quickly shut the window. As if on cue, a Steller's jay flew down and picked up the peanut's nutshell in its beak. Kurt's face broke into a wide smile, and uncovered his white teeth.

"Mr. Casey's blue jay!" he said out loud to himself. "I'll be damned." He started the car and drove off. Kurt couldn't believe the bird still stayed in the area. The person who owned the house, old Mr. Casey, moved out to *America*, to lower forty-eight, as the Alaskans often referred to the rest of the United States where his daughter lived in Arizona, so she could take care of her aging father. The house on the hill overlooking the Pacific Ocean stayed fully furnished and now rented by Margot herself. The bird, a leftover from Mr. Casey's days, stayed loyal to the place that saved his life, when Mr. Casey found him lying on the ground, and out of its nest. The mother fled the nest, and so there was no point returning the young one back up to the tree crown. Instead, Mr. Casey took the bird to his house, where the half-feathered young bird stayed, being cared for and fed every two to three hours by the old man. Mr. Casey kept sugar cubes that he iced in his freezer, and placed it one by one to the cage for the bird. When the time had come, and the bird developed full wings, and beautiful black and blue feathers, Mr. Casey released him back to the nature, hoping that one day, the bird would find love of his own, in his variety, but the blue jay stayed nearby, and nested on the nearest tree, where he watched Mr. Casey. And so the relationship between the old and the one, a human and an animal continued, and Mr. Casey drove to town to pick up a bag of unsalted shelled peanuts. Every day the Steller's jay came, flying low and landing onto Mr. Casey's palm to pick up a shelled nut and bring it on a tree branch, where he would crack it with his beak and eat it. Mr. Casey fed him every day, and when the time came, and the old man was moving to live with his daughter in Arizona, he cried and whispered to his feathered friend, "I have to go, but you stay here. This is your home; it'll always be your home."

Kurt knew all about the special relationship, because Mr. Casey shopped at his store, and always came down for a good chat. The bird stayed, and found a new friend, at least for now, for this summer. Kurt headed home, looking forward to get out of his dirty clothes and to take a shower. Alfred was waiting for him curiously to hear the news about the fire. Kurt looked forward to give him the good news, and to tell him about Leaf and the wolf puppies. He once again, he pressed his foot down, and sped up on the wide open road.

The next day, the images of fire trucks, firemen and water splashing over the trees, filled out the front pages of the Lingit News, as Margot poured herself a fresh cup of black coffee in a wide-mouth deep jug and carried both the newspaper and coffee to the garden table on the outdoor patio. The warm breeze came up from the ocean, and the sound of flying seagulls echoed through the late June's air. Margot's lips dipped into the black liquid, as she her eyes gazed over the fiery images on the paper. Another image showed spruce tree ignited in flames, torching and crowning the trees around it.

Fire crews gain, but the threats remain read the main headline. Underneath was a colorful photo of a single firefighter with a hose, working to mop up a section of the forest, just after the flames were killed. Margot reached for a toast, and took a bite. As she chewed the piece in her mouth, she brought the paper closer to her eyes and muttered to herself, "Kurt...That's definitely Kurt Groeneweg." She returned the paper on the table and placed a plate on the top, to prevent it from flying away in the summer breeze. Taking another sip of her coffee, she looked toward the waves in the distance. "This guy is everywhere...," she whispered to the ocean.

Margot's curiosity returned back to the newspaper as she continued reading.

...The wildfire sparked by lightning the night that it happened... The fire crew managed to put it down...no damage to the civilians

and their properties. The city has banned the upcoming July the 4ᵗʰ fireworks... Margot continued reading a quote of one of the firefighters, "Once you get a fire that is torching and crowning, that's the danger, because it quickly jumps from one tree to the next."

The wild animals most likely fled before the fire spread, as their instinct kicked in, was the last sentence of the report.

"Thank God." Charlotte put the papers on her lap and finished her toast and coffee. She stayed seated and tilted her head toward the Pacific Ocean, closing her eyes, listened to the waves and the breeze and the seagulls. There was no place she would ever want to be at that moment. Grateful, she doesn't have to look at other people, overhear their contestation, or see other houses and cars. At this house, where it was built, she felt she was as far away from the civilization, as possible. Except, the road let right behind it, and could take her to town in minutes. Margot let herself be carried away with the sounds of nature, freeing her spirit on that sunny morning. She relaxed her mind, and brought her feet up on the second empty chair by the table.

§

She must have fallen asleep, because when she opened her eyes and looked at her wrist watch, both of the hands were lined up in the middle, and over the number twelve. She let out a deep sigh, and her thoughts took her to Alfred and the German lullaby she heard him singing. Margot couldn't get it out of her head, and instead of asking Kurt, his older brother, she decided to go and visit Charlotte Groeneweg.

Margot went to the old fashioned telephone with the circular dial; she placed her index finger through each opening and turned the dial around until she finished the eleven digit number. To call out of Alaska required dialing not only the ten digit number with the area code but also a *one* for the United States. Margot smiled thinking she didn't know it the first time she called her mother and father, frustrated at the busy tone and the automated voice teller announcing that the number she dialed is incorrect.

A soft voice answered on the other side of the receiver. "Hello, this is Edith?"

"Hi Mom." Margot lips curled up and two dimples showed on her cheeks.

"Margot! It's so good to hear you. How are you?"

"Fine."

"Is everything going all right in the land of the last frontier?"

"Yes, Mom, things are good here. How are you and how is dad?"

"Dad's drawing right now. He's all cooped up in his room." Edith paused for a few seconds, before she add jokingly, "Isn't he always drawing something?"

"Yes, I guess he is."

"Mom?"

"What is it, Margot?"

A long pause entered the line between the women. Should she tell her mother why she picked this town, what really let her to visit such a remote place, all the way across the States?

"Margot?"

"I just wanted to hear your voice. It gets lonely here. I guess I'm so used to a city rush that sometimes I don't know what to do with myself." Margot hoped she sounded sincere. She was never a good liar. Both women, each with a telephone receiver by her ear, the younger one standing in the kitchen, with her back leaning onto the wall, looking out the open French door into the blue ocean, the strands of her red hair moving into the breeze, the older woman sitting down in an armchair, the fingers of her left hand restlessly pressing onto the golden pendant on her neck, with her forefinger and thumb consciously feeling the raised rose on the round plate of gold.

"Margot, my dear, you have my mint permission to do whatever you desire."

"Thank you, Mom. I love you."

"I know you do." Edith replied quickly and then hung up.

Margot snatched the black and white photograph of the young woman, wearing a pendant necklace and reached for the car keys on the wall table next to the house entrance. As she took steps down the large natural rocks laid out as a path to her car, she felt a tug underneath her feet that almost brought her down on her knees. Her heart started racing, and her mind counted the seconds, hoping for a sudden stop. This was Margot's first real earthquake.

"Oh shit!" she looked up against the sky, her mind racing; one quick thought after another made itself loud, get out of the house.

I'm out of the house! Margot's mind screamed back. *You are out in the open. Damn right, I am.* There are no electrical wires above your head. Thirty-three seconds, thirty-four, Margot continued counting, and then just like that, the ground stopped shaking. She looked up, and whispered out to the universe above her, "Thank you."

Her legs still trembling, she sat in the car and drove off. Being from the East Coast, she wasn't used to nor was she prepared for the ground to shake unexpectedly underneath her. But she chose to travel to Alaska, and Margot knew that something like this could happen. She just wished it won't happen for a very long time again, at least not, while she is there. Out the open window her eyes overlooked the powerful ocean. She thought of tsunami and her stomach turned sour and goosebumps appeared on her arms. Margot shrugged her shoulders and step on the gas.

She parked her car in front of Kurt's grocery store and walked inside to use the internet.

"Having trouble to get online in your beach house?" She recognized his voice behind her back.

"No. Just came to town, and thought I would check my email."

Kurt smiled and showed her to the computer room. A separate room, but joined to the store, that had five computers. "It's only busy during the summer season."

Margot looked around and replied, "I see that." Four out of five computers were occupied by tourists. She sat down and her finger typed for the recent seismic activity. While waiting for the site to download, her fingers impatiently beat onto the desk.

"6.3?" she read the number out loud.

Kurt leaned over her shoulder and replied, "Yeah, it was a good one!"

"What? Are you serious?"

"Yeah." He leaned even closer and she could feel his closeness to her. He read the headline, "64 miles in depth, 25 miles away from Lingit." He looked at the map next to the text.

"It's by the Haynes volcano."

Margot was shocked, but wanted to hide it. "Is the volcano still active?"

"Is it active?" Kurt repeated and the tone of his voice showed amusement. "Well, let's see…" He said and bit his lower lip. His eyes looked directly into Margot's. "…the last time the Haynes volcano erupted was about 3000 years ago."

"Oh. So it's not active!" Margot replied with relieved.

"Umm, it's called stratovolcano…"

"What's that mean?"

"It means, that the volcano is built up lava and ash…It means that stratovolcano is the most deadly of the volcano types."

"So it's a ticking time bomb!?"

Kurt shook his head and with a soft voice replied, "Look, no one really knows when it can become active again. But one can't live every day in fear of what if.."

Margot looked into his piercing blue eyes. "I know," she said quietly. "I don't think I've experienced so much commotion in such a short time my entire life. Wildfire, earthquake, I just hope the nature will be kind for a while now."

Kurt laughed as he glanced over at the several tourists, furiously typing their messages on their emails. "Welcome to Alaska." he replied casually. "You came here to write about birds, now you can add on to your journals."

Alfred showed up and nervously paced until Kurt went over to him.

"What's wrong?"

"M...mother."

"Of course...our mother." Kurt looked at Margot. He winked at her and exited the coffee room.

She overheard him ask his younger brother, if he needed to go to Charlotte's house. What an opportunity to see, where Mrs. Groeneweg lives, Margot thought immediately. She logged out and grabbed her purse and rushed out the store, noticing Alfred standing behind the cash register, while Kurt's car peeled off the pavement up front.

CHAPTER 9

THE HOUSE SAT ON A WIDE piece of land, at the outskirts of Lingit. The paved road ended with the last public street lamp, and then the surface changed to natural rock and dirt and narrowed up on the hill, with two curves. On the top behind the tall brushy grass, stood Charlotte's house.

Soft, light rain, almost invisible to the naked eye, brought the smell of the wild rosebuds alive, as Margot passed their deep pink-purple colored blooms alongside the back of the house. The two-story building had dark wooded shingles on each side, and large, many large, three folded windows on the top floor. The bottom had one oversized piece of glass, probably leading from the living room, she thought. Attached to the property laid a spaces garden. Green plants of dill already measured about two feet up in the air and half foot to the sides. Next to it were planted basil, parsley, and in the second row what looked like leaves of yellow and perhaps green zucchini. By the fence the young piece tried to climb and carry its products and finally on the sunniest spot, right by the wall, undoubtedly the warmest one from the entire vegetable garden, were metal round circles, of three stacks one above another and green plants that rooted through them. Margot recognized them as tomato plants. Shasta daisies with their huge, white petals and yellow centerpiece and tall green stems reaching up to five feet tall spread across the other side of the garden. Margot quietly passed over to the front of the house, aware of the danger, Kurt or his mother may see her lurking outside. What would she answer them? Why did she come over, why did she follow Kurt? As these questions filled up her mind, her eyes saw the majestic, enormously rich rose plants that overtook the entire front side of the house and porch. There were blooms of bright red, and dark red colors, white, and yellow and pink and orange. Margot's heart sank, because she realized she knew the reason for Charlotte's obsession. She hesitated whether she should tell the only person, who was directly connected to the roses. She lowered her hat, her hair neatly hid underneath it, and her face covered with large dark sunglasses. Thinking she achieved a typical look of a tourist, who does not want to get sunburned or recognized, or photographed, she passed the front of the house, as her nose caught a very sweet, inviting smell of homemade meal.

"Yummy," she said to herself, as her stomach grouched and her saliva longed for the familiar food. The smell of cooked potatoes and dill, mixed with the meatballs, brought over memories of Edith and her Sunday's lunches. A very good cook, Edith knew how to add just the right amount of cumin seeds to the sauerkraut and always remembered to mix in the caper sauce for the meatballs. But it was the sweet aroma of the dill that made her potatoes so tasty. For a brief moment, Margot almost forgot that she no longer was at her home with her father and her mother, but that she tried to be unrecognized in quest of finding the missing pieces of puzzle the main reason, why she came to this small town. The more she saw, the more she learned the more she was sure, she made the right decision to come to Lingit. As she passed the fence, she saw a woman in the window. Could she see her? There was no one walking outside, certainly not past the Groeneweg's house. This place truly sat on the outskirt of town, the opposite direction from Margot's rented cottage. She shied away and stared on the dirt and rock road when she quickly marched to her car. The words of her father echoed through her ears, *secrets, everyone has one. What's yours?*

 She drove slowly; there was really nowhere to rush. The road was wide open, with the ocean on the left and the mountains on the right. Margot took her hat off and sat it on the passenger seat next to her, and rolled down the windows. Should she call Edith and let her know she had found for what she was looking for, or should she wait, for a different time to let her secret out. And is there such a time, a better time? And what does it even mean, if anything at all? She crossed the railroad tracks, feeling the shocks of her car going over the iron rails. The road split into a fork, and she steered sharp to the right, taking a way she never took before, and kept on driving. Her restless mind persisted on, pushing one thought after another, shouting over her inner voice. The car's engine roared and downshifted, as the tires climbed up a steep narrow path. There were no road signs, no mailboxes, no electrical wires, just a road, tall grass, trees, and yet Margot still stubbornly persisted on getting up the hill. If there is a road there must be something. So what's up there, where does this down beaten path lead to? She liked to explore, her adventures soul pushed her forward her whole life. One of the reasons why she got to Lingit, and another, that tied her adventure with the past of the Edith, her stepmother. An unexpected, unplanned and unimaginable truth that hid behind it, yet, Margot wasn't scared. She didn't confine in Edith, because she was afraid her stepmother's mind would stop her from going further. *Don't wake up the sleeping dog*, she would most likely say.

The top of the mountain opened up to a spectacular view. She stopped the car and walked outside. The air temperature dropped and the breeze got stronger, but she didn't mind. A perfect place for a lighthouse, or somebody's house, she thought. Margot felt she was standing on the top of the world, her eyes gazing at the deep, wide, endless ocean, and the tiny town, with scattered houses down below, and the mountains behind, tall, steep and rocky. She spread her arms to the side, tilted her head back and shut her eyes. The electrifying energy went through her body, the sound of the wind and waves brought on a liberating feeling. Her mind finally came to rest, as joy entered her body and she felt a tingling sensation all the way to her fingers. Margot took a deep breath and yelled out of her lungs, "I'm alive!" the nature carried her voice through the grass, trees, water and mountains and repeated it in an echo several times. She laughed and her face broke into a wonderful smile. The warm feeling of sensational liberation overwhelmed her and brought tears into her eyes. She now fully understood, why a woman like Charlotte, with a tainted past, picked a place like this come, to live, to finish the rest of her life. The eye of the beholder could be very easily attracted to all the beauty around. The human mind could easily forget about the rest of the world and its crimes, but one's mind could not forgive. Those two, forget and forgive had a different meaning to Margot. Unlike Charlotte, Edith has lived to fight another day, as least, that's what Margot always thought of her stepmother. But the passion and motivation behind Margot's decision to come here and to face demons of the past, has come to a breaking point now, her zest to get it out to let the truth be heard despite the sensitivity of the subject, it was everything Margot currently lived for. She's not going to back out of it. It was too late, and she was ready not to give up. She couldn't give in now because of Edith. A woman who came to her life after her blood mother died of cancer, Edith represented a lot more than her father's second wife. Edith became Margot's best friend, the only one, when she was growing up, and when Margot uncovered something so sinister, so hard to grasp, she couldn't wait to find out the missing pieces of the puzzle. It's been a long journey for her, that has taken many years, much longer, than she would have expected, but now, she has come to the last piece of the puzzle of the past. She created a movement, a circumstance, whether it was right or wrong, she was going to let for others to decide. Determined, Margot wouldn't anyone or anything to stand in her way. Her strength lay in her passion and the passion was what led her to Lingit. One thing she couldn't do is to reveal this to her boyfriend back in Seattle. He wouldn't understand. So she came with an idea to travel all the way to a remote place in Alaska to do a study about migrating birds. After all, what's a little lie? Maybe it's not a lie at all. She was a journalist, and as such, she wrote about birds. John Ford didn't suspect anything different. When she came to him to let him know, where she chose to go for the birding season, he was surprised and at first did some effort to talk her out of it.

"It's too dangerous for you to go out there…Six full months? Are you crazy? God know what kind of people live there…" he said with an upset face. And then he added with emphasis, "I'll go with you."

She told him, it's not realistic, because he has to stay in the office, both of them can't just leave the magazine to run by itself. Edith, being very sensitive and private in her nature, always had a hard time trusting people. When Margot found out about Edith's past, she fully understood and respected her stepmother. She loved Edith's authenticity and firmness of her opinions. She wished that one day, she be like her. But as of now, Margot was like most people and could only dream of reaching such a level of depth and inner braveness.

Margot hoped for a spiritual connection to embrace the emotional side of life of Edith. She wished the same for Charlotte, even though, she was hesitant to approach the old Groeneweg with what she has discovered. Something, that went far behind the conventional ways of life itself and beyond others' facades yet the cause so devilish, so evil, that no-one could ever fully understand. A trust was a precious thing, and trust stood in the beginning of all that unraveled more, than 45 years ago.

Margot got up and walked to the cliff, carefully keeping herself away from the edge; she leaned over and saw a burlesque picture of beauty. A snow white mountain goat and her baby stood alongside the steep and sharp edges of the rocky cliff feeding onto the green brushes that grew from the sides. A little over across there was a herd of them – little ones with the big ones mixed together, as if they were glued to the cliff, relaxed and happy placing their bodies against the sun that pushed through the clouds and now shined onto them. There was a ram, a huge animal with majestic antlers that curved on the sides of his head. Margot took the camera off of her neck and snapped some photos from above. Then she returned to her car and slowly down the steep hill and from down below she stepped out of the jeep and took more pictures in just black and white film. The spectacular site freed of conflicts and filled with serenity motivated and inspired her to rush home and put her thoughts in writing, so other people can see and read about and hopefully give something for someone else.

Margot switch the film in her camera back to the color and photo documented the enormous field of the water fowl birds. The beauty of nature around her brought the deepest emotions in her. Feeling overwhelmed, she placed the camera into her lap and sat quietly behind the wheel. Nothing, but the sound of ocean waves washing in the rhythm over the rocky shore, and the sound of her own breath accompanied her. Joy entered her body and soul and she felt grateful for everything she had, realizing moments like these won't last forever. She learned a thing about herself. She didn't know she was such a softie. If she had not come to Alaska, and stayed in Seattle and continued with her cosmopolitan life, she may have never discover this side of her. Glad, she found serenity within herself made her feel better on her body and her soul.

Joy; such a simple sensation and feeling, yet how many people really fully experience true joy? Margot thought of people she knew in her life circle, that probably never experienced the real, pure joy. Those individuals lived by materialistic things only, undoubtedly by their own choice, characters lost in vain, and greed by the current society. How will she feel when her time here is over, and she will have to return back to the big consumer world? One thing she was sure of, she won't be the same Margot. Hopefully, she would be better, not for the acquaintances around her, but mainly for her own sake. She placed the camera on the passenger seat and drove off to charming Southeast town of Lingit, near the mouth of the Caribou River and surrounded by the thick-forested islands of the Inner Passage. With her windows down, she smelling a foul odor, thinking, it must be the ocean, or maybe the river. It was only after the Jeep's tires stopped rumbling on the rocky dirt road, and got onto the smooth, flat surface of the black tar leading to Lingit that she realized the foul smell is still in the car with her.

"What's that?" she asked out loud, and quickly looked around her car. "That smells awful."

Margot pulled on the side of the road and stepped out of the car, checked the back seats and down under on the floor and reached with her arms underneath both front seats and still couldn't find anything old, or rotten, like forgotten food, which was possible, although highly unlikely for someone like herself.

"Hmm. That's strange," she mumbled to herself and shut the Jeep's door.

And then when she made a step on the concrete she felt the mushy, sticky substance on her shoes.

"Of course!" she said victoriously, and started laughing. Her sneakers were covered in an animal waste.

"Bear poop, maybe?" she asked, but no one answered.

The image of her cartoonist father came to her mind, and his words swished though the air, *"Funny shit happens, and it can happen to you."*

"You're right, Dad, literally."

"It takes a strong character, and I'm not talking about a strong person, as far as muscles, I'm talking about a person with inner strength, and values, a good person with morals and one that can stand on his own feet and stand by his word. It takes one to become a person like that. Whether it's your life that changes you, the surroundings, people, circumstances, it doesn't matter. What matter is what you do with yourself. If you can stay true to yourself and in what you believe and follow your own path, no matter what, it's not about victory. It's always and only about your own inner success. Not very many people understand that. And not very many people can achieve that in their lifetime. But everyone can laugh and bring laughter into their days on this Earth; life's too short and you need to bring humor to your life, otherwise life is not worth living. Life without humor is only half way lived."

The young photographer heard her father's voice, as if he stood right by her. Margot walked over to the grassy area and tried to wipe off as much shit from her running shoe, as she could, while still carrying a smile on her face. She was glad; she didn't have to meet with the bear, realizing, she didn't carry any bear spray or gun on her. Margot didn't like guns, and even though Kurt had urged her to carry one with her, especially when he saw her by the lake by herself, she answered she wouldn't have known what to do with it. He laughed and offered he would teach her, and she refused. So, when she came by his store to get groceries, he handed her a bear spray. Not being used to a carrying a can of spray for wildlife while she walked around, she left it at home.

"You're a city girl," she whispered to herself and bumped her inner side of palm against her forehead.

The scattered bodies lay on the public beach, kids running around, building sand castles, tourist ladies covering their faces with overly large fabric and straw hats, people getting ready to celebrate summer solstice, the longest day in a year, that will fall on the Saturday. Margot looked forward to the local event and fireworks, even though she didn't know how the animals would like the fireworks. Her mind was sharp and clear, but her body just wasn't used to so much walking and waking up early, not sleeping enough; even though she bought dark curtains on her windows, she still somehow couldn't stay in bed past six in the morning. She still had some work to do, meeting her deadline, and submitting her articles and photos to John Ford she let out a loud sigh, as she passed the last house on the main street.

"What's that?" She slowed and stared at the fenceless back yard of the house. The family that lived there placed out an inflammable low to the ground swimming pool. An adult sow moose found her way in, and lay down in the water, cooling her body in the Alaskan summer. Margot stopped and grabbed her camera. The moose looked directly into the lens, as if it knew it was being photographed.

Later that night, Margot wrote her headline, *"A picture speaks a thousand words"* and attached the photo – a moose chewing on the grass, while lying down in a wading pool, cooling off. It brought on a feeling of liberation and harmony. An image so simple, yet beautiful and funny at the same time. It was a human hand that laid down the pool, and the next time it can be a human hand, that can bring down the animal. Margot shook her head at her last thought. She pressed send and shut the laptop screen.

A stream of water poured into the deep bathtub, while she brought a glass of chilled white wine in the room and got undressed. The bubbles created tall white foam, the smell of and vanilla and lavender scented the air. Margot slipped in the soothing bath and took a sip of wine. She knew, she would have to step up her game, and to speak directly to Charlotte. She just didn't have plan, how to do it.

CHAPTER 10

❦

The Iconic Coca-Cola Truck with its red trailer and large white written letters across and the original small, glass bottle painted on the side parked in front of Kurt's grocery store. Margot has always liked the image of the good old American pride; she found something nostalgic in it, just like paintings of Campbell soup, the everlasting art of Warhol, preceding its time and prevailing into the future. A driver walked out and opened the oversized sliding door on the truck's side and loaded cartoons of drinks onto his dolly and wheeled them inside the store.

The look at the small, thick glassed bottle of cola reminded Margot of Edith. Ever since she could remember from her childhood, Edith has always picked and bought cola in the original bottle. There was never a plastic bottle or even an aluminum can in Edith's household. While other kids brought their lunches to school, and some carried aluminum cans of Pepsi, Cola, Fanta or Mountain Dew or Seven Up, Margot tasted cola for the first time in her life out of the can and she immediately spat it out of her mouth. The memory of the image brought smile on her face, as she now walked through the Groeneweg's store. How could the same drink taste totally different? She tried it from the plastic bottle and shared the same opinion as Edith. The only way to consume Cola is from the glass bottle. The sugar, the rich dark flavor stood out, and excelled from the brother and sister varieties in cans and plastics. Edith later confined in her, and told her, that the small glass bottled liquid reminded her of home, back in Europe. That's how she remembered cola tasted when she was young. She had it sparsely, since the family was poor and could afford only the basic food items, yet the taste stayed with her for all those times, and her tongue could not be fooled by anything else.

Margot picked up seven bottles of the shelve and placed them in her cart. Albert saw her first and greeted her with an enthusiastic smile on his face.

"H..hello Margot!"

"Alfred, how are you?"

"F...fine!" he replied shyly with his eyes staring on the ground and his head forward and his back slightly hunched over he reached for the bottles and marked them up on the cash register. He reached over on the counter and opened a glassed cake cover and placed fresh raspberry filled doughnuts and apple strudel slice into a bag for Margot. He looked at her with his large blue eyes for a split second, before he shied away.

"Thank you." Margot said warmly.

Alfred bagged her groceries and passed over a flyer for a summer solstice party.

"A party?"

"Yes. T...the longest d..day in a year! It's fun."

Margot read the invitation, barbecue and live music and fireworks. "I'll be there. But you have to promise you'll dance with me."

Alfred blushed and shyly turned away. Margot grabbed her groceries and as she passed through the isle the iconic truck was already gone.

On the way back to her rented cottage, she passed the same wade pool, but this time the pool was empty, and the image felt somewhat sad, without the moose, or children splashing and cheering around. Where were the owners? Who owned the house? Margot realized although she's been in Lingit for month and a half now, she really hasn't spoken to many locals. The only people were Kurt, Alfred, the guy from the curtain store, and the owner of the Longnose Sucker, fish restaurant.

§

Her soft lips touched the white frothed foam from whipped milked topped with a little bit of cinnamon, just the way she liked drinking her cappuccino. While never leaving her eyes from the newspaper article about the upcoming solstice festival, she reached for a doughnut and took a bite. The tart raspberry filling melted in her mouth, as she chewed the sweet dough. Then she took a bite out of the strudel, and made a pleasing sound, "Mmm, it's so good." She indulged herself, and spoiled herself on that warm summer morning.

Margot read about the yearly event to climb Chetan Mountain, where people gathered at midnight to celebrate the longest day of the year. Although her legs weren't used to climbing steep hills, for the nearly two months she's been in Alaska she felt much stronger, and much more healthier and decided she will join the climb this year, together with locals and tourists. She ate the last piece of the strudel, which again reminded her of Edith, who baked every weekend including strudel and Edith's favorite sachertorte. Edith's home-made strudel smelled like cinnamon and vanilla, and the taste of apples and walnuts and raisins wrapped in a thin layer of dough finally sprinkled with a powdered sugar remained Margot of home. Sometimes Edith added a little bit of rum, and when she placed the strudel in the heated oven, the whole house smelled like sweet and heavenly. And Edith's sachertorte tasted rich in chocolate, apricot jam and vanilla and always got compliments of her neighbors, who tried to recreate Edith's recipe but were never able to perfect it. She finished the rest of the berry doughnut and told herself she'd better go for a run in the afternoon or perhaps in the evening. The light stayed out, and hours didn't matter anymore.

 A cottonball flew across the air and softly brushed over her nose, causing her sneeze. Margot looked up and thought it was snowing. The wind came in strong, and made the cottonwood trees shed their cotton, and now the air filled with hundreds of small white pieces. Margot got up and went inside the house. She took out the colored film and switched the camera to black and white and ran out to capture the summer snow. The tall cottonwood trees lined the back of the dirt road behind her house, and stood about 130 feet tall, with widely spread branches, and thick trunks. The trees had to be quite old. She wondered whether the owner of the cottage planted them there.

A chipmunk loudly announced his presence on the lowest tree branch as he hopped across from the thinnest part with leaves to the trunk and with a few wide jumps he descended onto the ground and quickly made it across the road. The chipmunk's bushy tail – bigger, thicker and longer than his body – wiggled against the sky and his large eyes stared at Margot. The little cute creature's mouths chew vigorously something as his small lips moved while keeping a safe distance from his only human companion. Margot looked at the last piece of doughnut she held between her fingers. She lowered her arm and the chipmunk got up on his hind legs and straightened his back and extended its neck. His eyes seemed to get bigger and wider as his little nose sniffed the sweetness between Margot's fingers. Then almost fearlessly the animal proceeded to her and with a quick snatch of his front paws he took the piece, shoved it in his mouth and brought his bushy tail up and against his back and jumped back across the road and disappeared into the nearby brush. And then in a brief moment the chipmunk appeared again, his cheeks stuffed with the possession as he chewed quickly then made a loud sound until he disappeared into the tall grass at last.

Margot was used to city squirrels that occupied the nearby park by her place in Seattle. She liked going for a run in the evening, just before the dusk, when the park cleared of the mothers and their children, and off the business people who came there to eat their lunches and sit and talk pleasure or do business while soaking in the sun, or just looking at the green grass and trees around. There were the newspaper readers, or the more casual and relaxed book readers, that took their shoes off and sat or lay down in the grass. But in the evening, different kind of people visited the park. The lovers strolling down the path holding hands, whispering to one another, their faces beaming in happiness, the young and old, the lonely people, the dog walkers, and runners, that sat all day somewhere in the office now enjoyed the freedom the park has offered them. The squirrels didn't care about who those people were, social status, gender, age, whether they were happy in their lives or where going through the sad times. The park squirrels had their own characters that put on for the human characters to show off they own the park, the grass and trees, the wooden benches, the little man-made ponds, the street lamps and the tree roots that lifted parts of the paved paths throughout the downtown park. These city squirrels were mean, fearless and they would bite Margot's finger if she handed them food straight from her palm. They would put on a show and demand to be watched, to get an attention of the spectator. They would steal sandwiches from paper bags, or from toddler's strollers, these squirrels cared only about themselves. Margot has known many people she could see as these squirrels, annoying and overbearing, never asking, just demanding for themselves.

Margot knew of many people whose personalities closely resembled these squirrels. There were too many selfish people nowadays. Margot has learned that in and around Lingit these little, fast-paced, brave and loud creatures are not actually squirrels but called chipmunks. Smaller in size, undoubtedly swifter in movement, able to survive in long winter months thanks to their developed tails, which they used to protect their bodies and retain heat during the coldest months in Alaska.

A chirping noise brought Margot back from her thoughts, as the persistent little furry Alaskan chipmunk emerged from the grass and cheerfully jumped across the road following the edge of the rocks and dirt that separated the shallow ditch knowing his way around, owning this property, the chipmunk finally disappeared from Margot's view and for that morning. She returned to reading her newspaper, the forecast sounded promising for the mountain marathon.

"Why not to try it?" she told aloud to herself and got up and walked to the house. Minutes later, dressed in T-shirt, shorts and no shoes, she ran down the beach and alongside the ocean, her bare feet in the warm sand. Soon, she felt pain in her hamstrings; she found it sure wasn't easy to run in the sand dunes, which made the workout that much more intense, but she loved it. She continued, her eyes staring into the distance ahead, seeing nothing but water and sand and tall grass up the beach by the road. The beach could not beat running through the city park. Margot didn't have to avoid any passing bicyclists, kids, or even domesticated pigeons, that were so used to humans, they appeared they would rather be stepped on than move out of your way; strangely humans had to get to the side to avoid collisions, not the overpopulated birds. Sweat broke on her forehead and her lungs short of breath signaled she wasn't in such a good shape as she thought. She finally stopped and bent over; pressing her arms on her knees, she coughed and then stood up and faced the ocean, placing her hands on her hips, and breathed deeply, opening her lungs and letting the salty air inside through her mouth. All the joys of a private beach, she thought. When Margot heard the cottage came with a non-public beach, she couldn't wait to rent it, to move in. What a treat for a city girl! She smiled as this thought reappeared in her mind, while the waves in front of her gotten bigger and stronger together with the wind that blew from the south.

This entered another world, her soul joined higher sense of herself as if she has found herself to finally understand who she was, who she'd been, who she'd become. And then she saw a person in the distant waves, a dot in the ocean, at least so it seemed from Margot's view. As the waves rolled, the person appeared and disappeared, almost moved like a puppet on the water. Margot stepped closer, and when the ocean splashed her feet, she felt that even on that sunny morning the water was cold, perhaps too cold. Who would go in? Who was that person? She brought her right hand and shielded her eyes from the sun. The largest wave came from behind and the surfer stood up firmly and held on and rode it for a long distance, a master of waves, the king of the here and now, Margot had a sudden regret she didn't have a camera on her to capture the beauty and art of these very moments.

"I'm Leaf."

Margot curiously raised her eyebrows and her face broke into a nice smile. "Margot." She reached out for a handshake, but Leaf opened his arms and gave her a hug. She instinctively shrugged.

"Saw you got worried there for a while, watching me in the waves," Leaf said jokingly.

Margot quietly nodded.

"The ocean's cold and quite unsettling today, but I love it!"

"I can see it." Margot replied.

Leaf gazed into the infinite waves and let out a loud sigh, before he said with a nostalgic voice, *"Love has no boundary."*

True, Margot thought, how so very true. She watched Leaf's trembling hands and his leg that carried a huge scar.

He noticed she was staring at him. "Went to Vietnam and got malaria, but I shot myself being drunk here one night. That can't get anymore ironic, can it?" They both laughed out loud, then Leaf added, "I think I've seen it all by now." A long pause passed between them, as they sat in the sand, a few seagulls cruising the air above them. One of the birds had a crippled leg that he couldn't fold back to his body and it just hung there, the end of its toes twisted. Leaf pointed his arm against the sky and shouted, "Look!" Margot looked up against the sky and saw the seagull, while Leaf said, "He's just like me. A one-footed cripple."

"I disagree. You wanna know what I see? " Margot protested her head tiled up, watching the seagull. "I see a beauty; his injury didn't slow him down, nor to made him less of a bird." She giggled and looked at Leaf, thinking whether he's going to get her double sense of humor. And he did, because his face broke into a wide smile, his eyes shyly low to the sand.

"I only believe in a few things in life," Leaf continued.

"What's the first one that comes to your mind?" Margot asked curiously.

"I believe an ocean can stop an argument." Leaf looked deeply Margot in the eyes and winked at her. Her lips parted as she took a breath, but before she could reply, Leaf leaned over and gave her an unexpectedly tight hug. Then he abruptly got up, took his surfboard and walked away. Margot looked behind him, his long hair braided in a wet ponytail bounced on his back, as he limped through the sand.

Scars. Human scars, visible on the surface, or the inner scars, slit and embedded in someone's souls, the invisible, yet the most painful scars, someone can carry. *Pain.* Everyone who is alive, will experience pain in some form. Physical or emotional. Which one hurts the most? *Mind.* The human mind, the master of the orchestra, the one, who can trick the human being and take the pain away, for a while, a while that's worth of living.

Margot got up and brushed the sand that stack to her body away. She kept on running, alongside the endless beach, running away from her scars, from her pain, from her own mind.

And then a soft, distant voice whispered to her, *"Appreciate yourself."* And Margot gasped for the air, as she was getting out of breath, her tights feeling the pain, her mind reminded her of the scars, she carried deep inside, when the soft angelic voice spoke louder and shut her pain when it said, *"Appreciate yourself and honor your soul."* She stopped, her chest moving violently up and down, she coughed several times. Margot turned and looked behind the long flat beach.

"Appreciate yourself," she whispered toward the Pacific Ocean. A memory of her childhood and a voice of her mother brought an overwhelming feeling to her. "Mom?" Margot whispered still facing the ocean. "I miss you."

One thing Margot always had feared was that the older she got the memories of her mother would slowly fade away, and would become more distant and blurry, as if they never happened and were only imagined. How can a five-year-old child preserve and keep the moments of past and carry them into a future? Photographs, letters, camera recordings? She had lots of pictures, only some handwritten notes from her mother, and no visual recordings. But for some reason, the soft voice of her mom stayed with her, in Margot's mind, in her soul and she wished, she hoped, the voice would never go away. When her mother died, a part of the child's soul died too. And when Edith came to her life, the part of her soul had returned, and Margot believed it was her mother, who brought them Edith Altman. And now, it was Margot's turn, to do something for Edith, as she felt, her own mother would do the same for her.

The first time Margot noticed something sinister about Edith's behavior was when they were in a nearby park, where Margot played with her friend after school. Edith would take her there, and sit on the bench, a book in her hand, staring on the pages, but Margot noticed she was not turning pages, was not reading the book she held in front of her. When she came over and tilted her head to look what's on the pages, Edith would abruptly shut the book and laid it in her lap. Then a couple of boys, about the same age as Margot, came to the playground. They got on the merry-go-round, and one of them spun the wheel. The kid's laughter dominated the air, and Edith's eyes stared at the boys, but her face didn't show joy; her eyes saddened, as her lips parted her hands with a slight tremor. Then both of her hands covered the face and eyes, as her chin lowered to her chest and Margot saw tears sliding down her stepmother's face. She wanted to jump off the merry-go-round, but it spun too fast for her, and she was afraid to let go of the grip of the cold, iron her small hand wrapped around. Her fingers clutched the pole, and she felt the pain in her fingers from holding onto too tight.

"Stop the wheel!" she yelled at the boy. But he ignored her. "Stop it. Stop the wheel!" And then from the corner of her eye, she saw Edith get up and rush to her. Later, when Margot asked why she cried, Edith told her the boys reminded her of someone from the past. The eight-year-old girl didn't understand, couldn't understand, the meaning of the Edith's past.

The second time Margot noticed something sinister about Edith's behavior was when she got a glimpse of her in the bedroom, the door slightly opened, Edith didn't hear her to come home early from school. Edith held a picture in her hand, talking quietly in a foreign language, before she started singing a song that sounded like a lullaby. Margot was eleven years old. The girl tempted by the moment, wanted to open the door and step in and look what was in her stepmother's hands. As she took her steps on her tiptoes, a loud slam of the door behind her back jerked her body and prevented her to proceed any further.

"I'm home!" the cheerful voice announced. Edith quickly returned the picture back to a small wooden box and shoved it under the mattress.

"Hello? Edith, where are you?" The voice came closer. "Margot! What are you doing here?" her father asked surprisingly.

Margot never got to see what Edith was looking at, nor did she understand the words of the soothing lullaby.

The third time Margot suspected something odd was when she was much older, and much, much more curious, than the little girl few years back. That's when she came upon a golden chain with a round pendant with a single rose. The chain was small, and would not fit around an adult neck, not even a child. She thought maybe it was a wrist chain. She placed it around her wrist. On the back side of the half-rose pendant were engraved initials E.A. Margot knew, they stood for Edith Altman. But why would she not wear her jewelry? Who gave it to her? Was it Margot's father?

Margot dug deeper, and over the course of a few years she slowly started building her puzzle. A piece by piece that didn't fit in, she collected, placed and replaced, and tried again, until the puzzle started making more of a sense, she so desperately wanted to uncover. Edith wasn't the only one, now Margot had her own secret, she promised herself to keep hidden, until she has the last missing piece, for which she knew she will have to take a flight, she would have to travel and meet with a certain person, and the thought of it gave her goose bumps.

And now, Margot ran back, fighting the wind that whipped against her, her mind unsettling, her legs giving up under the dunes as her bare feet took another step toward the house on the top of the hill, overlooking the Pacific Ocean.

"*Secrets. Everyone has one. What's yours, Edith?*" a voice nagged in Margot's head.

§

The chill of the night awoke her. Young Edith opened her eyes and stared at the half peeled paint on the ceiling. The wide opened curtains on the window let inside enough light from the full moon, which created various shadows in irregular shapes on the walls of her hospital room. She shrugged and made two fists, folding her fingers inside her palms, feeling the cold fingerprints. She moved the thin blanket to the side of the bed and got up. Her arm reached for a knitted cardigan that she placed over her shoulders as she walked out in the empty hallway. The young mother was trying to find a nurse, to ask her to bring her another blanket. Edith walked through the corridor, when she heard few laughs coming from behind a closed door. *Laughter*, such a simple, human thing. Yet, when was the last time she heard someone laugh? When did she let out the healthy, good-hearted laugh out of her lungs? At least someone was having a good time, even though the world was under the pressure of war, that some said was coming to an end, yet the end was so far away, that it seemed impossible, it would ever come to a fulfillment. As Edith continued walking through the corridor and the chill went all the way through her bones now. She rolled up the collar of her cardigan. Where's everyone? What kind of hospital is this? Edith turned to the left wing, and there she saw a woman walking against her. When the two passed one another, Edith fell as if the coldest, harshest frost came over her. She exhaled and could see her own breath. The other woman looked up and their eyes met.

Both brand new mothers, in one hospital, and Edith yet felt as if the time stopped, and her own life betrayed her, a feeling she had no idea where it came from, but she could swear, she never felt more confused as in that very moment, while passing a complete stranger, another mother, but the energy and her eyes were telling a different story.

The other woman disappeared behind the closest door, but Edith couldn't get rid of the terrible feeling that this stranger brought onto her. What was with her? She was never the one, to be too sensitive. Edith shook her head and sped up, when she saw a glimpse of a nurse, who walked across in the distant, cold hospital corridor. The other new mother had dark brown hair that touched her shoulders, was parted to the sides, and wavy, like folded ribbons. She had a long, narrow nose and pencil-thin lips. Her high cheekbones and sharp, pointed chin made her face look narrow yet still beautiful. Just like Edith, the woman had on a bright red nail polish. She was about the same height and about the same age, perhaps a few years younger from Edith. Their eyes met, as the women passed in the hallway, and Edith noticed a glimpse of sadness in the other women's blue eyes. She didn't expect that, because the woman carried herself very well and looked nearly perfect. What was her name? Did she have a boy or a girl? Was her child born on the same day, like Edith's? So many questions went through her head in that split second when she passed her. And then she realized, this was the same woman she saw through the gap of the open door, feeding her infant.

"Can I help you?" a voice came from behind her. Edith turned and stared closely at the old, wrinkled nurse. The nurse frowned at her. "You're not supposed to be wondering here through the hallway in the middle of the night."

"I'm sorry." Edith replied quietly.

"So?" The old nurse raised her bushy, unkempt eyebrows.

"So, I just wanted to find someone to ask…to bring me an extra blanket. I'm cold."

Later, in the early morning hours, Edith rolled restlessly in her bed. Two blankets twisted between her tights, she still could not feel comfortable, or warm. She lay on her side; a pillow between her arms as she rested her head down, tears came down her rosy cheeks. She could not carry the pain inside any longer, and had to let it out. The only reason she kept on going, she kept on fighting the life, the only life that was given to her, was her newborn baby. The child represented her future, since the past was cruel to her, and left her alive, but her husband dead, her parents no longer with her, no siblings, and no cousins. She had a friend, but the friend lived far away, on the other side of Germany, and Edith wondered whether the friend was even still alive. Maybe it was time for her to find new friends. With a newborn, she could start over, not telling anyone about her past, rather concentrate on the future. If there is any future, as the current world is in turmoil of fighting for a survival.

Edith wondered why she was still in the hospital. Why wouldn't the doctor let them go home. He urged her and told her she must stay and a week past and then ten days marked on the calendar and the young beautiful Edith still remained in the hospital with her newborn child. Her boy was healthy, a nurse brought him in to her multiple times a day and night, to feed and those were the happiest, precious times for Edith. But the nurse also came in to take her boy away, to rest and even Edith pleaded to her, to bring a crib to her room, the nurse refused, telling her the doctor had all the newborn babies in one room.

"You don't listen," the old, wrinkled bushy eye brow nurse said loudly. "The baby rests in a nursery."

"But I'm his mother."

It's been ten days she gave birth, her baby boy was healthy, eating, sleeping and she couldn't find a reason why the doctor did not allow her to go home. When she asked, she was met with silence. When she came back and asked again, the doctor told her the baby needed to stay longer under his supervision, at least for another week or two. Why? She demanded. But the doctor got called and had to leave her room. She was alone, in an iron bed, as she started to wonder, whether the doctor is honest with her. She didn't trust the old, bushy-eyed brown nurse. Could she trust this doctor?

"Edith? Edith! Where are you?" Adam's voice woke her up. And her dream went away in an instant as Adam came into the Margot's child's room and found his wife Edith on Margot's bed. He sat down, as he leaned over Edith's shoulder and kissed her on the lips. She didn't say a word, just took his hand and brought it closer to her chest.

"Are you okay?" His eyes looked into hers for an answer. After a pause, Edith finally said, "Yes. Of course, I am."

"Did you have a bad dream? You twitched and turned and mumbled something in German…" When she didn't say anything, Adam joked, "Sure it didn't look anything like you dreamt about a *blast from the past?*"

Finally, Edith smiled, and the corner of her lips curled as Adam kissed her hand.

CHAPTER 11

CHARLOTTE STOMPED ON THE BRAKE pedal, as she neared the railroad crossing. The wooden tracks were just pulling down, and two red lights flashed vigorously at her eyes. Charlotte stopped and shifted to a neutral and pulled up her emergency stick. Something, her older son Kurt complained about every time she put the car in neutral, a habit she learned from her own father, a habit of her European youth. The freight train announced its loud honk and the air carried it for a mile ahead. Charlotte rolled down the glass and rested her elbow out the window. The outdoor breeze softly brushed over her face and brought on a feeling of comfort. She listened to the train's wheels coming closer, beating on the tracks as the first wagons passed in front of her eyes. The long train, usually consisting of more than thirty carriages hauled on empty, rushing to its destination to be loaded with gravel and sent out further along. Charlotte sat in her car and closed her eyes, and listened to the sound of tracks as her mind took her forty-five years back.

The rhythmic beating of the iron wheels against the iron tracks slowly faded into the distance, as Charlotte found herself in the middle of the officer's private ball, accompanied with a chamber orchestra, where the drums took over, and basses hummed deeply, and cellos wept with a nostalgic sound of sorrow mixed with the sound of human voices as young Charlotte passed through the crowd of cigar smoking officers in their uniforms, and polished high black booths. Tables full of food with a centerpiece of a roasted pig, potatoes, sauerkraut, sausages and wiener snitzels, and roasted ducks lay out on a long table. The officers were circling the room, sipping cognac, some humming to the rhythm of the live, chamber orchestra. A surreal world surrounded her as one of the women in a long, black gown came to her and gave her a wide smile.

"Charlotte, this is officer Kalbfleisch. This is Charlotte Groeneweg."

Charlotte smiled and politely shook her hand with the officer, whom she immediately disliked, just like his last name, she thought of him as a butcher, getting hands on all the calves, and slaughtering them. She quickly wiped her right hand into her dress and shrugged. While the chatty woman continued, "Charlotte will be going to America soon. Isn't that right, Charlotte?"

A distant honk, and then another, that came clearer and much louder brought Charlotte back to her reality. She looked in the rear mirror and saw a line of cars parked behind her. The railroad crossing was now open, and the impatient drivers behind her couldn't wait to move on.

"All right, all right, I'm going. I'm going now!" Charlotte muttered nervously, as she stepped on her brake pedal, and with her right hand pulled down the emergency brake, she then shifted her stick and stepped on the gas. The wheels of her car loudly peeled from the road and left a cloud of an exhaust fumes in the air.

Downtown Lingit was decorated with an upcoming summer solstice even. There were banners announcing live music, barbecue, a mountain marathon. Charlotte stepped in the beauty salon and was immediately greeted by one of the locals.

"Charlotte! I haven't seen you for ages! Where have you been?" the cheerful hairdresser stared at her. "Have you been hiding in your house?"

Charlotte replied with the coldest, indifferent tone her voice could produce, "You just answered your question."

"Well, what are we doing today? Do you want me to cut your hair, make you look pretty for the summer solstice parade?"

Charlotte looked at her with a cold, stone face. "Just the manicure today."

"Of course, have you thought of a color?"

"It's red, as always," Charlotte replied. As she sat in the saloon chair, she looked at the ladies around, thinking, how much she doesn't fit in. After so many year, nearly a half century in this country, and yet she still felt like a foreigner. Her late husband often told her, it's her own mind, that on the outside she is just like any other woman in Lingit. "God, I hope not. It's almost an insult," she replied one time, and then they both burst into laughter.

Charlotte knew well, what lies in the power of listening. She's always been a great listener, never distinguishing among people, and always patiently listening to everyone that had something to say. Did she agree with other people? Usually not, but she knew being polite and listen wouldn't hurt anyone. And so she did, she listened to the ladies now in the saloon, chatting about their gardens and how much one potting soil produced better, larger, redder tomatoes, than the other, she listened to the various voices around her, as Petra was making her hands smooth, and pretty, putting a deep red nail polish on her naturally long nails. The women around her were various ages, from mid twenties, to late fifties and the old German knew them all. Regulars, at the beauty salon, where no gossip was left untold, Charlotte got updated on everything that had happened in their small seaside town, even though she herself, hated gossips. Charlotte, being sixty-seven years old, didn't look her age. She's always taken a good care of her skin and ate well, never really getting used to the American way of cuisine with its fried fast food; that kind of food, if it could be called that at all, Charlotte avoided religiously. As the youngest of the women, twenty-six year old beautician Petra worked on her hands; Charlotte couldn't but notice how the young girl already started showing signs of aging due to an overexposure on the straight sun. Even though Petra just talked about the most amazing moisturizer, her skin was dry and dull and had dark patches. She wore a no foundation, just mascara, eye-shadow and a lipstick. But she probably thought how beautifully tan she was; after all, it was summer. Charlotte was never fond of tanning. Ever since she was a little girl, she preferred the sky with the clouds that way she didn't have to wear hats to shield her skin from the X-rays, and that was when the sun was not harmful as it was nowadays. How will Petra look, if she lives to be sixty-seven years old? Another woman, that could not shut her mouth, was the thirty-something hairdresser. Her nails were fake, too long, and painted with the brightest pink one can imagine. Betty's hair was teased up high, over permed and she probably used a whole can of hair spray every day to make it stand and hold together like that. Betty's crow-nest had various colors, from deep brown, to red, to nearly rusty orange, Charlotte had no idea how she can have so many customers. She would never put her trust with her hair to someone like Betty from Lingit, in Alaska. Betty wore a spandex top, a tight tank top with a deep V, and every time she leaned over a customer, she basically rested her large breast on the shoulders of various women, who came to have her hair done. Betty's mouth was framed by a red pencil and glazed over with an orange-red lipstick. She put so much pink blush on her cheeks, and wiped it to the sides; she looked like a hot red tomato. Is this the fashion of the nineteen's? If so, Charlotte let out a deep sigh, she is desperately and inevitably behind, and there is just no way, she can ever catch up to the modern days of fashion. Betty's mouth, a natural born cannon that fired a word after a word, faster than a Napoleon, overshouting the stereo that was on in the corner of the room. Charlotte had read somewhere that an average, educated person uses about three-thousand words a day. Whoever wrote the article hadn't met Betty from Alaska. Charlotte watched her mouth, and noticed, the woman did not pause once, she didn't have to inhale, or exhale, she just fired her words out of her red pencil framed mouth, and multi-tasked with her hands, chopping pieces of hair of the customer, while leaning her large breast tight in a spandex top over the poor lamb, that sat down to the master's chair.

"What do you think?" Petra asked.

Charlotte lowered her head and looked at her red nails.

"Do you like the color?" Petra asked impatiently.

"Yes. Yes, I like the color very much. Thank you."

"We could put some ornaments on the nails, like *the flag*. The fourth of the July is right around the corner."

"A what?" Charlotte knew what Petra meant, but could not believe her ears. The young girl had the audacity to ask if she wanted to have an American flag on her nails. The other women quieted and all stared at Charlotte. Even though she'd been in America for forty-five years, Charlotte still spoke with an accent. What the women didn't know, Charlotte turned up her accent up and down, depending whom she spoke to. She looked at Petra's big eyes. "I think this will do."

"If you change your mind–"

"I won't." Charlotte replied firmly, but with a smile. Before the door of the saloon closed after she walked out, she heard Betty say, "She's a woman scorned."

Was she? Was that how the local women see her, *a woman scorned?* Charlotte always had been driven by her own feelings, emotions and intuition. The people around her could influence her, but ultimately she has always done things in her life the way she felt they were best to do. She wasn't a woman scorn. If anything, she was a woman with a sharp mind, and an unusual wit, that only the closest people to her could recognize and see. She very much treasured her privacy, not because she was ashamed of something, but because the privacy was her own thing, something she could control. Only she could decide how much she'd let the world know about her.

Holton barked and wiggled his long, bushy tail and then ran toward her. The dog licked Charlotte's hand, and she scratched him on the top of the head as usual. He led the way inside the store and trough the isle all the way to the register.

"Holton, you know you can't be here," Kurt told the dog, who ran out the back door and stayed in the backyard. "Mama, you look pretty."

Kurt was glad to see his mother step out of her house and joining the society, even though it meant a brief visit with him in the store. Charlotte wanted to tell him about the past, and every time she failed herself, not because she was weak, but because she didn't want to hurt him. When she looked at Kurt, she saw a beautiful soul, a soul of a kind man, with a firm head on his shoulders, an intelligent person, sort of innocent, stripped of the unknown. But he had a past he shared through his mother, a past that tied both of them to the old continent. Strong ties, stained by a burden, a part of their lives, a part of their fate.

I'll just have to hold on to her secret for a little longer, she told herself. Even though she was a woman of decisions, she had no idea, whether she ever would find the right time to tell him, if the timing would ever be right, to let her son know, what her biggest secret is. Kurt had blue eyes, Charlotte had brown eyes and her late husband Jack had green eyes. Alfred got Jack's eyes, green. The eye color of the child is inherited by one of the parents. Yet Kurt, never asked, never questioned where his blue eyes came from. Was he not aware of that fact? Perhaps he wasn't, maybe he was. Ignorance is bliss. And Charlotte decided on this day, she's going to nurture the ignorance of the bliss a little longer; a benefit of the doubt.

When the horrible accident happened, and the fishing boat got stranded in a cove, while the weather turned and brought on heavy clouds, pouring rain, and devastating wind, that raised the ocean waves several feet high, the captain did exactly what was required from him. Even though he no longer served on a commercial boat, carrying passengers, he still remained loyal to his captain's duty and took care of his two friends, before he was the last one to exit the boat. But the water already filled in the cove, and the boat got stuck, and there was nowhere to escape. Charlotte always thought what could have been the last thing her beloved husband saw, before he died. Was it the devil itself that ended his life and drowned him in the salty waters?

The second time she became a widow, she no longer believed in justice. Circumstances of life built in her inner strength as she slowly shielded herself from the society. Charlotte was left with two sons, one strong and healthy, the other a cripple. What sins has she caused to deserve to live, to live with a pain, until the day she dies? Kurt had a bright future, he put himself through an expensive education, got a lucrative job in a big firm, and when Jack died, he returned home to help his mother to help his younger, crippled brother. Charlotte told him she didn't want him to sacrifice himself for them. He was surprised by the choice of her words.

"You've always told me I need to be understanding of other people's needs," he replied.

"That's why I came back." Kurt added with emphasis.

"Mama?! What's with you today? Are you okay?"

Kurt's voice brought Charlotte back to reality and to her present. She looked at her son then lowered her head and her eyes saw the open back of potato chips. "Kurt, you shouldn't be eating these...You know how much bad stuff they put in them?"

"I know, Mama. I know I should be eating only the original flavor, where the ingredients reads "potatoes, veggie oil and salt."

"That's right. What does it say on *this* bag?"

Kurt turned the bag and saw the thick, long printed text in black and white that described the sour cream and onion-flavored chips. "But I can't help it. These are my favorite." His face broke into a nice smile, with two dimples on each side of his cheeks. He helped her with the groceries in the car, and kissed her on both cheeks before she sped up the road and across the tracks to the outskirts of town, where her shingled house and her roses with sharp thorns shared her secret.

Once inside, she placed the old, vinyl record on the gramophone and watched it spin, until a beautiful sound of uplifting, soft music came out the of the vintage antique phonograph. She brushed her red nail polished fingers over the quality dark pinewood for the box that spun the record, and then set her eyes on the real brass horn as she moved over to a side table, Charlotte poured herself a glass of cognac and sat down in the old, deep armchair. The music took her deep inside her thoughts. She had always believed that singing and chanting and music can be very important for everyone's soul, because hearing connects us to the universe, and the universe further connects all things. She listened to the beautiful built up, a piece that had four basic harmonies as she took a sip of her favorite cognac and once again her youth unraveled in front of her eyes.

The very same music spread through the hospital hallway through the open door of the doctor's office. The mid aged doctor had already grey hair and deep wrinkles on his forehead. The night before he visited the other, elderly doctor that worked on the same floor as Sigi. He asked him, "What's the point of life?"

And the old doctor replied, "The point is, you've gotta make a point. Make your own point."

Doctor Sigi's eyes were red, and tired from lack of sleep. He turned a page in the calendar and mumbled to himself, "March 15, 1944, one more week to spring." A nurse knocked on his open door and walked in, bringing him dark cup of steaming coffee. She looked at him with a concern but didn't say anything. He pushed the calendar out of his way and moved a folder with dark, black bindings closer to him. He turned the first few pages, and bluntly stared at the handwritten name in dark, black ink. *Altman.* The doctor took a sip of coffee, and instantly felt the hot liquid burning his inside trachea, as the coffee descended to his empty stomach, where it burned even more. He got up and walked to the door, shutting it. Then he sat down, and reached into his white coat and took out a black fountain pen. He started writing, slowly, making notes into the heavy folded diary. When he was done, he placed the fountain pen back to his white doctor's coat pocket and shut the book and placed it in his drawer, after which he double locked it. He leaned back onto his chair and placed both of his arms behind his head. He shut his eyes and listened to the opera aria coming out of the old gramophone. The words sung in Italian about a mother and her child, a life un-lived, an unfulfilled future, but there was hope, and hope was what kept the mother going for another day, month, year…

Charlotte went for a walk outside in the hospital courtyard, to shorten her day, to stretch her legs, to get some clean air into her lungs, to look at the sky and tree crowns, looking forward to spring, looking forward to her future with her newborn son by her side. Upon returning back, she heard the opera music, and curious, she stopped by the open door and watched the doctor, who had a head full of gray hair, despite his young age, contemplate above a black folder that was laid on the table in front of him. He wasn't aware, she was watching him.

Charlotte leaned onto the wall and listened to the opera singer, and aria well known to her, about a mother and her dead child. Why would the doctor listen to something morbid like that in the section, where new mothers gave births to their children? Even though the singer sung in a foreign language, whoever was a fan of opera knew the lyrics without learning how to speak Italian. And then she heard the clapping of the footsteps on the tiles and the door shut next to her.

When walked back to her room, her eyes met with another woman, who intently stared at her. She had brown hair, lighter color than Charlotte, but nearly the same haircut, with the ends just above the shoulders, she was her height, and about the same weight. The women could have been sisters. Charlotte guessed the other mother could be maybe slightly older then herself. She's seen her around, and just like Charlotte, this mother has been in the hospital longer, than usual. She wondered why? Was her newborn sick? She hoped that whatever the reason, both, the mother and her child would be okay. Did she live in this town? Did she have visitors? When the women passed, Charlotte's shoulder and arm nearly touched the other woman's shoulder. She smiled at her and her lips moved, and Charlotte could read she greeted her in whisper. Charlotte passed her and turned around, but the other woman already disappeared around the corner.

She returned back to her room, and soon after a nurse brought her baby boy into her arms.

The vinyl finished playing, and Charlotte opened her eyes in the present. She caught a glimpse of her face in the mirror on the wall and took a sip of cognac. She tilted her head back and swallowed the golden liquid. The cuckoo clock on the wall loudly announced the time.

§

Margot sat on the patio, enjoying the beautiful summer day; she lay on the lawn chair, in her bathing suit, her head covered with an overlarge straw hat and sunglasses, her lips with a soft touch of pink lip gloss, when something tickled her leg. She jumped up and saw the same chubby chipmunk came back to visit her, and carried a pine cone in his mouth. He did a little dance in front of the only audience he had, together with loud chirping sounds, and then the little thief disappeared into the tall grass. Margot's face broke into a wide smile as she extended her arm and reached for a margarita she made earlier with fresh limes she got from Kurt's store. She wondered how the locals did it during the winter here, since the citrus was so expensive to buy in the summer. While taking a sip of the tequila drink, she heard the chipmunk again, going loud and the tall grass moving back and forth. She licked her lips, where a piece of mixed sugar and salt remained from the drink, and laid back on her lawn chair.

This was a life she could get used to. Before she thought she'd get bored, but on the contrary, even now, just hanging out, doing nothing, felt pretty great to her. She didn't miss seeing other people. Maybe if she could do this every day, then maybe, just maybe she would get bored, but for now, this moment for quite tranquil and perfect for her. Margot already had plans for later that afternoon, which she was rather nervous about, but now, she could just lay here, and have a moment to herself. But, she came to Lingit for a reason. And the reason would not let her mind rest. Even though she was happy to have found the person, she looked for so long, and devoted her time to unfold the pieces of the past; she thought she would find a little rest for herself. Instead, her inner voice grew louder, and more impatient, as she knew, she would have to face her encounter sooner than later.

Margot finished her drink and walked inside the house. The clock on the wall showed it was ten minutes past two in the afternoon. She'd better get ready for her trip. After she showered, Margot stared at the clothes she laid on her bed. Having a no idea what to expect, Kurt's voice arose in her mind.

"Pack lightly, and dress in layers," he said to her the other day, when he invited her to go bear viewing.

"I'll take care of the rest," he added. What was she thinking when she agreed to go on such a trip! The only time she encountered live bear was at the zoo, and the two were separated in a safe distance by an iron cage. She snatched the bear-spray and shoved it in the side, easy to get to pocket on her backpack.

Margot prepared her camera and took extra films, colored and black and white, got dressed and checked the time on the wall. She looked forward to the trip, being a natural adventurous soul, but still had butterflies in her stomach. A double, loud honk came from the outside. Margot grabbed her backpack and walked out of the house.

"Are you nervous?" Kurt asked when they got to the small, private airstrip, where a float Beaver plane with a pilot awaited them on a wide opened lake. Margot shook her head, but before she could reply, Kurt jumped in, "Margot, don't be nervous. It's fun. You'll see."

She knew he tried to encourage her. "I'm not nervous," she said firmly and stepped from a wooden deck into the plane. Kurt wanted her to sit up front and next to the pilot, so she can get a better view and take pictures. Frederick "Fritz" Martinson shook Margot's hand with a firm steady grip and gave her a wide, bearded smile. The heavy, rumbling engines of Beaver plane lifted them in the air and into the wild; a territory that can only be access via plane or a helicopter. Soon, the view underneath opened wide and offered a spectacular view of the Chetan mountain ranges, thick spruce forests, high saddle blue water lakes, long, thick and narrow rivers, that intertwined into one another. There were majestic waterfalls, coming out with a huge force from the top of the mountains, overlapping and splashing over rocks bigger and smaller, and boulders that were sticking out half of the water and proudly into the sky. Margot took many pictures, and gasped over the beauty that lay in front of her eyes. There were mountain goats on the sharp end of the tall, steep rocks, a heard of adults and their babies, together feeding on the green bushes that pushed through the rocky terrain and grew on the sides.

The view from above changed from green fields and trees to rocks then to snow. She focused her camera and zoomed in onto various crevasses of the mountains down below, onto which the sun shined and created a beautiful illusion of shadows, which from high above looked like human bodies, dancing, hugging, and making love.

Margot took pictures in color, and then switched the film to black and white, to make the shadows stand out. She thought of a hug, such a simple gesture yet so powerful. A hug had no religion, skin color, age or gender, and it doesn't require money. It was easy to do and always brought on emotions. Margot thought of how people didn't hug enough anymore. Everyone rushes, she tried to remember the last time she hugged someone. Fritz suddenly lowered the plane, and got as close as he could over the flat surface of the mountain, that opened to a stunning view of a glacier. It suddenly dawned on her that they were going land on that glacier. She turned her head and looked at Kurt. He smiled and winked at her. The deep blue eyes were expanded in front of their eyes, and the sharp sun made it difficult to see. Kurt handed her a special sunglasses before they stepped out of the plane. Margot felt the chill from the ice, but because of the strong sun, she wasn't cold. She deeply inhaled, thinking this is the cleanest air she's ever let inside her lungs.

"It's called Ticasuk glacier. The name comes from Native American language by Inuit people. The Eskimo meaning can be translated to *"where the four winds gather their treasures from all parts of the world, the greatest which is knowledge."*

Margot shut her eyes and spread her arms to the sides. The quietness and spectacular beauty of that place made her very emotional. But she didn't want to cry, definitely not in front of him.

She looked behind her and saw Kurt and Fritz taking out backpacks. She walked to them and asked Kurt what they were doing. "What?!" she gasped and her face showed a total disbelief. "What do you mean, we're going to pitch a tent here? HERE?" Margot did a three sixty turn on the ice. "I thought we're going bear viewing!" she continued furiously.

"We are. Tomorrow morning," Kurt replied.

"What?!" Margot looked at the pilot, who was walking back to the plane.

"Is Frederick leaving us?"

Kurt turned and looked at his pilot friend. "No, Fritz is not going anywhere," he said with his relaxed voice.

"Why didn't you tell me, then?"

Kurt paused and looked at Margot. She was furious, but she still looked pretty to him. "I didn't tell you on purpose, because if I had, you'd do exactly this. You'd freak out on me! You packed stuff to last you a week!"

"Are you making fun of me?" Margot asked.

"No. I wouldn't do that... Margot!" he took her hand, but she jerked it back. "It'll be fun. I promise. You'll see."

Margot watched as the men pitched two tents. She was still mad at Kurt for not telling her in advance. Who stays the night on the top of a mountain, on a top of a glacier? And why are there only two tents? Is Kurt going to share one with his pilot friend? Oh no, definitely not. That's not going to happen; she's not going to sleep in a tent with him. When was the last time she went camping? She couldn't even remember. She was never a Girl Scout, and her father wasn't into camping; she was an only child, so there was no sibling she could go backpacking with. Margot looked intensely at Kurt. If he thinks, that she's going to share her tent with him, he is so wrong! Who does he think, he is?

"There you go, princess!" Kurt smiled at her and pointed at the pitched tent. There's just no way, she's never going to share her tent with him, he thought, that's just not going to happen, ever.

She lay in her tent but could not fall asleep. Even though it was a deep night, and her watch showed eleven thirty at night, there was a complete light outside. And because she was on the top of the snow-white glacier, the light from the glacier made it even lighter, and much brighter outside. She felt bad for giving Kurt a hard time before, but she wasn't the type of girl that would like surprises. And she hated to admit it, but Kurt was right about her. If he had told her in advance, they were going to overnight in the middle of nowhere, on the top of a glacier, she would not go on this trip. Margot unzipped her sleeping bag, put on boots and opened the tent. He sat by the portable stove, a steaming mug in his hand. He smiled at her and waved at her to join him. Margot realized she's never seen him mad.

Kurt's kind blue eyes looked at her, when she sat down next to him.

"What are you drinking?" she said.

"Grog. Would you like some?"

She smelled the inviting aroma of dark rum, cloves and lemon spices. Margot slowly sipped the hot liquid, and soon felt it in her stomach. She felt tipsy pretty fast, due to the height there were in, the alcohol worked much faster. Around one in the morning the light finally dimmed, and the moon shined above them. The only thing Margot regretted was that the stars above them weren't much visible.

"The stars are still there," he said and looked up.

"We just can't see them much at this time of a year," he sighed.

"Groeneweg," she said suddenly.

"Yeah?"

"Is that German?"

Kurt paused for a brief second, biting his lower lip. "No. It's Dutch." He could see a slow surprised shift in her face, even though she was good at hiding it. Kurt noticed a pattern that repeated with Margot, she was definitely a girl full of secrets. And now, she is the one, asking him questions. "Why do you want to know?"

She shook her head and shied away with her eyes. "No reason." She didn't want to lie to him. But it was too soon to tell him. She couldn't do that here, on the top of an ice mountain. Instead, she tilted her head back and stretched her arm toward the open skyline. "It feels like I can almost reach the stars from here."

"It does, doesn't it?" Kurt looked up. "Life is really simple, but some people insist on making it very complicated." The fresh air carried his words across the mountain tops.

"I couldn't fall asleep."

"Is it the height?"

"No. I think it's the quietness of this place. I'm so used to some city noise, to hear cars pass by, or ambulances, or drunks signing in the streets..." They both laughed.

"Thank you," Margot said suddenly.

"For what?"

"You know..." She lowered her head. "For this all."

"You're not mad at me anymore?" he teased her.

A loud snore came from the tent where the pilot Frederick "Fritz" Martinson slept.

"Sounds, like someone's deep where the foxes say goodnight," Kurt said.

Later, Margot pretended she was asleep, when he entered the tent. Kurt was very quiet, and very considerate; she didn't know a man like that before. And then she heard him whisper, "Good night, city girl."

He fell asleep fast, but Margot's mind raced. If she were in town, she would get up and go for a walk. Ironically, she couldn't do it here. She didn't want to wake him up. A slight chill went over her body and she shivered.

"Good night, Kurt," she whispered and looked forward to the next day's adventure. She felt, it's going to be a big one.

CHAPTER 12

Margot Woke Up To The Sound of the plane's rumbling engine. She tilted her head and saw an empty sleeping bag next to her. Margot unzipped hers and stuck out her left arm out and looked at her watch; five till nine in the morning. She unzipped the tent and a very bright stream of sun nearly blinded her, she shielded her face and reached for the sunglasses.

"Good morning," Kurt greeted her.

"Morning," she replied. The air was crisped and the sky was so blue, there wasn't one cloud on it. She looked around and felt an immense joy in her heart. She survived her very first night on the top of an Alaskan glacier.

"Coffee?" Kurt handed her a hot steaming mug of black coffee and a sandwich.

"Thanks."

She watched the men as they walked back and forth from the plane, loading everything in. "Can I help you with anything?"

"No. Everything's almost done. Did you sleep well?"

She had. In fact, she hadn't slept like this in a long time. Fresh air made her pleasantly tired. Margot nodded.

"Ready?" the captain spoke through the mike.

"Can't wait," Margot replied, looking ahead through the Beaver plane's glass.

The pilot lifted his thumb up, and so did Kurt. The helicopter detached from the snow and into the air and into a brand new adventure.

"The weather couldn't have been better," Fritz said amusingly.

"What a spectacular view," Margot gushed while taking photos of their plane's shadow reflected on the snow peaks. Just like the ocean, the mountain ranges seems to be endless, the view of three-hundred and sixty degrees of pure wilderness. And then the gust of wind made the plane go into a slight turbulence and Margot's heart started beating fast. "That was scary!" she let out a sigh.

"That's nothing." Fritz assured her, smiling carelessly.

"I guess that's nothing for you," she replied. Her stomach felt like a knot.

Kurt leaned forward and touched her shoulder. "It's always windy through this passage."

That didn't make her feel any better. She set her sight on the beauty around, rather than the turbulence, if that's the last thing she would ever see, at least, she was looking at something beautiful, a pristine, goddess, pure nature. The pilot made a turn and then they started descending over the snow, and later over the rocks, and then the forests, and rivers became their company all the way to the biggest, strongest river, that flew threw a valley.

"That's the place, we're going to," Kurt announced.

After they landed, they were welcomed with a rushing wild sound of the river. The air was surprisingly much cooler, perhaps because they were in a shade. Kurt handed her a back pack, and he put the larger, heavier one on his back. Fritz Martinson stayed behind, close to the plane.

Margot immediately found the terrain to be a huge challenge. Even though she wore the appropriate boots, upon Kurt's insistence, the river rocks were covered with a slippery moss.

She followed Kurt's steps and tried to avoid falling in the water. Large forest plants, with heart-shaped flowers and lavender color grew up high among fern foliage and thick alongside of the river, and gave out a specific, sweet aroma full of vanilla, or lemon-ginger in the air. She couldn't think of anything but spices.

The green plants added to humidity and Margot could see her own breath. The trail switched from slippery rocks to soft, brown forest grounds, but didn't make it any easier. There were thick roots laid out in front of them, and Margot had to navigate carefully not to get her legs twisted between them. The trees stood tall, and thick and wide to the sides and the majestic spruces were covered in cones. Margot thought of her chubby neighbor chipmunk, and how many cones he could fit in his mouth and how happy it would make him to be here.

Kurt turned around and saw, she is a little behind. He stopped and waited for her to catch up to him.

"Are you doing all right?"

Of course, she was, this was easy for her. "Yeah, I'm fine."

They mostly descended the first half of the hike. There were wild mushrooms popping out of ground, and Margot regretted she didn't know much about them.

She used her fingers instead of brush this morning, and re-tied her high ponytail. The brush got left behind in her bathroom, since she had no idea she would be staying overnight. She wore no makeup, and she already used Kurt's lip balm and sun block. She tasted the honey flavor of the lip balm on her lips.

He pointed toward the steep hill, "That's our last challenge, after that, we're almost there."

Margot liked a good challenge. To get on the top of the hill, each had to climb almost like a goat, but she wasn't scared. Using both hands, they held onto the branches and boulders. Margot felt the burn in her hamstrings. She had no doubt she would feel it even more tomorrow morning. But today, she was on a hike, in the middle of nowhere, with someone she barely knew, someone whom she kept her secret hidden, and wondered, if he had any idea, who she really was.

She felt her heart pounding, as she wiped off the sweat from her forehead. This was harder, than she thought, but the reward that awaited them up top, was well worth it. Kurt stretched his arm and she held on tight, while he pulled her up and over the huge gap between the boulders, the last steps that led up to a wonderful, wide-open view of the valley down underneath them.

"Not bad for a city girl, like you," he teased her with a smile, when both stood on a flat surface of the mountain.

She sat in the grass and took off her back pack. "Don't call me that."

"What? But you are a city girl."

"Not when I'm here." She drank the energy drink he put in her bag. When she didn't hear him respond, she looked behind her, and he was gone. Her heart jumped as she jumped to her feet. "Kurt?" she yelled after him, and then saw him bent down, on a patch of meadow in near distance.

He got up and walked to her. "Thought you may like these." He handed her forest strawberries, still attached to their green stems and leaves.

"Oh, no way! Thank you!" Margot's face broke into a beautiful smile. Kurt sat next to her, gazing at her pretty face. What was on Margot's mind? She seemed lost in her thoughts for a brief moment.

"You're so quiet, all the sudden. What are you thinking about?"

"Just, that if it's possible to handle this much beauty around, and then come back to the reality. I think I'll be a different Margot, after I return to Seattle."

She smelled the little wild red berries first, which made Kurt laugh. Then she placed one forest strawberry in her mouth and closed her eyes. "Mmm, there is no like flavor like a forest strawberry... It reminds me of my childhood."

Kurt looked at her and his face expression changed. He kept quiet and Margot opened her eyes. "Have some."

"No, they're all yours. They are really called wood strawberries, not forest strawberries."

She insisted and he took one and lay down next to her in the grass. They both stared at the blue sky, now accompanied with smaller and bigger scattered clouds. The breeze blew softly and made the stables of the tips of the grass move.

"Where did you spend your childhood?"

"East Coast. That's where I grew up, in upstate New York."

"When you have a bad day, what's your refugee, how do you treat your soul?"

"You mean, what do I do to make myself feel better?"

"Yeah."

"I listen to music. It's my therapy."

"How do you relax?"

"I get out of the house, and go for a walk, or drive somewhere, where I'm alone. And then I just stare at the nature in front of me. The ocean, mountains, trees. And I hear their music, the ocean's, the mountains', the trees'."

"Sounds to me, it must be a pretty big orchestra."

"Yeah, it is. And it pulls on my heartstrings and makes me feel better. I guess, what I'm trying to say, I need to feel serenity, it's important to me."

"I had a hunch about you," said Margot.

"You did?"

"Yes. I had a hunch you are a romantic."

"East Coast, hmm." He broke a stem of a straw grass and bit it in between his teeth.

"What about you?"

"Me? I was born here, and grew up here, and then I got tired of this place and wanted to get out, go out some place else. Any place…" He let out a sigh. "So I went to the Atlantic University and after that I got a job in a big corporate world…" He let his words slowly disappear into the air.

Margot ate the last strawberry, but the sweet taste stayed in her mouth and she all the sudden feel nostalgic. She felt for him, she felt guilty of what she knows, and he doesn't and she can't tell him, at least not now, and definitely not here.

"Are you ready to see some bears?" he got up and stretched both of his arms and she got hold of him and he pulled her up. Margot started to feel her legs. After all, she *was* a city girl, not used to using her muscles plus all that running she did the day before on the beach. She promised herself, she'd better get into a better shape, if she really wants to hike the mountain on the solstice day.

They walked across the large meadow blooming with various shapes and colors of wildflowers, and then they met a mountain hair, that wasn't scared of them at all, and Margot got some beautiful film stills of the hare, which looked like he posed just for the two of them.

"Look!" Kurt shouted and pointed his hand toward the patches of grass that were laid down.

"Oh, no way!" Margot cheered.

"Sow moose and her two babies stayed here overnight." Kurt said, but Margot already knew it. She took pictures of the imprint in the grass where moose had lain overnight and next to it were two, smaller imprints where the babies slept. And then a curious ptarmigan kept her eye on the only two humans, the two hikers that passed nearby her, trying to protect her young chicks.

They got to the river, and Kurt told her they need to cross it in order to get to the place, to see the bears. They both took off their hiking boots off, and Kurt carried hers and his, as barefooted they entered the cold water. Margot felt an immediate chill that went through her entire body.

"Make it quick over the water," Kurt shouted at her from the other side of the river.

"It's easier said than done!" she shouted over the rushing streams.

"Come on, you can do it. I know you can!"

Just don't wipe out, not in front of him, Margot told herself, as she navigated through on the other side. The water was cold, very cold, and the chill traveled through her body, all the way to her bones. Her bottom feet turned red and somewhat stiff.

"You gotta make it quick. The longer you stay, the harder it gets," Kurt shouted from the other side of the river.

The sun reflected through the clear water and made it even more difficult for Margot to watch her steps. The slippery rocks were sharp and covered with green moss and green plants. She tried to do her best, lifting her red, nearly frozen tights and making larger steps. Then she got angry, the anger built up inside her, *"Goddammit, Margot. Don't give him the joy of you falling in the river. Oh, my god, it's cold!"*

Kurt reached out, and she held onto him. He finally pulled her through the deepest end of the rushing river. "Good job!" he cheered. And Margot looked up and her foot slipped on the underwater rock and as she fell in, the backpack slipped from her shoulder and quickly floated down the rushing stream.

They sat in the grass. Margot soaked up the sun and felt much better, while eating and drinking some hot coffee from the Thermos bottle. She dried her socks and hiking boots, and there was no point of going over the loss of her cloths and the backpack. She laughed at her clumsiness and she was grateful, Kurt took her camera and carried it across the water himself, probably knowing, she would wipe out.

"People always chase after something every day," Kurt said. "I was one of them, and I just got tired of it. I didn't understand myself anymore. Is this who I was? I wasn't happy. I lived an expensive lifestyle, thought I had friends and beautiful people around me. It took me a while to realize that in the big world I completely lost my own identity, who I am, who I'm supposed to be. Many people had bad characters, but it was upon me to find out. And then one day I finally told myself, I stopped chasing and I made a change, and I let things come to me, rather than to chase after them. It was the best decision I've made for myself."

"I met Leaf the other day on the beach," she said quietly.

Kurt looked up and his eyes came lit with an enthusiasm. "Leaf is the kindest person I know. If you need help, go to him. He'll never reject you. He's almost self-destructing to the point of his own disdain."

"The will to live free like him...it's pretty admiring." She finished her coffee.

"It's an extreme. Not everyone has the capacity to be like that," Kurt replied. "But yeah, more power to him."

And then Kurt took out a bar of Swiss milk chocolate and Margot's eyes got big as he handed it to her.

"Yum." She opened the bar and put a piece of the velvety sweet chocolate into her mouth, "Mmm, it's so good."

Kurt's eyes kept looking at her, when he said, "I thought you may enjoy it. I was afraid you'd bail out on me."

"What do you mean?"

"Ahh, I just wasn't sure whether you'd be for so much wild adventure."

"You doubted me!" Margot said surprisingly, and put another piece of chocolate in her mouth. Then she realized she forgot to share the goodness with him, and moved the bar in her hand to Kurt.

"No, I'm fine."

"Have some. I'm not going to eat it all by myself...I mean, I could, but–" She smiled and lowered her eyes to the ground.

"It's quite a hike to go see the bears," Kurt interrupted her, as he took a piece and let it melt in his mouth. "We're almost there."

"Hmm, I wonder..." She put on her hiking boots.

They descended the second part of the hike, which didn't make it any easier. Many times she had to hold on to the twigs or rocks or roots lifted from the ground, to get down to another river. Kurt and Margot entered a deep forest, and the air immediately cooled down.

"You got quiet, now," Kurt said, as he walked behind Margot.

"It's kind of scary here, don't you think? We're the only people here, in the middle of nowhere...What if...what if a bear showed up right here, right now?"

"I carry a gun." Kurt's words echoed through the tall spruce trees.

Margot abruptly stopped, turned and faced him. "You have a gun?"

"Of course!" he said and spread his arms to the sides. "Do you think I would take you on such a hike, in the middle of nowhere, without carrying a gun?"

"Where is it?"

Kurt moved his shirt up and uncovered a black bolster around his belt on the side of his hip. A brief moment of quietness seemed like an eternity between them. "You have to have one. It's for protection," he finally spoke.

§

The late afternoon was totally worth it, when they got the wooden bridge and deck, a viewing place, built up high above the wild, rumbling river, surrounded by trees on each side, and huge rocks, and caves from the cliffs of the Indian River that accompanied the waters.

To Margot's surprise, their pilot was already waiting on the deck. The pilot waved at them, and at that moment it occurred to Margot, that's the reason why he stayed behind, why he didn't join them on the hike. He could take his plane all the way here, he could fly and land somewhere near. She looked at Kurt, and he could read her face, and Kurt was the first one, who spoke.

"Yes, Margot, we could have taken the flight here, but I thought, it would be nicer…perhaps more enjoyable for you to hike, instead to fly to the Indian River.

"I almost drowned in that damn water!" she replied furiously.

"But you didn't…"

"I was lucky…."

"I think you did pretty good…"

"I lost my backpack, I lost my personal things, I will never see them again."

"No, but you didn't lose your camera. And that's the important thing. You got tons of pictures, and saw lots of things, you would otherwise miss if you took a flight here..." When she didn't say anything, he continued "Besides, it was more fun to see a city girl tackle water crossing, climbing the hills and sliding down on her butt..."

She bit her lower lip, and gave him a straight answer, "The city girl likes a good challenge. There's a lot, you don't know about me, Kurt."

"You sure are secretive."

They walked down to the viewing deck. The sound of the rushing water over the boulders was loud, and overwhelming. Kurt pointed his finger to the left side, where the natural stone caves accompanied the woods, and there was a grizzly sow and her two young cubs. The sow walked slowly on all fours, moving her head to the sides, her huge paws with long, sharp nails and her shoulder blades moved into the slow, almost hypnotic rhythm. Her nose worked overtime, sniffing the air, and smelling the humans, her only spectators. The two cubs behind played with one another, nipping at the other's front paws, wrestling and chasing after one another. There was a large, male grizzly, and the sow felt the place no longer safe for her cubs, so she decided to take them away from the water and down the stream. She was older and probably knew the strong, male grizzly could attack her young ones and eat them. The male grizzly walked into the water and stood in the shallow part right close to the small waterfall. Salmons emerged from the water, and jumped high in the air, while the bear made a minimal movement, waiting for its next fish to catch in his mouth, the patient bear waiting for his next meal. He caught a silver salmon and quickly with his paw held it and used his mouth to skin it alive.

He munched on the fish's skin, full of protein and oils, the most nutritious part of the fish, and when he was done, he no longer was interested threw the rest of the meat on the shore. He repeated this tirelessly, and soon the carcasses laid on the rocks attracted the younger, less experienced bears, which ate their meat. Two eagles joined them and landed on the shore, picking up the pieces, or whatever the bears didn't eat, cleaning between the rocks, snatching and satisfying their stomachs.

And then something spectacular happened when an Alaskan blue bear showed up. Margot had heard the legends, and hoped to see one for herself. And now it was her opportunity to take photos of the majestic animal, who had a standoff with the local porcupine, and neither of them were willing to give up their rights to the fish, and stubbornly waited one for the other, the blue bear roaring and showing his teeth, standing on his hind legs, and the porcupine showing off his needles, the bear was cautious, not to get too close. It was the bear's instinct that he kept a safe distance from the much smaller, animal.

The whole experience felt very special, there were no other people, except the three of them, and the nature down below was all theirs. Margot lost track of time, as she tried to capture the moments on her camera. This was a true animal habitat, this was their territory and world, and Margot was just a visitor, a quiet, cautious one, honored to be able to attended the feast of the salmon fish, and be a part of the yearly rituals. This was an epic trip, well worth every second of her time, as she would forever be grateful, that Kurt took her on, and took her in and showed her a little bit of his part of the world. But there was a duty, a sense and purpose, and the inevitable reason, why she came to this state.

The Beaver plane once again went up in the sky with them, this time, heading home. Margot's body felt tired, but her mind and her heart filled with richness, and memories, she'll forever cherish, as she held onto her camera and couldn't wait to send some pictures home, and some to John Ford at Natural Bird Magazine.

The sky still very bright, with an occasional cloud, was their highway to home.

"What's the first thing you're going to do, when you get to the house?" Kurt asked her.

"I'm going to take a very long bubble bath." She replied and the corners of her lips curled up into a wonderful smile.

§

Margot stood in the kitchen when a knocking noise made her head turn. The blue jay was back, and he wanted his treat. She reached into the pantry and took out a shelled peanut. The bird stood behind the window and watched her impatiently. She opened the window and he snatched his prize and flew on the nearby tree branch. Margot opened the chilled bottle of white wine, and lit a large jarred vanilla candle. The soothing aroma soon filled in the bathroom, and intensified as he poured vanilla extract to the tub.

She let her skin soak with the snow-white bubbles, as she took a sip of the wine and leaned her back against the tub, she shut her eyes. Margot didn't care about the things she lost in the backpack. Those were just things, cloths, she could replace. Maybe she took it too hard on him, maybe she didn't. Would she do it all over again? She smiled and whispered to herself, "Hell yeah, in a heartbeat."

CHAPTER 13

"Edith Altman, Wake Up...wake up now!" the unfamiliar, rasped voice rang in her ears. She felt a sharp pain in her head; a throbbing migraine had invaded her brain. She took her inner strength and opened her eyes, a blurry vision of a faceless woman wearing white uniform hovered above her, making Edith even sicker. In the gray light in the room there came another voice of a different tone, and a slightly upturned accent, that belonged to a man. Then a very intense, sharp pain entered her right arm and she screeched on her bed. She felt no more pain, her vision sharpened and the voices became clearer, stronger and closer to her.

"You are quite a fighter, Edith," the male voice said first.

Edith looked up and saw a devil's face, staring into her eyes, so closely, her right arm crossed across the chest, and her right hand covering her left side of the chest, as if she wanted to protect her heart. The evil eyes took possession of her entire body, she inhaled for air, but her lungs couldn't but suffocate under the pressure above her. She took remaining strength and screamed from the top of her lungs.

"You're not real, you don't exist!" she shouted.

Adam held her in his arms, "Jesus Christ, your heart's beating so fast," he said. "Shh, it was just a bad dream. That's all. It's all right now, everything's all right." He whispered to her. She pushed his right arm away from the grip, and then she touched his left armed and pulled it away from her body. Edith got up and walked to the bathroom. The door loudly shut and Adam listened to the stream of water she turned on. She sat down on the floor and brought her knees together. She thought of the words she read earlier that day.

"Dear mom, I've found the last piece of the puzzle, at least I think I have. It's very important, you come and visit me here to confirm my findings. Love you, Margot."

Edith hated puzzles. Anything that had to do with the secrets, with the research, to find and to put together, she kept herself away from. It was her conscious decision not to clutter her mind with things like puzzles in the newspaper, crosswords and likes similar to train your mind, to sharpen your brain. Edith Altman hated to solve and resolve, and she had the best reasons for that. Margot, on the other hand, had a spirit of the power to look into the unknown, a curious mind that hungered for answers. The first time Edith became suspicious of her stepdaughter trying to crack her past; she decided to keep it to herself, until she is sure, that's the case.

She slowly let little pieces of trait for Margot to find. Edith was good, not to make them obvious, she very much put an effort in the detail of her work. An old, black and white photograph, that fell on the floor, and nearly under the bed, just the corners of the thick, rough-edged print paper showing a golden, necklace with a rose pendant in a wooden box, in the second drawer from the left, but the drawer casually half opened and the wooden box laid on the top of freshly washed and neatly folded laundry...If Margot decided to play a game with her, Edith was in. She wanted to know, how far her stepdaughter is willing to go and how much of the puzzle she is able to put together.

Edith got up and splashed her face with the cold water. She looked into the mirror and pressed her lips together. Then she gently wiped her face in the Egyptian towel and returned back to bed. Adam was sound asleep, snoring loudly. What a carefree, blissful soul.

Edith brought the blanket closer to her chin and shrugged. A chill went over her body. A demon of her past still haunted her, and she could thank Margot for it. She knew, she had no other choice, but plan a visit to the land of the last frontier. She hated that idea, she really did.

§

Charlotte sat on a very uncomfortable chair; the legs were uneven, wobbling underneath her weight. She held her hands in front of her, with her palms up, while the other woman deeply studied her lines. The air was very warm, and the town cheered with the newcomers, mixed with the locals, to celebrate the longest day of the year, the Summer Solstice. Kurt wanted her to get out of her house, and have some fun with other people. Charlotte's ironic sense of humor led her to a psychic's tent. And now, sitting on a cheap chair, she stared at the woman with a gypsy scarf tight closely over her head, large, thick golden loops in her ears, smudged black eyeliner and long, fake deep purple nails that currently cut into Charlotte's gentle, clean, and soft palms.

"I see you've been hurt in the past, I see you are a deep thinker…and I…" Charlotte suddenly jerked both of her palms from the psychic's grip.

"Would you like to do Tarot cards instead?"

"No."

"I think you should," the psychic insisted.

"Read the Tarot cards for me," she said.

The woman quickly shuffled the cards in her hands. The back was done in purple printed ornaments, intertwining together; they were the same exact color as the psychics overlong, fake nails. Charlotte didn't like the color or the fakeness of the nails.

"You have secrets; they are a part of your past," the woman said, looking at the Tarot cards on the table.

Charlotte pressed her lips together and frowned, her heart beat fast inside her chest. She felt restless. She reached into her purse and placed money on the table on the top of the cards, quickly got up exited the psychic's tent.

The outdoors atmosphere cheered with children's laughter, as kids ran around freely, and adults enjoyed the sunny afternoon, there were food stands with hot dogs and reindeer sausages, the barbecue smell spread through the air, and mixed with the sweet aromas of funnel cakes topped with fresh berries. Kids eating ice-cream and snow-cones of various crazy colors that left stained lips green and blue. A live music where the largest open garden had beer and wine, local artist playing music on the stage, singing, the summer in full bloom, the longest day of the year, and the sun would stay on the sky nearly the whole twenty-four hours on this day.

Charlotte walked through the crowded downtown and sat on a bench overlooking the ocean. She watched the white caps coming and washing over the sandy shore, and the soothing sound of the waves, and then the music again entered the air from the stage in the distance when a little boy came to her and showed her a sea shell he found in the sand. "Look." The boy extended his open arm toward Charlotte.

"That's very pretty," she said and smiled at him.

A mother's voice called for the boy, and he quickly turned and ran away. Charlotte looked after him and the image opened a wound in her memory as she suddenly found herself young, back in time, when war was coming to an end, and the future of her and her baby boy was uncertain. The present mixture of kid's cheer, live music slowly faded away as the ocean waves pushed to the front and brought on their strengths coming to Charlotte's ears louder and stronger with every tide that washed on the shore. She shut her eyes and let the waves take her to her past. The sound of waves persisted and now mixed with the sound of horn that echoed through the wild, unsettled ocean.

Young Charlotte stood on the front deck of a large ship, a baby in her arms, wrapped in blue and white blanket, surrounded by other occupants, and their families, and luggage as they all said goodbye to the old continent and anxiously awaited the long route to get to the better world. The expectations were high and very uncertain, but the hope they carried joined them together, and where was hope, there was will. And the twenty-one year old Charlotte and her one year old son looked forward to the future, and the new hope that was given to them. As she stood on the deck, surrounded by people who waived at their loved ones who came to say good bye, she kissed the sleeping baby in her arms and moved the soft blue and white blanket higher to his chin, covering the golden rose pendant.

When she was at the hospital and a nurse brought her baby he had a pendant hidden and wrapped in the blanket. A golden chain, short, for a small child, and a round pendant that had an ornament in the shape of a single rose flower. Charlotte asked the nurse where the jewelry came from, but the nurse didn't know. When she asked the doctor, neither he had an idea, so, at least that's what he told her. She kept it and asked around the next day, but to no avail, the mysterious pendant belonged to no one. So she kept it. She kept it and thought maybe an angel brought it to her, maybe a message from her husband Klaus…Everything didn't need to be explained or had a reason, she simply thought. The baby didn't mind the necklace, and Charlotte liked how it looked on him. Little Kurt smiled a lot, and when he was happy, Charlotte was happy. They spent a month in the hospital and finally the day arrived and Charlotte could go home. The bittersweet thought of home she used to have back in the day, and now it was just the two of them. She lived in a small flat, a single room, with a joined bathroom on the floor that the other two flats used.

When an offer came to her, through a friend of another friend, Charlotte didn't hesitate. Even the thought of leaving her home, the only one she had ever known, didn't hold her back. She had to start over, and a new, foreign place, far away on a new continent sounded just like a perfect plan. The world was going through turmoil; the war was coming to an end. The only thing she really care about was to have a better future for her son. She agreed and entered a new adventure. She stepped on a ship that was bound to New York. She loved the idea. But deep inside, she was so scared, often crying herself to sleep at night. She'd lived through so much already, and survived. Charlotte promised herself, no matter what, the life she's going to make is going to be a good one.

A good person was awaiting them at the New York's harbor, the older man spoke her language, for which she was grateful. She stayed at his place, and the family of four was gracious to her. She stayed in the big city for a year, and surprisingly fast she came to accustom and adjust herself to new things around, learning the language was not easy, but she practiced for several hours every day with the kids of the family she stayed with. And then one day, when she was working at the harbor, she met a man, a fisherman, who came on business all the way from the west coast, and beyond, he said his life is in Alaska and Charlotte was enchanted by his stories of the nature and the ocean, and she said good bye again, this time to the big city for an exchange for yet another adventure, and joined Jack in Alaska, and he became the father of Kurt and raised him as his own, and because she asked him, he never told the older son he wasn't his biological father. She made a home in a small town and learned to like it. When Alfred was born, her life became richer and she felt the family couldn't be happier. With two sons and a husband, Charlotte Groeneweg lived one day at a time. Such a life didn't last, and the first tragedy came with

Alfred. He fell from the stairs when he was three years old, causing him to stammer. He developed slower, and they knew he was always a little behind. She felt the fall was a curse from above, because she was lucky until then – she had survived and had good things coming to her life. The second time the tragedy stricken was on a stormy night, in a fall, when her husband drowned on the fishing boat. The boys were still small children, and Charlotte became a widow for the second time.

The second time the tragedy strike, Charlotte thought someone had sent a curse on her. When Kurt was born, she couldn't feed him, the doctor told her, not to worry, and he told her he would find a way and keep her boy alive. She stayed in the hospital for a month, while someone else nursed her newborn child. Charlotte was afraid to ask questions. On the last day, when they brought her Kurt, the necklace appeared, and she thought, it was a gift. A good present, but now, she thought it was cursed. She took it from the Kurt's neck and placed it into a wooden box. Then, on an early spring morning, when the fog covered Lingit, Charlotte Groeneweg went outside to her yard and dug a hole, where she buried the necklace. She placed new soil over, and planted roses all over the place in front of her house. On that early spring morning, she forever buried a tie to her past.

Wet drops spattered on her and brought her from her thoughts. Charlotte opened her eyes and Holton dropped a wet tennis ball to her lap. She smiled at the dog and scratched him on the top of the head. "Go get your ball," she said as throwing the tennis ball into the ocean.

"Hello, mama." Kurt joined her on the bench. "What a beautiful day." He looked at his dog, battling the waves trying to get to the ball. He tiled his head and looked at his mother. "I'm glad you got out of the house."

"I've been living in this town for over four decades. Can you believe that? Where did all that time go? I feel so old."

Kurt reached for his mother's hand. "You're not old."

"My sweet Kurt." She looked at his eyes and kissed the top of his hand he held in hers. "Where's your brother?"

Kurt bent down and took the ball from Holton's mouth. He cleaned the sand from the wet surface, but the impatient dog jumped up and snatched it from his hand, then ran away to the ocean, carelessly jumping through the white caps.

"Alfred's at home, just keeping to himself, as usual."

The kid that brought the sea shell to Charlotte was back, now playing with Holton, making a total mess of himself. The dog jumped in the air and then shook his wet fur all over the boy, and then Holton barked and the boy threw him a ball and the dog chased after it.

"You used to do that, roll around in the wet sand; the sand was everywhere, in your hair, in your mouth, ears. You never wanted to go to the bathtub and allow me to get you cleaned. Remember those days, when we had our first dog, Rex?" Charlotte asked with a soft voice.

"I remember some. I definitely remember good old Rex."

"You've always had this tremendous drive in yourself. And now you are stuck here, in this small town, cut away from other civilization...Don't you miss being around the big corporate world on East Coast?"

Kurt thought of his answer. Did he miss the outer world that used to mean so much to him? "No, I don't miss anything from that past," he said firmly. Only Charlotte could see a slight hesitation in the tone of his voice. She knew, he practically sacrificed himself, to return to Lingit, to take care of her and his younger, crippled brother.

Sacrifices. At some point in our lives, we all have to come to terms and in one way or another sacrifice something, in exchange for something, or someone else. Kurt placed his arm around her shoulders, "I love you, Mama."

Charlotte leaned over and kissed his cheek, but didn't say anything.

"Have you thought of going back to Europe…going to visit Germany?"

"No. Why would I do that?"

"Why? It's still a part of who you are. It's a place, where you were born, and where you grew up…"

"It's in the past now. I don't look into the past. You know it. I live for today and what's tomorrow going to bring…" Charlotte shrugged her shoulder, "Nobody knows."

"I thought of going over and travel a bit." Kurt said with a sad sigh.

Charlotte's face instantly froze and her posture stiffened. She removed Kurt's arm from her shoulders and looked deeply into his blue eyes. "Why would you do that?"

"Why? Isn't it obvious? My mother is from central Europe, and I thought, maybe, just maybe we could have a trip overseas…" He looked back at her, and suddenly regretted having this conversation.

"That girl, over there, she looks familiar. Don't you think? Do I know her?" Charlotte said suddenly, staring at a woman in a straw hat and a summer dress. Holton stopped playing with the boy and ran to the girl. "I think I've seen her somewhere before…"

Did Margot see them? She was preoccupied by greeting the wet, dirty dog.

"It's getting too crowded for me here," Charlotte said as rising.

Kurt and watched her to walk away.

§

Margot looked up and saw Kurt sitting on the bench by himself. He waved at her and she waved back before throwing the ball to Holton. Kurt got up and walked down to the water and joined them. The dirty, happy mutt stained Margot's pretty dress with his large, wet paws.

"Sorry about the dog. He is such a mess."

"Oh, I don't mind. I'm getting use to the fact that every time I see you, I lose some piece of clothing."

"Ah, the backpack that went down the river…" Kurt smiled at her. "I'm sorry about that, too."

"Where's Alfred? I haven't seen him lately. Is he okay?"

"My brother? He's fine. He's kind of like my mother, avoids big crowds. And believe it or not," Kurt pointed his hand toward the people ahead, "This is crowded Lingit."

Margot smiled and nodded. "Was that was your mother on the bench with you?"

"Yeah. She is a character."

"How so?"

"Umm, Charlotte Groeneweg lives in her own world she'd created for herself a long time ago."

"What kind of world is it?"

"I'm not sure. I don't really know. Sometimes I think my mother has a lot of secrets. Deep, and scary…Maybe I don't really know her that well,…my own mother…"

They walked side by side on the beach, with Holton running around them with a tennis ball in his mouth. Margot looked up at Kurt and pressed her lips firmly together, and smiled mysteriously. "You know, how it is, when you meet with people," she said. "It can set your mood for the moment, or for that day, sometimes you know what to expect. Like when you meet with a friend you know, and you tell yourself, *'I'm going to laugh,'* or other times, when you meet with a stranger and the stranger sets a mood, gives you a certain vibe, you don't like. At the end, it's up to you, how you're going to deal with it."

Kurt paused and picked up the ball Holton dropped in front of him. He threw the ball as far as he could, and the dog chased after it, water splashing to the sides from his wet fur.

"Even though she is my mother, sometimes I really think there's a lot, I don't know about her. Sometimes she gives me the creeps."

Margot suddenly stopped and stared at him. He looked vulnerable and his face saddened. The words of her own father came to her mind. "You know, my father always says that you need to bring humor to your life, otherwise life is not worth living…" She took a deep breath and continued, "That life without humor is only half-way lived."

"I think I can agree with that," Kurt replied and his face cheered up and showed a genuine smile.

"So what do say, are you ready to run to the top of the Chetan Mountain?" she asked.

He looked surprised; he didn't expect Margot to join the run. "Sure. Are you?"

"I'm ready."

The sun was up high on the sky, a beating heat, and now it also came from down below, as the concrete warmed up and the people gathered under the hill, the marathon announcer fired its fake gun in the air and the spectators cheered for the runners. Margot's tan body gleamed in the shorts and tank top she wore, as she tackled the uphill battle surrounded by couple hundreds of other eager runners. The hill's ground was soft, and mushy, and got softer under the feet and running shoes, creating mud on the lower portion of the Chetan Mountain.

The heart inside her chest beat faster as her lungs gasped for more air, the hill proved to be a challenge for her. Kurt attended the race, but she lost the sight of him, there were just too many people, and they pushed one another like hungry vouchers to get faster, sooner to the prey, in this case, the top of the hill, a very steep climb. Although the bottom of her running shoes had good traction, many times she felt like mountain goat, using both of her arms and her hands holding onto the hill, her fingernails stained by dirt, and her forehead covered with sweat.

There were kids, with their mothers and fathers, singles, and couples, young and old, all together with one goal, to reach the top of the mountain, not for a price, or money, but for fun, for the joy of the day, the longest day of the year, when the outdoor light never leaves the sky, the only day, that's rightfully called a Solstice day. The slippery grass got stomped by the enthusiasts, over and over again, until the dirt prevailed and covered most of it. People stood on the sides and cheered loudly, their hands clapping, some whistled and some yelled when they got a glimpse of their family members among the crowd. The hill beamed in various colors of T-shirts and jerseys. The mountain came to life for only one day a year.

Some runners already gave up and exited the race, while those with the athletic bodies kept on running; Margot had no doubt that the latter attended the race every year. She wanted to get on the top, for her own inner satisfaction. She pushed harder with every step uphill. Some people had trumpets in the audience, others had drums. Loose dogs ran underneath the legs of children and adults, the wind that picked up and became stronger, brought over the smells of the barbecue stands.

A familiar voice came upon behind her, "Hey, city girl!" Kurt got next to her.

And before she could answer, another familiar tone showed up from the other side, "Good to see you here."

"Leaf!"

Leaf winked at her.

"I thought you have an injured leg!" Margot said honestly.

"I do, but nothing would keep Leaf away from Solstice run! It's my town, it's my run!" "Have fun!" Leaf yelled and disappeared among the other runners.

The rugged terrain's steepest part was the last portion of the hill. Margot looked up and saw the fastest runners going down, a much more difficult task than climbing up. She stretched her arm as far as she could to reach an overlapping boulder, and pulled herself up, bringing her right knee to her chin, but she didn't have much strength in her upper arms and couldn't bring her left foot up. The slippery portion of the hill underneath her legs totally bogged her. She got very irrigated, when suddenly she felt someone touching her butt and lifting it up.

"Come on, Margot, you can do it."

"Kurt! Get your hands off of me!"

"Not until you get to the top."

She pulled herself up and looked down at him. He made a quick step and joined her in a second on the top of the mountain. He smiled and gave her an unexpected hug. She hesitantly wrapped her arms around him but didn't hold tight like him.

"Am I forgiven for touching your lovely behind?" he said.

She looked at him with her lime colored eyes, "I'm gonna need to think about that."

"Okay. We still have to get down." They both looked down below. The colorful crowed looked like a field of ants. The spectacular view from the top offered wide ocean scenery.

She could see the entire town that seemed smaller now, than a shape of her own palm. She seized the moment thinking; this is probably her first and last time standing on the top of the world, in the land of the midnight sun.

Margot felt great she was able to climb the Chetan trail about two thousand feet above the sea level and 2.2 miles in length.

"Good job, Margot!" Kurt cheered her up.

"Thanks. I'm really glad I made it up the hill," she said while she lowered her sight to the downhill in front of her feet. "I can feel my legs burning. I don't think I got this much physical exercise in years!" she added humorously.

The descend wasn't easy, especially on her knees, but she didn't give up. She found joy in the movement, in the nature and in the people around her, the alluring atmosphere of happy faces, laughter, encouragement and accomplishments. Margot found it easy to get inspired here in this small, seaside town. In fact, she felt a strange attraction to this place, as if she was meant to be here, meant to come and visit it and now, she was actually doing it.

The sweet, sugary aroma of the cotton candy watered her mouth with saliva. She took a piece of the bright pink color in her fingers and let it melt on her tongue. The artificial color stained her hands and lips. She looked over at Kurt. "I feel like a kid."

"There's nothing wrong about that," he replied, and she noticed his blue lower lip from the blue cotton candy in his hands.

"I can just sit here and do nothing. And it makes me happy. Is that normal?"

He looked at her and paused for a moment. Kurt's face got serious, as he shifted his sight from Margot's face to the ocean. He kept quiet. She looked at him and for a brief moment regretted, she cannot confine in him to let him know, why she came to Lingit. This wasn't the right time or the right moment. Will there ever be? Will she be brave enough to face the reality, does she have what it takes to bring the last missing piece of the puzzle she's been working on for so long, to make it complete? Is she going to hurt someone by going back to the past, to reveal what's left unsaid? Is it fair, ethical, necessary? What has she brought onto herself?

"Margot? A penny for your thought?" Kurt's piercing blue eyes looked at hers.

She shrugged and got up from the sand. She brushed her tights. If love also means compassion, then she has to carry on, for her stepmother, for Charlotte, for Kurt, Albert and for herself. Margot had her mind set, determined, with a goal. She made a decision; she needed to carry it out. It was too late to back out of it now.

CHAPTER 14

*ATTRACTION. A WORD WITH A **Meaning** of many shades, variations, shapes and melodies. What is a desire to attraction, and can one be without the other? Do we desire to attract or do we attract to desire? In the animal world, the males fight over to win the females, the strong desire to mate and attract is pure and innocent, but it's also violent, and the males who lose bleed their wounds, so the attraction can also destroy, but the desire persists and they keep on going for the next mating season, for the next hope, a chance until they no longer can, but survive. It's the desire and attraction to their own demise.*

Animals in nature don't see the attraction as physical, to them, it's more the attraction of scent, vibes, an allure the female gives give out to the male she attracts. It's a primal lust and I sometimes wish this would apply with people, sort of like a beauty within, beneath the surface, when one's eye needs to look deeper to recognize the higher self.

I yearn for such a harmony, but doubt I'll ever find it myself. Could it be the same with people, can humans attract to desire and then destroy for they longed for?

Margot stopped typing, and reached over for a glass of white wine. She felt the chilled liquid going down her throat; she quickly finished the glass and hoped to feel the buzz soon.

She crossed her arms behind her back and stared at the screen. John Ford told her to submit a new story for the magazine. She attached the photos from the trip she took with Kurt. With that thought the corners of her lips curled into a soft smile. The bear viewing experience and the night spent on the top of the glacier changed her inside. She used to feel a lot of anger, especially when she worked in the city, surrounded by the rush of people, bosses, managers. For the past two and a half months she slowly transformed into a new Margot. And the old Margot like the new one a lot more. She gave herself to nature, she stripped the layers that she used to treasure so much and so deliberately, not letting others to get to know her better. But now, she became a vulnerable Margot, still slightly melancholic, but much happier than ever before. She thanked this little town, this trip, this life experience for it. She thanked Kurt in her mind. But she was afraid to speak out with her words.

Margot downloaded the images of grass, where a sow moose and her two calves slept overnight. Perfect maps of folded grass, that persisted even after the animals exited the site.

She mailed it to John Ford at Natural Bird Magazine and let out a loud sigh. She knew he would call, and when the landline rang on the kitchen wall, where the telephone was mounted, she already stood there, waiting, with her third glass of wine in her hand.

"Hello?"

"Margot!"

"Hi John."

"What the hell did you just send me? What's this? I can't use that. I..I just can't print this!"

Margot had to put the receiver away from her ear. She took a deep breath and let out a deep sigh.

"Did you even read what you wrote?"

"Yes, of course, I did," she said and he sensed her ironic tone of voice.

"Have you been drinking?"

Margot looked at the nearly empty bottle of wine on the kitchen counter, her lips parted and then shut. She didn't reply to John.

"Hello? Margot? You still there?"

"Yeah. I'm here. Look John, I thought the pictures are beautiful and you can use them."

"Pictures of grass? I mean, what am I even looking at?"

"It's an imprint of a cow moose and her two babies." Margot twisted the rubber cord around her forefinger. She pressed the receiver closer to her ear, but the other side of the phone was quiet. "That's where the sow moose had lain, that's where they all slept."

"Hmm, I don't get it," John Ford replied with a distant voice, and Margot felt sorry for him. "How's the local beach?" he asked sarcastically.

"It's nice."

"Yeah? What did you do there?"

"I just sat there."

"You didn't go surfing, or for a swim, or on a boat ride, nothing? Nothing at all? You just sat on the beach?"

"Yeah, I did."

"That's boring."

"No, it isn't. I sat in the warm sand, and overlook the ocean and I thought how small our existence is, how little we are, with our lives, and with our worries, and with vanities, and pettiness. And how little we laugh in our lives, and how little we appreciate the good things, good friends, and how little we express love to one another. I thought of how much everyone rushes to get somewhere, to get up in the morning, to rush to get to work, to rush from work, to rush to get groceries, cook dinner, rush to go to bed, rush to get and catch on sleep, only to rush again in the morning. And the whole circle repeating insanely to the point when one day you stop, and the reason you stop is because you die." She paused and took a deep breath, and then she continued with emphasis, "And I sat on the sandy beach, and overlooked the ocean and I told myself, you know what? I want to disconnect from my fake friends, from the rush in my life, and for once in a life, I want to feel alive, and I want to be alive. And so I did just that. I sat on the beach on that beautiful day and I lived."

"When are you coming back?" he asked her suddenly.

"I don't know, yet." She replied distantly.

"What? You've been there for two months now. How much longer are you planning on staying there?"

"When you're busy, times go by quickly. And I've been pretty busy here…"

With a strong, angry voice John Ford replied, "You're in the middle of nowhere on an island!"

"It's a peninsula," she corrected him, and then said firmly, "I have to go now."

"No. Wait!"

"Bye, John." Margot hung up. She poured the last glass of wine and said to herself, "Bottoms up."

She crashed on the living room sofa, but her mind wouldn't let her rest. She returned to the day on the glacier. When Kurt and she sat around the portable stove, drinking grog at midnight, and the sky was bright blue, and light was all around them. The warm, aromatic spices of dark rum, and cloves tickled her nose, as she drank the hot liquid.

"What's your daily affirmation?" Kurt asked softly.

"A what?"

"How do you encourage yourself to keep doing, whatever you're doing. You know what I mean…"

Margot took a sip of the hot, inviting aromatic liquid. "I don't have one."

"Really? I find it hard to believe."

"What's yours?" she looked deeply at him.

Kurt stared at his cup, then he bit his lower lip and raised his eyes and looked intensely at Margot. "I try to go by my guts. And also I remind myself I need to trust my inner compass that I have here." He placed his right hand over his chest, where his heart is, then he paused for a second, before he continued, "I know I need to trust my inner compass that I have in my heart."

"That's beautiful," Margot replied.

Kurt has been on her mind since the first time she met him at the grocery store. A man, who sacrificed his life, his lucrative career he had in New York, only to return to the forgotten small town in the big Alaskan land to take care of his mother and his brother. Kurt has a strong character and charisma, and there was a lot of love in his heart. She also thought he has a gift to recognize and separate all the rotten ugly characters that he had met on his way in the big world.

Margot admired his strong will, it was alluring to her. She knew of people who would no matter what do anything just to climb on the top and throw others who put their trust in them into the lion's den.

She didn't want to hurt him. He had no idea why she came to Lingit. Margot chose to find out the last piece of puzzle that belonged to her stepmother Edith. Now, she was closer than ever, and she made a promise to herself carry on until the end. She is a fighter, it's in her blood.

Although she never liked playing mind games, those kind of teases where one person talks, but really doesn't say anything, rather let's the other person guess, instead of being straightforward and honest, Margot became the one, who played the game now. The only way to get out of it is for her to finish it until the very end. The moment when she told her father Adam popped up in her mind.

"Humans haven't really evolved that much. We drink coffee to wake us up and then we take sleeping pills to put us to sleep. It's ironic." Adam told his daughter.

"The mouse goes where the cheese is," Margot replied to him.

"Yes. But it's the curiosity that kills the mouse at the end. Are you sure, you want to go there?" He asked cautiously and placed his arms around Margot's shoulders.

"Yes. Yes, I'm sure. Sometimes you just have to take a risk." Chardonnay made her pleasantly tired; she adjusted the pillow below her head and stretched her body on the sofa. As Margot's eyelids got heavy, she muttered under her lips, "The world out there is cruel."

※

Young Edith woke up to a rambling beating of large rain drops on the window, the wind strongly swished through the open seals in the corners of the wooden frame. A long, angry lightning, flashed on the night, dark sky, and then another much stronger with cricket arms and legs that spread wide to the sides, accompanied by roaring thunders. Edith left the curtains opened when she went to bed. Just a few hours ago the night sky gleamed with beautiful bright stars and she had a perfect view from her hospital bed. The calmness and peacefulness of the sky disappeared and the devil took over the night.

The apple trees outside in the courtyard fought the force, but the weakest branches couldn't but stand the brutal storm and cracked and fell and flew away in the wind on the ground, the first green leaves still attached, a spring unfulfilled for the future blooms and apples that the branch could have delivered. Edith suddenly felt a profound loneliness in her heart. She's been in the hospital for nearly a month now. She'd demanded answers from the doctor and the nurses, but none replied to her clearly. Why was she still there, why wouldn't they let her and her baby boy go home already? She had no visitors; the war took all she ever loved, her husband, her parents, her sister, and her child alive. If there weren't for the baby, she wouldn't have fought so hard to live. The baby meant everything to her, and for the newborn's life she carried on, she kept on going, breathing, and living for another day.

But now, she had enough of the lies the nursing stuff have told her. She's made up her mind, she is going to take her baby in the morning and leave this place, for once and for all. The brightest of the lightings, flashed through the window in front of her, and reappeared several times accompanied with the scariest thunders. Edith got up and walked to the curtains, sliding them together tightly. The golden chain and a half-circle rose pendant she wore on her neck reflected in the glass's window and Edith stared for a brief second at herself, then she looked behind the image and out the window a shadow of a creature passed on the sidewalk, slowly turning its dark face toward Edith. Was that the devil himself? She shrieked and firmly shut the curtains together. Her hands trembled as she returned to bed; she muttered under her lips, "The world out there is cruel."

Edith awaited the nurse to bring her the baby to feed, she felt anxious, after the stormy night, she wasn't able to really fall asleep and the restlessness showed in her fingers. She nervously tapped the tips of her right hand on her knee, when the doctor entered her room. Edith tried to read his face, but the grey haired doctor Sigi kept his eyes low to the ground, and the thick, black frames of his glasses didn't allow her to see much of his face from the profile.

He shut the door behind him and walked over to the simple desk and pulled out a chair. Edith finally looked him in the eye. There was no emotion, no expression; the doctor's eyes had no depth, as if he wasn't a human being.

"Mrs. Altman...Edith, I'm afraid I have bad news for you." The words came out of his thin lips, and entered her small, hospital room and traveled like a sharp bladed knife that pierced straight through her young heart.

She couldn't move, her entire body froze at the moment, and she became paralyzed with fear and the impact of the sentence delivered to her.

The doctor continued, casually, as if this was a routine conversation. Edith watched his thick, dark eyebrows move, the only movement in his face, more of a tick, as he said, "Your baby boy has died."

"What?" She felt her lips move and heard her voice enter the room now, but her body remained very still, her fingers clawed to her knees.

"I'm sorry, Edith."

"No! No, that can't be! How could he die? He was just with me yesterday. What happened to him?" Edith's body went into a panic, and tears rolled down her cheeks she felt the most atrocious pain inside her heart. A disbelief and complete despair and surrealness of the moment set in, and then she looked the doctor in his eyes and felt tremendous anger as she got up and threw herself at him and started beating him with her hands into his chest. Edith screamed out loud from her lungs as the doctor tried to pull her arms away and behind her back. Two nurses entered the room and fought her strengths, prevailing when a sharp needle entered one of her arms. Edith lost control of her limbs and her strength instantly dissolved under the influence of the clear liquid that the beasts injected inside her broken body, inside her broken heart. Her mind now clouded with the darkest thoughts spread across her brain, her cheeks became pale, and her lips cold and dry and crusted in the corners, pressed firmly and then parted but weren't able to pronounce any words. The sharp migraine struck her every nerve, the brown and grey lines appeared under her tired eyes as the beasts laid her on the bed.

She felt her loose arms hang over the edges of the cold, hospital sheets, a puppet obeying the orders of the soulless, heartless monsters leaning above her. She turned her head and her blurred vision enlarged the numbers from the desk calendar that stood on the stand next to her. She muttered the numbers with her slurry, slowed speech, nineteen-forty-four.

The world shut down around the young woman as her body gave up and gave in to the ropes that tied her to the hospital bed and overtook the possession of her being.

Edith opened her eyes and bluntly stared at the calendar on her night stand next to her bed. "Nineteen-ninety." She moved a strand of her hair from her eyes and wiped the sweat out of her forehead and moved on her back, covering her face with her left forearm. Edith pulled herself up and walked to the bathroom. She turned the water on and washed her face, letting the lukewarm drops slide down over her high cheekbones, and some over the lips, and down on her chin and neck. She watched the clear drops, that could have been her own tears, except there weren't salty to make a wet lines as they continued down her chest in between her breasts and disappeared behind her V-neck blouse. She reached for a brush and combed it through her thick, naturally curly hair. She kept her youthful haircut, cut under her chin, and parted to the sides all her life. Her father's genes passed onto her, and at her age, nearly seventy years old now, she had very few grey strands. The chestnut color of her hair made her look much younger. All Edith had were memories of her parents, the past, she was so afraid to go back to, and so she visited it only in her dream, involuntarily, her mind, the suspension of disbelief she so much forced to fight during a day, entered and prevailed, until she woke up. Reliving the past was very hurtful to her. She heard the garage door open and the engine of a car came closer until it shut down. She swung around slammed the bathroom door. Edith slid the glass door to the shower and turned both faucets on. The water from the shower beat on the tub.

She leaned closer to the wall. Adam came home early from work, he always did on Fridays. For the past eighteen years, Friday night was their date night. They started this tradition after Margot left for college. Only on a few occasions they weren't able to keep the date, but then Adam made it out to her. A knocked on the bathroom door made her jump.

"Edith?"

"I'm in the shower," she yelled, still fully dressed, her back pressed against the wall.

"Just making sure, you're okay."

She heard his step sound on the tiled floor moving farther away from the door, as he exited the bedroom.

Edith let her clothes fall on the tiles as she stepped in a shower and let the water clean her body, her hair, she thought of how great the shower is, to take away what's on surface. She could put on a face and a nice dress and her lips would curl into a smile, even though the pain inside her heart would be no different. Adam didn't have to suffer with her. She wouldn't want him to. Her past was separate from his, and he deserved the better Edith, the happy Edith, because, he truly made her a new woman. She lathered the white foam from the light scented shampoo in her hair and let the water do the rest. She looked forward to the dinner with him.

The female signer looked like a diva in the dimmed light, standing next to the piano, dressed in a long, black dress that had silver linings on the edges of a deep open back and neck, and its sleeves covered the young artists slim arms all the way to her wrists, and every time she moved, the silver glitters took on various shades of colors in the restaurant's light. The jazz singer moved slowly to the rhythm of the song, as the male pianist occasionally lifted his eyes from the keyboard glancing over to her. The restaurant was full of people of different ages, and ethnic groups, people dressed nicely and ladies wore their jewelry and flowery perfumes mixed with the men's colognes in the air and from time to time a scent of a freshly grilled steak and dill potatoes entered the air.

Adam took her hand and leaned over and gently kissed her rosy cheek. After all these years, she was still in love with the man, as he was in love with her. Edith knew, she was a lucky girl. After the life played its cruel prize upon her, for whatever reason, spared her soul and took everyone else's, a miracle came in a form of a good Samaritan, who helped her back on her feet, to rebuilt what remained to gain strength to fight on.

"You fight for what is your own; you fight when you have to."

The angel sent her to America, with a single piece of luggage that was made out of carbon thick paper, and had two silver flip on flip off safety pins. Adam represented everything, the love of her life, the light, the purpose to be; at times she felt she didn't deserve him. She leaned closer to him and whispered into his ear, "You're my best friend. And you're still very handsome."

He wrapped his arm around her shoulders and kissed her on the lips as the jazz singer finished her song and the last tones of the piano accompanied her voice. The hands of the people in the audience clapped, and the young singer glittered in her gorgeous nightgown as she bowed and smiled. And then as she tilted her head and shifted her eyes, all of a sudden, the sharpest of pains pierced through her heart as her eyes met with the elderly man, sitting by himself across the room behind the table in the corner.

Edith shrugged and let go of Adam's hand as her face gained an expression of a righteous shock.

"Edith, what's wrong? Are you okay?"

"Excuse me for a second," she heard herself say, as her she got up and stood on her feet.

"Edith!" Adam called after her, but she was already half way gone across the restaurant.

The singer's strong voice united the people again, as they quieted down, and let the pianist and his beautiful muse entertain them for the night.

Edith looked at herself in the restroom's mirror. "That can't be him. No way. It's not possible. How old would he be now?

Ninety?" She heard a flush from one of the stools and realized she wasn't alone there. Edith quickly splashed her hands with water and pumped some soap into her palm. A woman joined her at the long, dark marble sink. She smiled at her and Edith politely returned the smile looking at the woman in the mirror reflection.

"I always like the smell of the vanilla soap they use here. Isn't it lovely?"

"What?" Edith stared at the woman's full lips that were stained with a bright orange red lipstick.

"Don't you love the smell of the soap here?"

"Oh, yes, of course. It's lovely." Edith waited for her to exit, before she straightened her back, she pulled her shoulders back, raised her chin up high and with a firm voice replied to her own self in the mirror. "You're falling to pieces. Pull yourself back together, Edith Altman!"

As she returned to Adam's table, she looked one more time at the old, single seated man in the corner. Her mind played a trick on her. There was no way this could have been the doctor that came to her hospital room to tell her that her baby had died. She hoped that man no longer was alive. For the sake of others, if not for her own.

Adam greeted her with a warm smile. "Hi." He stood and pulled her chair from the table and waited for her as she sat down. "I missed you."

The waitress brought them food, and poured more wine into their glasses, as they ate and listened to the jazz. Edith turned her head one more time the direction, but the corner table was empty now, and she thought, maybe, just maybe, there was no one there seated this whole time, only her mind and her sight played a trick on her.

Later that night, when Adam was sound asleep, she quietly got up and opened her drawer, and slid her arm inside underneath her folded cloths, and took out a wooden box. She opened it and took out the golden chain link with the half-round pendant and kissed it. She felt the rose petals on her lips. They were cold, oh so, very, very cold. Edith carefully placed the pendant back and shut the drawer. She walked over to the kitchen, and picked up the phone, listening to the dial tone for a brief moment, before she pressed the numbers and the ring tone entered her ear. Edith let the phone ring for a long time, before a sleepy voice picked up on the other side of the receiver.

"Hello?"

"Hi baby."

"Mom? Are you okay…is dad okay?"

"Yes, Margot. Dad's asleep, and I just couldn't fall asleep… Did I wake you up?"

"No, it's not even that late here." Margot leaned over and looked the clock on the kitchen wall. "It's only ten thirty."

"I forgot. You're four hours behind. Funny, how far away you are now."

"It's four hours from East Coast, yeah I'm on Alaskan time…"

"I'm just missing you. It's a lot quieter here without you." Edith said softly and truthfully.

"Mom?"

"Yes, dear."

"Did you get my email? The last one I sent you…"

Edith paused, before she replied, "Yes and I will *see you* soon."

"Thank you."

The women spoke for a few more minutes, a pleasant conversation between two beautiful souls, not related by blood but very strongly bonded through their lives and fate that tied them together. A mother and a daughter. One, who came from the old continent, the other who waited for her on the new one.

Margot hung up, went to the bathroom, brushed her teeth, and combed her strawberry colored hair. Barefooted, she walked to her bedroom and threw herself to bed and shut the light. Before she drifted for the night, the words of her article from earlier that day came to her mind and mixed with her father Adam and her stepmother, Edith.

Attraction. A word with a meaning of many shades, variations, shapes and melodies. Attraction is Adam and Edith.

CHAPTER 15

EDITH **D**IDN'T **W**ANT **T**O **L**IE to herself. She was scared but determined to face the inevitable. She looked at the folded cloths she laid out on bed in front of her. Margot had told her to bring casual clothes, something she feels comfortable wearing, and leave the expensive at home, if she doesn't want to lose it. The most expensive item, that couldn't be measured in the amount of money, was the golden necklace and pendant. She placed her clothes in the luggage and sat on the bed. From underneath her pillow, she took out the necklace. She clutched her fist and shut her eyes. Goosebumps appeared on her bare arms.

"I can do this. I must do this, for once and for all," she whispered to herself.

If there weren't for her stepdaughter, Edith's life would continue in its normal pace, day to day, and her inner demons, her past and her youth would be hidden from the rest of the world, just like she wanted, just like she decided a long time ago. But Margot entered her life, and she no longer was the little girl, Edith met the first time, Margot's father introduced them. A lot has happened since, and the two women became best friends, and when Edith found out, what's Margot's curious mind was up to, at first she got very furious at her, but never told her. Just like Margot, Edith had a secret, and she kept it hidden. Now, Margot invited her to visit the Alaskan peninsula. She told her Edith needed a vacation, and she has a surprise for her. Edith felt, the surprise will be bittersweet. She didn't want to disappoint her stepdaughter.

Edith knew of no one who could relate to her secret. How could anyone? One thing she really wanted to know, and that is how did Margot find out? Edith thought of many different scenarios but always came to the same conclusion; Margot didn't hear anything from her. Edith treasured her past, and never let anyone on the new continent know, what lay deep within her soul.

Time has allowed her to deal with her pain. Is it possible that Margot found a connection at her work? On her many travels? Edith knew, she will find out soon. She quickly finished packing her luggage and checked the time on the wall. Adam will be home in about two hours, and then they will drive to the airport. A guilty feeling washed over her. Edith has always tried to be honest with him, and now, she couldn't tell him more, and it slowly tortured her inside.

She would never thought that she would live to be seventy years old. At least not when Edith was twenty-four, leaving the hospital, on that unusually cold, and breezy Bavarian morning. Alone, no baby in her arms, and she thought the world came to an end, her life ended at just twenty six years old, she had no one. A simple one room place, she shared with a friend, a joined bathroom on the common hallway for the two remaining flats on the same floor. She didn't see her future, young Edith thought she had none. Little she would expect, her life would take on yet another turn, and give her a new chance in a land, she only dreamt of.

That's why now, at seventy, when she looked in the mirror, she thought of all the years, that she buried in the past, and now, the time has come to face the unknown, to overcome her own challenge, and she didn't know, whether she is strong enough and what it takes for her to stand face in face even to see Margot. She thought she may never forgive her, because if she's going to tell her about her own past, than it better have the conclusion, she so much long to deserved.

Edith put on her favorite music and sat down into a deep, old, armchair. She watched as the vinyl span around on the old-fashioned gramophone. She poured herself a glass of Adam's cognac and sipped the liquid slowly. The soft tones of the music soothed her soul, her heart, as she listened to soft tones of violin playing joyfully and then the music swelled and strengthened with the symphonic orchestra adding dynamic piece and taking over, while the violin shut down, but not for long, returning back with a fast tempo, letting the sound flow through the air and out the brassed horn of the vintage phonogram.

Later that evening, Adam stood close to her, touching her hand, kissing her on the lips, before she exited through the airport's security and into her gate. She thought she would never live this long, and what on Earth's was she doing now? She headed on a flight in the middle of nowhere, in the far away land of Alaska.

Soon after the takeoff, she covered herself with a blanket and tried to catch on sleep. When she wakes up, she would see Margot, and everything will be fine. Maybe she just imagined this whole thing. Maybe her stepdaughter didn't have any agenda at all. What if Edith was all wrong about her? The life thought her not to trust people. Could it be that when she saw Margot going through her personal things, taking pictures of the necklace and rose pendant, taking pictures of the black and white photo of the newborn baby, that there wasn't a deeper meaning? She let out a loud sigh and moved the blanket closer to her chin. In a few hours she will hopefully find out. To travel across the states, from east coast to the west, wasn't such a simple thing to do. Edith was tired, she wanted to stretch her legs, put them up high. She was going through a crisis, where she wanted to scream, escape the people around her, the crying baby on the board that the mother could not quiet down, the flight attendant trying their best, to calm down the angry and irritated flyers.

Edith had no control, and she didn't like it. If she could drive a car to Alaska, at least she would be her own boss, she could decide when and where to stop, to choose her company around her, at least to some degree, but such a drive was too long for her, and it wasn't really practical. She popped a Valium in her mouth and ordered a glass of whiskey. The other woman, who sat next to her, gave her a strange look.

"What?" Edith asked and looked at her sharply.

"You shouldn't mix pills with alcohol."

"Excuse me?" Edith couldn't believe this stranger had to audacity to actually tell her what she should or shouldn't do.

"Sometimes you have to do what you have to do," she said and finished the whiskey. The baby kept on crying, but Edith's Valium kicked in, and the cries faded into distance, until they were no longer near her ears as she drifted into a relax, comfortable sleep.

§

The rain poured hard on the dried up soil that welcomed it instantly and soaked it in, so there was no water left on the surface of the rocks or the dirt. But there was enough water running down the edges of the paved road and down the hill, where it gained more strength, and took on loose debris and leaves before everything went down the gutter and underground. The large drops beat onto Margot's jeep, as she drove to the small airport on the outskirts of Lingit. She wore tight jeans, long, red rubber boots that covered her slim calves all the way under her knees and a white, long sleeve cotton shirt and a red capped raincoat. She parked the car and placed the hood over her red hair. She remained seated and just listened to the rain, thinking, she had no idea how she's going to pull through her plan once Edith steps of the plane. That's the thing about puzzles, planning and putting it together is one thing, but doing and going through is another story.

She watched the small commuter plane as it descended above the land strip and made a loop, before it touched down and landed in the uninviting weather conditions.

Margot covered her face with both of her arms for a brief moment, before she looked at herself in the mirror.

"Don't back out now," she told her own image, before she opened the jeep's door and her tall rubber boots stepped in a paddle down on the paved road.

"Everything's so green here. I didn't know that green color can be so pretty," Edith said, as she looked through the wet window out on the side of the road. "Does it rain often here?"

"This is the first big rain we've had, since I've been here," Margot replied without leaving her sight from the road, as she ran through a huge hole in the road, and the water splashed wildly to the sides. The rain persisted, as Margot helped to carry Edith's luggage into the house on the hill. Edith looked inside the cozy living room, and quickly asked for a burning fire in the wooden fireplace. Although she wasn't really cold, there was something homey and inviting to have a lit fireplace in July. Margot set a tea kettle on the stove, while she let her stepmother to look around. Edith stood by the large windows and looking out at the sandy beach and the ocean. The waves arose high, and the water was angry, unsettling, kind of like herself deep inside.

The whistling sound entered the air and made Edith look away from the deep, grey waters. She hurt it shut, as Margot poured the boiling water over the tea. The women sat on the brown leather sofa, the yellow gaze from the fireplace and the soft sound of birch logs cracked into the open.

"I can see why you want to stay here for the entire season." She tilted her head toward the glass doors. "This view is spectacular."

"Just wait when the rain stops and the sky clears. The sunsets are unreal here..." Margot said and Edith could sense something new in her stepdaughter's face. This was a different Margot.

"You don't have TV. How come, Margot? You? A TV fanatic?"

Margot giggled and bit her lower lip. "No, there's no TV here. I don't need one. There's so much to do outdoors, that when I come home, I'm tired, but not tired like I would be back in Seattle. TV is the last thing on my mind." She said and took a sip of her tea. Edith quietly watched her, and was amused and pleased at the same time to see Margot happy.

"Funny, what's two months can do to your inner self."

"I think you found yourself here, Margot. I really do." Edith said and Margot looked at her, but didn't say anything. Was Edith right?

"I find it *liberating*." She knew that's exactly how she felt. Liberated from all the head clutter the TV programs tried to push into their viewer's minds, commercials, products to buy, and then there were news, and every day violence. Only a fraction of the news was positive, optimistic or funny. And the anchors who put on their brave faces and read the evil news, as if they would read a consumers label of some type of food, and then switch into a different field, and genre and again talking mechanically, their faces barely moving, only the lips working overtime, and their voices delivering the dailies, and the anchors knew, they will do it all over again tomorrow morning, or at night, and the day after, because the world had so much to tell, and people always wanted to hear other peoples stories.

The only cable channel Margot would miss was the Cartoon Channel. She tend to turn it on late at night, when she couldn't fall asleep and watch *Tom and Jerry*, or *The Simpsons*, *Looney Tunes*.

"Margot?"

"Yes, Mom?"

"I said dad says hello. And yes, he's still afraid to fly." They both smiled at one another. Adam has never been on an airplane. Although he used various aircrafts in his cartoons and drawings, the man had never taken a trip into the sky.

Margot glanced over to the living room, where Edith sorted through various photographs, colored and in black and white that were laid out on the coffee table.

"These are so beautiful, Margot," she gasped over the images of the nature, forests, rivers, animals, and birds. Margot sat next to her and folded her legs under her chin.

"That's a Red Neck Grebe," she said as Edith looked at the bird that pose on the Wahya Lagoon, looking directly into Margot's camera. "And that's Northern Shoveler. They're all migrating birds. They come and go, have their young ones here, and fly away to Vancouver or Seattle for winter only to make the same trip again in the spring."

"Oh my goodness, look how cute she is!" Edith said softly, as she stared at the photograph of the young, red tailed fox. "It looks the animals just posed for you. These pictures are spectacular, Margot! I'm so proud of you!" she said and leaned over and placed her left arm around Margot's shoulder, while kissing her on the cheek.

"You're such a good photographer. You have an eye for detail and for the right moment. I bet to get these close ups wasn't always easy."

"No, often times it was a half day wait in the sun or in the rain or wind. Sometimes I got a glimpse of the animal, but it ran away before I could get a good focused photo." Margot took a sip of her tea and looked into the burning fireplace. The fire wasn't big, but she felt the heat and the nice, dry thin layered birch logs made the rainy day inviting.

"It's not like the fox, was waiting for me there. But you are not supposed to know the details behind the picture. That's the magic of the moment of the photo itself when it all comes together, and you look at the final print. All those days of waiting are all in this single picture."

Margot went into the kitchen and placed a dish of meatless balls in tomato sauce into the oven.

The women talked and laughed, and Edith felt proud of her stepdaughter's accomplishments that she almost forgot about her own past, of her son who been violently taken away from her, ripped from her heart, and vanished into the darkness. Until Margot awoken the evil spirits and brought them to life, once again, Edith would need to face the devil in flesh and blood. She promised herself she won't let anything show, until she was sure, that's why Margot invited her to Lingit. After all, this was a perfect place for the devil to hide. The end of the world, small hidden town, far away from major civilization, with a new start, while the past kept in secret. If the doctor is still alive, he must be over ninety years old, and probably weak in his body, but Edith thought, the devil's soul could still persist and be strong but could not hurt her anymore. Not now, not ever again.

There had been many sleepless night. Edith thought of the Bavarian doctor, who came to her room early morning, after the hellish stormy night, that had broken the branches of the apple tree in the hospital's courtyard. If Margot wanted to complete the puzzle of Edith's past, for whatever reason, perhaps to see her finally at peace with herself, she wasn't going to fight it. Ready to face the challenge, she flew to the last frontier.

The oven's loud been made Margot jump to her feet as she disappeared back in the kitchen. The women ate dinner, sitting on the pillows on the hard wood floor, in front of the fireplace, overlooking the angry ocean, and the rain beat to the drums, and the trumpets and the sad, melancholic tones of the cello, the wind that blew the rain drops against the glass. The scrapes of the silverware knives over the china plates.

"I'm so glad, you're here, Mom," Margot said after they ate, and Edith looked at her softly and took Margot's hand into hers. "Me too, Margot." Then she let go of her hand and let out a deep sigh. "Who would of ever thought, I would make it this far. Alaska, the land–" And then Margot joined her, and they both finished the sentence in two tones of voices, one young and strong, one old and with a slight German accent, "–of the midnight sun." Both of their faces lit with a brief smile as they looked at one another.

"Coffee?" Margot offered and didn't wait for a reply. She went into the kitchen and set two mugs on the counter. The aroma of freshly grinded beans dominated the kitchen's smell now, as Margot set the coffee machine for two cappuccinos.

She held a tray in her hands, as she returned to the living room her eyes glanced over Edith, sitting on the brown leather sofa, her head lowered, and her arms in her lap and her back slightly hunched over. As Margot set the tray with two cappuccinos, and strudel with walnuts and raisins and cinnamon sugar and vanilla bean, she baked earlier that day, before she drove to the airport to pick up her stepmother. She paused, because she saw Edith holding a black and white photograph in her hands. Margot thought she hid the picture in the book and set the book in her bedroom. Apparently she forgot, and now Edith stared at the image of herself, a young woman, with full lips, dark brown wavy hair, cut under her chin, and parted on the sides, her eyes full of life, a light blouse, with an open V showing her firm skin, and a necklace with a raised single rose dominating her neckline. Edith's fingers brushing back and forth over the rigged edges of the thick print paper, her lips parted, emotions showing on her forehead with wrinkles between her eyes, as her brows moved by the inner thoughts at that moment.

Margot quietly and slowly sat down next to her. "I love this picture of you. Hope you don't mind I took it here, with me."

"No, of course I don't mind." Edith set it aside on the top of the book, in which she found it. Now the book and her picture rested on the stand next to her right arm. Her past, present and her future all in that simple photograph.

"You know what they say...a picture says a thousand words. A black and white one shows your soul, while the colored pictures photograph your cloths," Margot said softly as she placed a piece of strudel with chopped walnuts and raisins, and hint of lemon, and rich in cinnamon and vanilla bean on a saucer and passed it to Edith.

As Edith finished the apple strudel, the mix of sour apples, walnuts and cinnamon melting in her mouth, she said, "Mmm, it's all very good, Margot. Thank you."

"I had the best teacher," Margot smiled at her. The memory of her youth resurfaced on her mind, as she spent nice time with Edith, who thought her how to cook and bake from scratch on the east coast, while her father Adam spent his time in his room, illustrating drawings for the Fenwick Press Sunday's papers. Suddenly, she wished for those times to be back, all those beautiful, peaceful moments of home and atmosphere, when she was a child. The smell of cinnamon will always remind her off Edith.

The large rain drops subsided, and only a soft rain fell from the dark clouded sky. The wind still blew strongly and made the unsettling ocean bring on large waves that crushed over the shore and rocks. All the birds were gone and the sand obeyed under the pressure of white caps that ruled over it. The tall grass and cattails swayed to the sides in front of the house's porch. The temperature dropped down to mid fifties. And then a first sunbeam cut through the thick, grey sky, a shy stream of light that persisted and got wider and stronger, with the help of the wind that sent the clouds away from the sun. And then across the beach and to the left of Margot's house, a spectacular double rainbow showed up on the open skyline.

Edith turned away from the glass door and called, "Margot…" She waved her right arm in the air. "…come over here. Look."

"Oh wow, that's beautiful! You see, I told you, the rain will go away." Margot quickly snatched her camera, and Edith opened the door and both women stepped on the wet wooden patio. Edith took a deep breath, the air fresh after the rain and the salty ocean opened up her lungs. She moved her chin up and against the sun that made its way through the clouds and now shined highly above the women's heads. Even the ocean now calmed, and Edith listened to the sound of waves whispering quietly and her eyes stared at the double rainbow, and its colors of red, orange, yellow and green. The crisp air brushed over Edith's cheeks and the wind made her velvet black and white scarf float behind her beck and over her shoulder blades.

She felt overwhelmed, every nerve in her body reacted to the beauty of the nature she was surrounded by. The rainbow on the sky still persisted, even though the rain was long gone, a gateway to a different world, *serenity*.

She felt a profound calmness as her body and mind were stripped of pain. She wished the moment would last, but a screaming sound of two seagulls now entered the space above the house, as the birds chased one another, because the one up front had a piece of food in its beak, and the other, smaller wanted it. Hunger made them enemies, as they fought over the piece of meat someone had thrown away. Their sharp, pointed yellow beaks screamed at one another, as their feet danced around on the wet pavement. One demanded the same thing from the other; to go away, to exit. And the stronger, bigger one got its wish as the weaker bird gave up and flew away empty beaked.

Later, when Edith lay in bed, sleep didn't come to her easily. The outside light confused her mind, and even thought she traveled a great distance, and made a four-hour time difference, her body wouldn't rest. Margot had bought thick drapes and placed them over the window in the bedroom, but the light still came through and didn't do the trick for Edith. She pulled the blanket to the side, dressed in pants and flannel shirt, and slipped her feet into the rubber boots and walked outside. The wind had dried the patio furniture, and there were no signs of previous heavy rain. Edith's brown curls moved into the wind as looked over the deep waters. She loved the sound of the ocean; she craved the sound of waves. She could easily picture herself to live here.

And then with that thought a creepy shadow clouded her mind. And she took her thought back; she would never be able to live in a place, where the evil lives. She has imagined a hundreds of times a situation where she would meet with the Bavarian doctor again. Anywhere in the world, her mind projected her with thoughts of various places, towns. If she ever met that man again, how would she react, what would she say to him, would she scream, cry or would she remained still, because all the screams and cries she had done in the past came unheard and unanswered.

Perhaps she is all wrong and this invitation is just a trip that Margot wanted her to take, to share some time with her, in a place where neither of them gone before. Maybe her beloved stepdaughter had no secrets, no surprises, and it's Edith's mind that tells her otherwise. But what if Margot really dug deep and went to places, where Edith has always wanted to go, but was too afraid of what she could find. A dilemma, with which Edith has struggled all her life. Pacific Ocean wept loudly around her with deep tones of basses, the voices of the bottom of the sea coming to surface and into the vast Alaskan air.

What really happened back in the hospital, where she gave birth to her only son? Forty six years ago, Edith had no answers, perhaps the time has finally come for her to know to lay the soul of her precious Rolf to rest, for once and for all. If the doctor lives and he's in this town, then she's going to face him and she'll demand the answers no matter what. Nothing would hold her back anymore. She stood up and quietly shut the glass sliding door behind her.

Edith leaned her back against the pillow and shut her eyes. This time, the sleep finally came, and the features of her face softened, her hands folded across her stomach, with fingers relaxed and legs covered with blanket, her lips shut together, and soft, green and purple veins showing through her skin on the temples, and under a few strands of her dark brown hair. Out the window, a light fog settled above the water and the sand, as the early morning pushed the night away.

CHAPTER 16

LINGIT'S MAIN STREET LIT UP with a parade of spectaculars, celebrating the Fourth of the July. A man with his lips pressed against harmonica in his hands, cheerfully entertained the crowd with a melody of rhythm cords that gathered around him, a hat laid out on the concrete road, with loose coins and some paper bills inside and around for the musician of the summer's afternoon. The man held its harmonica in his hands, sometimes covering a part or leaving it opened and just pressed against his bearded lips, he created high tones and low tones; he made the harmonica in his hands cry or laugh. Children of various ages running around, natives, whites and blacks and some Asians, whose parents own local restaurants, ran between the legs of pedestrians, sometimes bumping at the old ladies, all in good fun in the heat of the season.

Couples swing their hips and smiles appeared on their faces, their eyes hidden behind the dark sunglasses and hair tucked under the straw hats, baseball caps or just the foreheads of ladies hidden under the colorful visors that protected their skin from the bright sunlight. The bearded man wore no shirt, his skin burned from the sun; he knew how to play the small instrument and made it look easy and fun as he whistled various melodies of well known songs on his instrument, people joined in, and some sang along the harmonica, and the man behind it didn't stop, and the crowd changed after a while, some people continued walking, new ones stopped, and some sat down on the ground and crossed their legs and clapped their hands. Edith moved her wide hat lower to the eyes as she passed the harmonica man.

A native woman in her sixties, with her long dark hair, approached her. "I like you hat!" the native shouted.

"Thank you." Edith replied and smiled politely.

"You have a lovely smile. Pass it on!" the native shouted after her and waived. Farther away, where the paved road was wide and open, a bunch of young kids spread over the area and had crayons in their hands, drawing pictures of animals, and planes and sea creatures.

"There you are! Mom!" Edith heard a familiar voice.

"Hi Margot!" The women hugged and held it for a brief moment. The outdoor atmosphere boomed with positive energy and craved more hugs and kisses and smiling faces. The people united for one afternoon, one evening, all for good food, great fun and memories.

Edith thought how a mood of a person can change a perspective of another human being. The electrifying energy that someone can project onto another intensified with a certain mood, and it didn't matter if one knew that person or not. Just like the Indian woman a minute ago, the one who told Edith she had a lovely smile. Such a simple sentence with a powerful message was an instant mood fixer, an emotion that reflected in Edith's face, when she heard the words and smiled again. Edith needed to change an environment; she's been living on the east coast for nearly half a century!

The smell of boiled corn made the small children of a large family beg their parents and stop to feed their stomachs. The sad faces instantly disappeared when the kids' hands touched the corn on the cob or another's that dug into a bag of buttered popcorn. Even their little mutt dog got something in his mouth and meticulously licked his whiskers on both sides several times, before the kid fed him another piece of the greased popcorn.

"This town knows how to throw a party!" a random tourist shouted cheerfully as he passed them on the road. The smoke from the barbecue stands lifted up high and carried above downtown and into the open air. The ocean's calm waters attracted those who laid out their beach towels and folding chairs and carelessly spread their bodies on the warm sand, soaking in the sun and summer. Lingit in July beamed with newcomers, mixed with locals, and everyone on that day showed up with bright faces and smiles, happy in mood and enjoying the day off for those, who usually worked, now they could join the crowd and sing songs, play guitars, or trumpets and walk in the downtown parade. Very much like the solstice party a few weeks ago in June, this brought and united people again, no one argued, no one cried, only the two yapping little Chihuahuas that were tied up to a street lamp would not shut up, but persist on high pitch bark, until their owner showed up with a barbecued turkey leg in her hand, and untied the little vicious beasts, and bend over and gave each a piece of the delicious, white meat.

A little girl with long, blonde hair, the ends of her strands curled into rings, and with big round blue eyes, carried a blue shaved ice cone in her hand. As Edith passed her, she gave her a smile, and the little blonde girl stuck her tongue out at her, blue as a blueberry. Edith let out a loud brief laugh and stuck her pink tongue out at the little girl, who frowned and turned and walked away from her.

Margot stood at the native's booth, admiring the artwork that the old Indian woman displayed. Everything was handmade, handpicked and hand crafted. Different earrings of sizes and shapes, bright blue and dark purple colors, some had feathers some had little pieces of seashells, others were made with ivory, and decorated with miniatures little carvings. She took a pair of ivory hoops, that were carved into a dolphin's shape. She looked at her mother, and asked, "Mom, what do you think of these?" Margot placed them into Edith's open palm.

The earnings were light as a feather, and very beautiful. "I love them," Edith said as admiring the detailed artwork.

The native rewarded her with a wide, half-toothless smile, with chubby wide and flattened cheeks and very dark, eyes. She moved the round mirror closer to Edith, and Edith put the ivory dolphins on and smiled at Margot's image that reflected in the mirror.

"Thank you very much. The earrings are so beautiful," Edith said softly, and the American Indian took the bills from Margot's hand and placed them into a metal box. "Wait, don't go yet," Edith said quickly, and touched Margot's arm. She looked at bracelets and necklaces and made more purchases, because she liked the work and effort the Indian woman put into her works. Edith knew she could not find such exquisite pieces on East Coast, definitely not in galleries in her town. She bought the same bracelet for herself and for Margot, the native told them it's for protection, infused with a well being ritual and Edith believed her, because she wanted to.

A little farther down the road, a man painted portraits, more of cartoons than real images of faces in front of him. The women liked the humor the artist put into his drawings and sketches. They sat down and posed for their own, black-and white ink portrait. Edith loved the fast movement of the man's arm, watching his right arm moving over the white sheet of thick paper witch such an ease. The trumpets came alive in the background, and drums beat to the rhythm of the steps of the people, who joined the parade, as the crowd moved through the streets of Lingit. A little train for toddlers spun around on the hand lain tracks in a circle, while parents snapped their cameras of their youngsters. Next to the bright red, yellow, light blue and dark green painted open seat wagons was a merry go round. Kids could choose a ride on an elephant, a white unicorn, accompanied by bright lights that flashed as the attraction slowly moved around.

Away from the noise, surrounded by open space, an iron posts stood and behind them a live petting zoo, with babies and their mamas, chewing on hey, and fresh carrots and sliced apples, relaxed under a large built tent, in the comfort of a shade with metal buckets filled with water.

Adults and children kneeling down, reaching over the fence and petting the baby miniature goats, of various colors, somewhere black and white, some brown and white, some had sharp pointed antlers, while other's the older ones had the crown of their heads filed for the safety of everyone who took care of them. The small goats, never bigger than an average medium sized dog, would come to the fence, and curiously stare at people's faces, looking into their eyes, sniffing their hands, in search for more sweet carrots or corn or apples.

And then a tall, skinny, young man in light colored jeans stained with dirt on his tights and a half unbuttoned, black and white flannel shirt opened the gate, and let some adults and their kids in, so they could walk around the animals, and pet the baby cows, that rested in the corner on pile of soft hay, or be lifted by their parents to reach the white llama's neck and head, to touch its fur, but the llamas would turn and sometimes spit, and the parents didn't like it, and when one llama with very long eyelashes decided to spit on its admirer, the parent got upset and the kid cried, while another children smiled and laughed out loud.

Chickens with feathered legs ran freely and tangled under the people's feet, nibbled on the ground for scrapes of leftover food. And piglets with their pink bodies and curled tails chased the hens away. An all white male goat came to Edith, and pressed against her calves, leaning its body weight onto her, and she felt the warmth of the goat's skin on her bare legs, and leaned down and scratched the male's head between his antlers.

There was a separate area that held all the orphaned wild animals, that were found alongside the ridges of the road, alive, but their mama's dead, run over, or the babies abandoned, and good Samaritans who came forward and took them in protection and gave them to a local wildlife refuge group.

"Hey girl!" a familiar voice came from behind Margot's back, as she turned two arms folded around her shoulders and gave her a tight hug.

"Leaf! This is my mother, Edith."

"Oh, nice! Good to meet you, Edith. I'm Leaf." He quickly introduced himself and reached over and hugged the other woman.

Edith wasn't used to complete strangers touching her, but suppressed a shriek and politely and very softly hugged Leaf back.

"Leaf was born here—" Margot said.

Leaf jumped in and with a smile on his face replied, "Well, not *here* at the wildlife center. I was born in Lingit, and I will die in Lingit."

Edith looked at him curiously; checked out his long, braided ponytail and very tanned skin.

"Let me give you a tour," he said.

The women followed him inside the closure and passed around some printed signs that were hammered to the wooden posts and carried a brief information and breed of the rescue animals.

Edith noticed the man's limp, as he took a large step up to an attached caravan, he had to lift his left tight with both of his hands. He reached inside for a colored flyer and handed one to Margot.

"We welcome any donations. It's for the two baby musk oxens and a baby moose; our newest and most recent rescue."

Margot and Edith looked at the cutest picture of the baby musk, standing on a pile of straw, his mouth half open, his head slightly tilted to the side, and looking straight into the photographer's camera.

"Oh, of course we'll help and donate," Margot said and added, "this musk ox is so very cute."

They followed in Leaf's footsteps as he took them around and to the orphaned animals. There, in the corner and on the green patch of grass lay a baby moose.

"He's about a week old," Leaf said proudly. "I picked him up by the end of the road, close to the rail road tracks and put him into a dog crate and he drove with me on the back seat of the car. He was most likely abandoned by his mother."

"Why?" Edith asked and a shadow of sadness washed over her face.

"Eh, I don't know. Who knows, sometimes it just happens."

"Thank goodness you saw the poor little thing." Margot quickly added.

Alfred walked from around the corner, a bottle of milk in his hand.

"Alfred! How are you? I didn't know you help around here," Margot said then turned to Edith and introduced them.

Alfred opened the wooden gate, and they all stepped in. Alfred stepped up to the moose calf, and knelt down, and moved the bottle close to the calf's lips and it started sucking on it instantly. Margot slowly removed her camera from around her neck, not to disturb the beautiful site and took some photos.

"Oh how precious the little one is," Margot gasped and the features on her face softened and her eyes had a gentle glow in them.

"That's a real bonding, right there," Leaf said with a smile on his face, as he pointed toward Alfred and the one week old moose calf.

"Does he have a name?" Edith wanted to know.

Alfred lifted his sight and looked directly at Edith. "I c...call him Rex."

"Rex? Isn't it more like a dog's name?"

"Yes, ma'am. H...he reminds me off my German s...shepherd I had when I was a k...kid. H...he has the s...same c...color."

"The babies at the wildlife rescue also receive diet supplemented with offerings of fireweed, alder and willow," Leaf said. "Would you like to go pet him?"

"Can we?" Margot asked already making steps toward the tiny moose. All done eating, the baby got up on his legs and wondered around his enclosure, then he sank to the ground on the grass, folding his long knobby joints under him, as he stuck his long nose to the bowl of water blowing bubbles through his nose. Margot and Edith laughed as the younger one kept taking pictures; she didn't even notice Alfred already exited the closure. Leaf took them to another fenced area, with a pair of piglet-sized, two weeks old musk oxen just awoken from a nap.

"They will snatch anything into their mouth that is shaped like a nipple. They are hungry little beasts."

Edith and Margot made a very generous donation to the animal rescue and Margot told Leaf she would mention a note in a magazine she works for together with some photos she took that day.

They returned to the main strip and chose to have a late lunch on a bench overlooking the beach and the Pacific Ocean.

Margot got a baked Alaskan potato topped with chives, cheese and sour cream and Edith got a pork chop on a stick and garlic mashed potatoes in a paper shaped canoe. Soon the shore birds came in flying, begging for the food, some landed in the sand, and the white and grey gulls fearlessly approached their bench, stretching their feathered necks and long pointed orange beaks at the women.

"I can see why you like it so much here, Margot. It's a little charming town and the locals seem to be very friendly."

"It's not a bad place to live." Margot replied, her eyes mapping the salty waters in front of her.

"But wouldn't you miss Seattle's lifestyle?"

Margot took a deep breath and paused, she finished her food and set the paper cup aside, and rested both of her arms and elbows on the benches back before simply replying, "Maybe."

§

Later that night, when all the rush quieted down and the drunks went to their homes and cottages and hotel rooms, and the animals were driven back to their wildlife center, the city of Lingit and their firemen crew eagerly awaited the July the Fourth fireworks. The blue sky had several scattered clouds of off white, and pale grey color. And the crescent moon showed up on the horizon, but the sun still persisted on the unobstructed view of skyline. A lot of people showed up, their heads turned up in one direction, small kids sat on the shoulders of their fathers, and grandfathers, to get a better view of the red, green, purple and yellow shooting stars against the sky.

"Hey!" a little, young, yet very sharp voice yelled next to Edith. She tilted her torso and looked at the girl with long, blonde hair which ends curled into rings, and her blue eyes. She saw her several hours earlier at the fair. The girl, sitting on a man's shoulders, stuck her tongue out at her, again.

Edith smiled. "Hey, you, I've got something for you too!" she showed her tongue.

The girl giggled, her tongue still stained with a blueberry color. The man gave Edith a strange look as he made a few steps aside and farther away from her.

Margot hasn't seen Kurt all day, and thought he probably had to work the store all day, since Alfred helped out at the orphaned animal rescue. She knew he is one of the volunteers for the fire department and is behind the spectacular fireworks site. As everyone around her stared at the sky, she lowered her head and looked into the crowed, mapping the faces in front of her, and then behind her. The corners of her lips lifted and curled into a smile as she watched the woman with her two Chihuahuas. She now had the dogs under zipped cotton hoodie, two tiny heads with gigantic ears popped in and out, depending on the noise the fireworks did in the sky. And then the women moved to the side and behind her stood Charlotte Groeneweg. Margot's smile instantly disappeared from her face, as Charlotte pierced her with her eyes from across the crowd. The intense moment made her stomach jump and covered her bare arms with goose bumps. This was the first time she stare that woman right in the eye. Could Charlotte know who she is, why she is in Lingit? Could the old Groeneweg know Edith, who stood right next to Margot? Questions flooded her mind, as her hearing kept on bringing the cracking sound of the fireworks.

The woman with the two small dogs moved back and her wide, out-of-shape body covered Charlotte's away from Margot's view.

"What's the matter?" Edith asked, noticing a shift in her stepdaughter's body language.

"Nothing. Nothing at all."

With the last bright sparkles against the sky in a complete daylight, the crowd clasped their hands to thank for the spectacular afternoon, day and night before it slowly dissolved into various directions, people heading back to their cars, or walking to their houses and hotel rooms.

As Edith passed the oncoming traffic, the bell shaped sleeve of her blouse got caught on another woman's purse that she wore sideways and across her chest.

"Oh, I'm so sorry." The other woman gasped. And all three women came to an abrupt stop. Margot's face froze as she stared at Charlotte in front of her, trying to release the cotton fabric of Edith's cloths away from the claws of her purse. Although everything happened so fast, to Margot the moment lasted an eternity as if everything went into a slow motion.

The voices around her were inaudible, and faces and figures blurred as they pass them around.

"There. Oh, I'm so glad it didn't get torn," the other woman said with relieved tone of voice and smiled at Edith. Then she turned sharply and disappeared somewhere into the crowd.

"Didn't she sound German to you?" Edith said.

"What? No, I don't think so, mother."

"Never mind." Edith said and checked on her sleeve.

Everything at that moment became mechanical to her. She drove herself and Edith back to the house, as her stepmother felt tired after a long day in the sun. But Margot went back into her car and drove back to Lingit's downtown where she sat on the public beach, now empty, the sand chilled and the sun that went down behind the horizon. She checked her time, a midnight was approaching and the daylight dimmed, but the sky was still dressed in a blue color above her head. Kurt showed up and sat next to her, handing her a cold bottled beer.

"I thought you may want one."

"Thanks," she said and they both brought their knees together close to their chins, as they sipped on the liquid.

"I saw Alfred today at the wildlife rescue."

"He loves to volunteer for them. He lives for the spring and the abandoned newborns."

Kurt glanced behind Margot's shoulder at the stand that sold helium balloons during a day. The owner left it there, some balloons tied with strings to the handle of the stand, unattended.

"I have an idea," Kurt said and finished his beer. He quickly jumped to his feet and ran to the stand. He reached into his pocket and took out a Swiss knife and cut the strings loose and grabbed the balloons and carried them back to the beach.

"Guess what?"

"Oh no. I know what you're up to."

Kurt winked at her and sat down close. They used one balloon after another, sucking on the helium, laughing and conversing with their voices altered by the gas in their lungs.

Margot laughed so hard she felt her stomach muscles and the corners of her eyes watered as she wiped them off. This was yet another side of Kurt Groeneweg – a really good one, she thought.

§

Charlotte turned on the aria of her favorite opera on the old gramophone, lit a cigarette, and moved the glass of cognac closer to her as she sat down to her favorite deep armchair.

She took a long drag and held it in for a moment before she blew the smoke out of her mouth. Her head nodded to the orchestra as she shut her eyes and swung slightly to the rhythm of the melody. Then she raised her chin and opened her eyes as she reached for cognac and took a big sip out of the golden, smooth liquid. She let it roll inside and left to right with her tongue, absorbing the taste of the liquor before she swallowed it down her throat. She listened to the German singer as she sang a sad song about a woman who lost her child. Charlotte rested her cigarette on the ashtray, and pressed her back into the holstered fabric. She moved her gypsy scarf closer to her chin. Her pretty, natural long nails with a bright red polish dug deep into her chest, as the opera singers voice intensified. Charlotte took the last sip of the conga and heard the glass as she sat it on the table. She finished her cigarette and shut the butt in the ashtray. The woman licked her lower lip and then bit it, before bringing her lips firmly together as she drifted into a nap.

The aria continued and the singer cried with an angelic voice as the basses and the cellos and the drums beat hard, before her cries shut and the soothing melody of a violin entered its solo, the singer joined in and sang her aria. She passed the door by the doctor's office who had the gramophone on. As she walked, she glanced into the open door to a room, and saw a young woman, about her age, crying and hugging her own knees, as she sat on the floor in the corner.

Charlotte wanted to go in and hug her, she remembered her she saw her once before in the hospital corridor. What could have happened to her? Then Charlotte placed her right arm across her heart.

"Oh my God." She gasped and quickly shunned her sight away. "She must have lost her baby." Mother's heartache over her lost baby. She said to herself and with a fast pace she marched across the hallway and into her room and firmly shut the door behind her.

CHAPTER 17

EDITH WOKE UP EARLY, MADE herself strong black coffee, and after she drank the hot steaming liquid, she opened the glass sliding door and walked out on the wooden patio. She kept quiet, didn't want to wake Margot up. The time moved slowly for her, ever since she arrived to Lingit. She found the small town to be very charming, as much as calming, and she loved the freedom of walking outside and seeing nothing, but the sky, the ocean and the sand.

Barefooted, wearing her soft pants and a T-shirt with a zip up hoodie, she looked much younger then seventy. Often times people were stunned at her youthful appearance, her natural brown hair color, stripped of any grey, the genes, she could have passed on to her own son, if the fate wasn't so cruel and wouldn't take him away from her. She took a deep breath and let the salty, cooler air enter her lungs. Then she walked down to the water, not letting her feet get wet, she strolled alongside the beach, next to white caps that came and went and washed over the shore.

There were small, rugged sea shells with irregular edges scattered over, and half-way buried in the golden sand, she carefully jumped over them, not to get a cut in her feet. The wind blew threw her hair as she reached into her hoodie and took out a silk scarf and wrapped it around her head and crossed the end around her neck and let the rest of the scarf fall behind her back, and onto her shoulder blades.

The wind made her eyes watery and she regretted not brining her sunglasses with her that morning. She glanced over the waves and saw a silhouette in the distant waves. Edith stopped and brought her right arm up and opened her palm and stretched her fingers and brought her hand over her forehead staring at the person ahead. The silhouette stood up and glided over the calm waves, coming closer to her, like a messenger, hands balancing the body as the surfer rode the wave toward her.

His wet face broke into a wide smile and brought on wrinkles around his lips and eyes. "Good morning," he said enthusiastically.

"Morning," she replied.

"Would you like to try it yourself?"

"What?"

"The surf. I can teach you..."

"Oh Leaf, I'm an old woman. You know what they say, you can't teach an old dog new tricks!" she looked deeply at his warm, beautiful eyes.

He winked at her, took his surfboard and ran back into the waves, until he remained a distant dot in the ocean, Edith watched him as she sat on his board and waited for a wave that would bring him back to the shore. She thought a spirit like

Leaf could not live anywhere else in the world. He's found his home.

She walked back to the house on the hill – the only house on the private beach surrounded by tall grass, cat tails, some boulders, and few pine bushes that decorated the sides of the house. A loud, persistent chirping noise came down below her bare feet. She looked down and saw a squirrel. The small animal had a long, bushy tail that swung to the air, like a painter's brush and was longer than the animal's body. The squirrel kept staring at her, and then got up on the hind legs, folding the front paws on its tiny hairy chest and curiously looked at her human companion.

"I bet Margot has been feeding you."

The chipmunk listened and stayed still.

"Okay. You've earned your breakfast, but only because you're so cute." Edith walked through the open glass door into the house. She returned in a minute carrying a few peanuts in her hand.

"Mom, don't feed the chipmunk," she heard Margot's voice behind her back.

"Why not?"

"Look how fat it is already," she replied humorously.

They had breakfast on the patio, and Edith fed the chipmunk and then Margot fed the Steller's Jay who flew from a tree down on the window, demanding his treat. But despite the serenity around her, Edith could not find an inner peace. The heaviness of the matter she had on her mind weight heavy and she felt, as if she was suffocating slowly, but surely, sinking down. She looked over at the ocean. Is the bottom of the sea awaiting her?

The women took off on a road trip that Margot had planned for them. The promising temperatures were supposed to reach a staggering 85 degrees, a local tropical heat.

"Let's turn the air off and just roll down the windows," Edith said.

"Sounds good to me."

Edith leaned over and stuck her head out. The road that led alongside the coastal trail had a moderate traffic, most of the people exited to the side roads, where their summer rental cottages hid in the forests, each with their own private land.

Then the paved road abruptly ended and the gravel took over for the rest of the bumpy road. The car rode through the dust, that lifted around the car and made them to shut the windows and turn on the air.

After about five minutes of Edith's bones thoroughly shaken, not to mention her stomach, which felt like it relocated to her throat, Margot stopped the jeep. A vast open land awaited them, like a wide screen in a theater. The colors so spectacular, from the lightest green to the deepest green, and shades of brown, and the grayish white boulders that protruded from the land and stood up high against the blue sky dominating the wide-range view.

"Wow, this must be the top of the world." Edith said and the women stepped out and walked toward the meadow.

The wild flowers growing carelessly around put on a show of deep purple, pink, yellow and red colors and lured over various butterflies and bumblebees. The air was crisp and very clean, with no humidity and no mosquitoes and definitely no annoying flies.

"This truly is a paradise." Edith let out a sigh. "I've seen many different places, but nothing can quite compare to this."

"It's like the land is projecting its own, very beautiful aura at us."

She looked over at Margot, but she was busy snapping shots of the butterflies and bumblebees that landed in the centerpieces of the flowers in bloom.

She threw herself down, spreading her arms to the side, she blended with the land and smelled the fragrant pollen in the air and said softly, "I can die now."

"No. Don't do that, mother. No-one's gonna die today." Margot stretched her neck and looked over at Edith. As if the world paused and forgot the people they inhabited the Earth weren't always nice and polite. Justice wasn't always served and scoundrels at times prevailed, and life could be a burden. But not here, at this piece of land at this very moment, Edith's feelings were full of harmony and she could hear the busy bees not buzzing, but enchanted with tones, that have grittiness and fullness and unity. Except, she knew she will have to return to reality and this moment will not last, and she'll soon have to face someone who she thought would never, ever see again. If her stepdaughter went so far, and accomplished to put the pieces of Edith's puzzle together, and brought her past alive, then Edith told herself, she needs to be strong and go through it. If the Bavarian doctor was still alive, and hiding in this charming town, she could at least get some answers he has owed her this whole time. The morning he came to her hospital room, and told her that her baby body had died, those moments and words forever pierced her heart and had been haunting her since.

She felt angry, but after so many years, nearly a half a century, the anger within her no longer had sharp-pointed edges. Time has slowly filed them, and formed them into despair, something, she could not fix, she could not touch, she could not return back, ever again. What would she do, if she meets the person that destroyed her life? How will she react? The man would probably be weak, and perhaps even immobile, but the physical pain meant nothing to Edith. The emotional stall, however, never could be understood by someone like Dr. Siegfried Mueller. Was she the only one that had that happened, or where there others? If so, how many?

She never found the strength within herself to go back and visit her past. She had time to stop Margot, and she wanted many times, when she found out what her stepdaughter was doing behind her back. But then again, the thought of getting some answers, if possible, haunted her more than letting the past stay behind. So she never told Margot what she had found out, that her stepdaughter started uncovering her stepmother's European past. Perhaps she wanted to know before she died, and then she could die at peace, knowing what had really happened on that morning in Bavarian hospital.

Margot lay down next to her in the grass, and her hand touched hers and their pinkies crossed, as both women stare at the sky, each through their own dark sunglasses.

"You're awfully quiet now. What are you thinking about?" Margot asked first.

Edith hesitated, before she replied, "What other surprises do you have for me here?"

Margot tilted her head toward her, and let go off the Edith's pinkie. She sat down and brought her knees together and hugged her calves.

"You're gonna have to get up and come with me," Margot said and turned and raised her bottom from the grass and extended both of her arms and took Edith's hands and helped her on her feet.

She pressed the binoculars closer to her eyes, and felt the plastic on the top of her nose. Edith zoomed in and sharpened the image. There, on the top of the tall spruce, two eagles made their eerie. The wind that has always blown from the west, made the tip branches bend and flattened and the birds made it into their home. One adult, the other juvenile, a parent and its youngster. The large bird shook its feathers, black on the body and white on the head, while the offspring looked quite like an ordinary bird. Feathers brown with dark patches, like spots or freckles all around, and physically much smaller than his proud, majestic parent.

"How old is the baby bird? It looks so different; you'd not guess it's an eagle,"

Edith said, never taking the binoculars away from her eyes.

"I don't know. But because of the color of its feathers, he can be anywhere from a year old up to four, maybe five…"

"What? Are you telling me, the eagle as everyone knows, with black and white feathers, actually stays like this for the first five years?"

"Yeah, isn't that something? It doesn't become adult until it gets the specific colors, its characteristics, which define him."

The women picked forest berries, wild huckleberry bushes were full of the dark, semi-sweet berries, and then there were variations of golden and red raspberries, so big, and so sweet, Edith has never tasted better berries in her entire life. She moved closer to the bushes and stepped into something soft, and mushy.

"Ewww…is that…is that a bear's crap? Margot?"

"It sure is."

"And now what! What do we do, Margot?" Edith looked around.

"Don't panic, mom. You see, it's dry, it's old." Margot picked up a stick and shoved it in the poop. The bear, just like them, snacked on the berries that went through his digestive track and back to the nature itself.

"But aren't you scared?" Edith again looked around.

"I am, but I'm not really thinking about it every minute of the day. It wouldn't be any fun to enjoy the outdoors. We've got bear bells." She took the bell into her hand that was attached to her belt, "We've got bear spray." She pointed at the can on the side, easy to access pocket on her backpack. "The only thing I don't have is gun."

"Are you kidding me? A gun?" Edith said breathlessly.

"We are going to be just fine."

"I'm amazed and speechless." Edith shook her head. "What happened to the city girl?"

"The city girl? She's still here, just a little different now." Margot winked at her.

§

Alfred pulled the garden hose across the yard and pressed the nozzle. He liked the clear drops that fell on the roses and as lingering glittered in the sun. The corners curled up into a shy smile. Set to substitute the rain water, the sprinkler gently hydrated the roots and refreshed the flowers in prime bloom. The fragrant beauties shined in red colors, and their strong, green stems had long, sharp pointed thorns that his mother forbid him to cut off. He never understood why she wanted to keep the thorns, even when she told him to go out and cut some stems and arrange them in a vase at home. Charlotte Groeneweg always kept the thorns, and the bigger and pointed they grew, the more she adored them.

"What would the roses be without their thorns?" She once asked him.

Between two bushes, where the dirt parted the two strongest stems away, Alfred saw a fresh soil, with different color, a much lighter brown, than the soil that was used for gardening the rest of the roses. He turned the water off and knelt down. Carefully, not to get scratched, he moved his arm through the opening, and buried his fingers through the soil. The tips of his right hand instantly felt something hard. He pushed the dirt to the sides and a saw a top of the wooden box there.

Alfred jerked his hand back and twisted his torso, looking behind him. When assured no one was watching him, he once again reached between the stems, but this time his skin got caught and a long, hair thin cut pierced through his pale skin and the blood poured out of the wound.

"Ouch."

He persisted and took the box out of ground and brought it between his tights. There was no lock, just a simple clasp. He pushed it up with is thumb, and the lid still stayed closed."Alfred! Alfie? Where are you?"

The sharp voice of his mother made him jump. He hid the wooden box between his tights as he heard the footsteps on the front porch.

"Alfred! What are you doing in there?"

"W…watering the r…roses."

"Come inside. I need you." Charlotte stared at her younger son.

Alfred twitched, but couldn't get up, knowing the box is between his tights and he didn't want his mother to know, he found it.

"Now!" she yelled after him.

He waved at her and the blood spilled the other direction toward his shoulder, when he lifted his arm. Charlotte frowned at him and disappeared behind the front door. Alfred quickly shut the clasp and returned the box, pushing the soil back on the lid. His curious mind and big eyes now had a secret.

§

Kurt couldn't stop thinking about her. The night when they fooled around on the beach, like kids, having fun with the helium balloons was one of the best times he's spent with her. The glacier trip and the bear viewing trip were great, but only on the beach he saw the true Margot, the girl he felt he's known for years. He still heard her laughter, an infectious, cheerful sound that made his heart tickle.

He asked her how she would define love, and she replied, "Love has no fear." After the overnight trip, he saw her again, a few days later at the outdoor theater. The small town's enthusiasts had build the place with their own hands, using the forest logs, carving them into long benches with a back rest, sending the wood, making it smooth and comfortable to sit on, staining the surface with a clear polish to protect the seats year around above the open skyline. The locals, mostly fireman and volunteers and movie fans picked a large meadow, across from the road, on the other side from the ocean. They sat down tall metal poles that held the wide screen that projected movies. This was not America's drive-thru theater, where people could pull up and stay in their cars and eat and drink junk food, while they watch a movie. This was a truly place where people didn't come to stuff their stomach with popcorn or French fries, or greased chicken and calorie infused hamburgers. This was more like a European-style outdoor theater. The audience could walk to, sit down on the benches or lay out their beach towels and comforters right on the green grass. The movies that played were mostly old, black and white, from the thirties, and forties, screening Marlene Dietrich and Gary Cooper in Morocco, and Katharine Hepburn and Spencer Tracy in *Without Love* and then those, that were technicolored after they were shot in black and white, and with the new technology a man's hand colored the film and audience could see their idols hair color, like a beautiful Grace Kelly and Cary Grant in *To Catch a Thief*.

The open air would carry the sound from the screen out loud through the amplifiers. On summer nights, the theater would project cartoons for kids in the evening, and Tom and Jerries would come to Lingit, and from their screen overlook the young, eager spectaculars that listened and watched them with open mouth, and these cartoons faced the road, and the ocean behind and their stories would carry on through the air, above the theater, the road, all the way to the waves and high above to the sky.

The kids would stare at their magnified heroes as if any minute the illustrated figure could step off the screen and become one of them, in the audience. The benches, and the grass covered with blankets would empty and the screen's heroes would exit for the evening, leaving a blank, white canvas behind them, until the midnight screening, when adults filled in the auditorium, women wearing their perfumes, and lipsticks and long eyelashes, and men trying to impress them sitting closely, hugging their shoulders, or hips. And the screen would project, once again for a new set of eyes and ears, and the voices would mix in the air, with a different sound, because they were old, much older than the people who came to watch and listen. The night he took her to the outdoor theater they watched *Casablanca*.

She leaned over to him and whispered, "I had a hunch about you."

"You did?"

"Yes. I had a hunch you are a romantic."

The light outside dimmed, and the sky was clear for another hour, before it darkened more and the stars showed up for a brief moment in the land of the midnight sun. He noticed

Margot looked up and smiled at the stars, and he wished he could hear her thoughts, but only perhaps the universe could hear them, and the rest would nobody's business.

He still didn't know what to think about her. The girl to him had a mystery, a secret he didn't dare to figure out. She came to his town, saying she was a photographer for a magazine come to do a study on migrating birds. Rented a house on the hill on the outskirts, far away from any other houses or neighbors, on a private beach, that only one resident has always entered, Leaf, who has been surfing the waves there, and Leaf told him, he has a hunch about Margot. He told Kurt, he had a hunch about the city girl, that she came here for another reason, a smart fox, that hasn't laid out all her cards yet.

She didn't tell him her mother came to visit her. He was astounded when he heard Edith's accent. So familiar to his ears, he'd listened to it all his life, the voice so similar, the words pronounced almost identically, the same intonation, if he closed his eyes, and just listened, he could very well be listening to his own mother Charlotte. Kurt didn't say anything, he kept it for himself. Margot has never met his mother, and there was no point going into details. At least not at the Fourth of July parade.

While Kurt had been honest with her and answered her many questions, she'd been very quiet whenever he wanted to know more about her. She would quickly change the subject, turn away, or ignore his questions. This drove him crazy, and only deepened his curiosity about Margot.

"What do you do every day, that makes you happy, that fills you with joy?"

He asked her.

She paused and tilted her head toward the skyline and smiled and two dimples showed on her rosy cheek, before she looked back at him and with a firm voice Margot replied. "Every day I look at the sky. And I like how it changes, from morning, to noon, to evening. And before I shut the curtains I always look up and I never get tired of the images I see." She paused and then added shyly, "I guess that may be too ordinary for you…"

"No, not at all." Kurt said quickly. "I think that's a beautiful thing to do. The best things in life can be totally ordinary…." His face softened and he continued with a quiet, rhythmic voice.

"I've seen sunsets from the view of the planes and from the ground. I've watched the sun go down behind the horizon and hide behind the mountains east coast, and on the west side of the country. I've seen a sunset in Hawaii, when the water turned orange, and red and the sun slowly descended and blended in the distance, joining the waves, until it disappeared from the sky." Kurt said.

"What about a different continent?" she asked and looked into his eyes. "Have you ever seen sunsets in a different part of the world?"

"No. I've never traveled overseas," he said simply.

"You haven't, really?"

"No. Not yet."

Was it a challenge? Did she try to tell him something? If so, their words were left unfinished, because Alfred disturbed them, and needed Kurt's help.

〄

The month of August brought in different colors and nature and animals became well aware, the summer soon will be over. More rain fell above the ocean and above the peninsula, and then when the sky cleared, the air slowly became cooler and windier. The babies born that year had grown bigger and stronger, the birds' feathers developed, but still needed more time, two more months to grow to be able to make the long migration. Margot sat in the grass overlooking the Wahya Lagoon, now filled with many birds, of various sizes, colors and sounds. Families that stayed together or lonely ones that just cruised through the sweet water. She watched as their heads plunged down under water to feed on the green plants. Margot thought of the birds and sunsets, how many they have seen, on their flights in the sky, or on land in different parts of the world. The little nest that the ducks built in the spring was now empty, as the newborns exited into the water together with their parents. The green foliage of water lilies have grown on it instead and spread tall and thick all the way around, a private water lily island, that the birds created, a piece of art. They used the sticks and shrubs from the shore, where many of these flowers grew, and recreated their own private flower island. The open white blooms had yellow centerpiece. Margot zoomed in with her camera and snapped black and white photos.

Edith's been visiting for over a month now, Margot showing her around, all the beauties of nature and animals and plants and berries. She introduced him to Kurt, and he arranged another flight, much easier and laid back, for Edith. They flew above the town, and high above the ocean and then their pilot showed them the mountains and glaciers from, all from the bird's point of view. But when it came down to bringing the last piece of the puzzle, Margot hasn't been able to go through it. She grew closer to Kurt than she desired and knew this would make the truth come out much harder than she wanted. The worst thing for her was to hurt another human being. She didn't count on having Kurt enter her life, she didn't plan for it. But he was a part of the puzzle that she had worked so hard on to put together.

They had barbecues at her rental on the top of the hill, and Kurt brought over Alfred and the dog, Holton, ran around and chased the chipmunk who smelled the meat and wanted to snatch a piece. And then the blue jay showed up with his pretty dark blue and black feathers, and black mohawk and Holton chased him away, too. She listened to Edith, when she talked to Adam trying to persuade him to come over, but Margot's father made out his mind. The man has never flown in his life, and he wasn't going to make an exception at his older age.

Kurt had invited them over to meet his mother, saying the women Edith and Charlotte would like each other, when Edith said she came from Germany. But every time he started this conversation, Margot would shut down and her face would frown and she would look away and always come up with some reason, why they can't come over.

She knew she couldn't keep the secret forever. The time has come and the future was uncertain. The lives around her will change and the last piece of puzzle would perfectly fit in and forever be embedded in its entirety.

CHAPTER 18

§

The Autumn Showered The Seaside town bright with colors, the birches turned yellow, and the cottonwood trees looked like gold showered their branches, and the apple trees produced small, and prickly pale red and green apples, perfect for strudel or homemade apple butter, jarred and set in the pantry for the long, winter months. The first flocks of Canadian geese gathered in the sky and flew up high; from the view down below, they looked like a swarm of bees.

The wild, high bush blueberries and their scattered bushes in the forest were now ready for harvest and many families with their kids put on their raincoats and rubber boots and bent their backs to pick them up and make them into a canned fruit or jams or just eat them fresh on a homemade pie on Sunday mornings. Kids hung around the Lingit streets, their mouths stained by the purple berries, their fingers colored and their clothes destroyed. They were happy kids, healthy and very lucky, Edith thought, when she passed them on her way from a grocery store. The little angel, the girl with bright blue eyes, and long blonde hair that curled at the ends into gorgeous rings, was among the screaming bunch, and she once again stuck her tongue out at Edith. And Edith blew a big bubble out of her chewing gum, and the little girl for the first time smiled.

"You should smile more often; you've got a beautiful smile," Edith told her.

"Do you want to go to the mushroom festival?" Margot asked when Edith entered the house.

"Mushroom festival?" she repeated jokingly and smiled at Margot.

"Yeah. I thought we'd have some fun. It's called the Forest Fair Festival."

"What kind of mushrooms are you talking about?" Edith still had her youthful sense of humor, which Margot loved about her stepmother.

A week later, downtown transformed into stands with booths. This time the locals put on displays their products of wildflower, dandelion, and fireweed honey. Seedless jellies of huckleberries and marionberries, and apple pies, and apple jams and mushroom pies and jars of sliced and dried mushrooms for many winter nights and dill gravies. There were kids with blueberry lemonades, and adults with blubbery vodka lemonades.

"This town knows how to celebrate," Edith said and took a sip of the vodka infused blueberry drink.

"I love it here. Only wish Adam would overcome his fear of flying and got over here. He won't even drive such a long distance now. I wish we're younger…"

There were booths were kids could get their faces painted, and so the crowd filled in with the princesses, and the monsters, and the vampires and the zombies. There were adults with painted faces, unrecognizable, and silly and fun and the same time. Edit wondered if they were high on mushrooms and had to laugh at her own sense humor.

"What's so funny?" Margot asked.

"I was just thinking...let's get our hair done." She paused and pointed her right forefinger at a pair, a woman and a man with two colorful Mohawks.

"What?! No way!" Margot replied sharply.

The young punk boy who worked on Edith's hair had pierced lower lip, a ring through both of his nostrils, and when he talked and leaned over Edith's head, she noticed his tongue had an equally important jewelry. He said his name was Connor and he came to Lingit from L.A. A drifter, who had plans to travel through the West Coast all the way to Alaska and then cross the border and travel through Canada and on the East Coast and down to New York City.

Edith never judged people based on their appearance. To her, the character was the deciding factor, whether she liked or hated someone. In this case, she liked Connor.

He had tattoos all the way from his shoulder to his wrist, a full sleeve as he called it, and said there are more tattoos covering his young body, but felt it inappropriate to show Edith. She laughed and replied she was young once, and even though she didn't voluntarily stained her skin with a permanent ink, she had nothing against his tattooed body. Connor told her he wished his parents were so open minded like Edith, and told her if it was possible, he would take her to be his grandma. Edith was flattered and amused at the same time, but the word *grandma* made her feel so old.

Connor complimented her natural brown hair, stripped of any gray and natural curls and the thickness of her strands, and then he Grace in with a brush, and teased her curls and then he reached for a hair blower and used it like a vacuum, pulling her strands to the sides, and to the top of her head and after that the used tons of hair spray, and told her to shut her eyes and sprayed many cans of various colors onto her hair, until there was no natural brown color visible.

Margot glanced over and if her jaw could drop, this was the perfect moment for it.

"Holy shit," she said before her stylist told her to shut her eyes and did an equally important job on her naturally red hair. When the ladies were ready to go back to the mushroom festival, Edith gave a generous tip to both of their stylists of the day and gave Connor her phone number if he ever makes it on the east coast, she'll take him out to dinner. A date was set and Connor gave her big kiss on the cheek, and Margot pulled Edith out of the tent and onto the streets of Lingit.

They munched on elephant ears powdered with sugar and topped with fresh berries, sitting on a bench overlooking the beach. Kurt passed them on the lower portion where the white caps touched the sand, together with Holton, who chased his ball. He looked over at them, but didn't recognize them and kept on walking. Margot thought it was hilarious, that he even didn't take a double look. But the dog picked up their familiar scent and stopped and sniffed his nose in the air, lifting his head higher and turning his neck to the side, where the women sat on the bench. His feet rushed through the sand dunes and away from Kurt and the water, and Kurt yelled at him, but the dog kept on running until he reached Margot's bare tights and wiped his wet tongue, and slobber and wet nose onto her sun-kissed skin. Holton begged for the food, and Edith was the first one who gave up and torn a piece of the funnel cake for him.

Margot greeted him first. Kurt's face turned into a wide smile and he placed his hands onto his hips and his eyes reflected humor and gentleness at the same time. "I'll be damned. I'd never guess you two would go for it." He pointed his finger at the women's new hairdos. "You both look fancy and so glamorous."

The unusually warm autumn air brought a lot of people outside, and although the waves of the ocean were too cold now for swimming, people laid out their folding chairs and towels on the sand that the sun heated for them, and just listened to the whispers of the deep ocean, or read their magazines and books, or had their walk mans on their ears with their favorite music. And those, who preferred to be more active, joined the fair, and made their purchases to support locals. As the evening approached the newly built stage started filling with musicians and a small, chamber orchestra. Kurt took his dog home, and brought over Alfred. He asked his mother, whether she would join them downtown, but she declined. He knew not to put pressure on her, and let her be with her roses, and her thorns, as she listened to the old gramophone through the open door and windows, as she sat on the covered porch having her cognac and a cigarette.

The musicians were dressed in casual clothes, there was no need for ties, and suits and polished black dress shoes. They had a special audience for a night, with painted faces, and crazy hairstyles. There were fairies sitting in the front row, and Mickey Mouses in the second, and Alices from the Wonderland and Tin Men and scarecrows. Edith looked around and liked what she was seeing. The freedom of expression the people chose for that day reminded her of Halloween, except this was much better, more spontaneous, and infused with all the berries, and vodkas and wild mushrooms. Even Kurt and Alfred got some decorations in their hair and on their faces. They all played their roles for that day, and evening and the air filled with harmonious atmosphere and united them together.

People sat and rested and didn't have to talk. All united, they all communicated through their eyes. The sound of music entered the air a two-way communication for those who performed and the others who listened, a conversation between two sides that didn't require any words. The sonorous tones, full and deep and rich, filled the atmosphere. And at that moment the purpose of life was simple, to enjoy every minute before the music ends, and people leave and lights shut down and quietness sets in.

For the next half hour, Edith gave herself fully to the orchestra in front of her. Her mind and her body let in the melodies and she enjoyed herself. The music let her forget for at least a while, everything that has bothered her, it fixed her mood, her emotions and liberated her soul. She shut her eyes and lightly swung her shoulders to the sides, her arms and hands relaxed and rested in her lap, she slowly moved her chin up and down and tilted her head to the side and raised her eyebrows with the angelic high tones of the violins.

When the music was over, the crowed cheerfully clapped and the musicians smiled, pleased with their results. Then people stood up and left their seats and headed for their homes. The women said goodbye to Kurt and Alfred, before entering Margot's jeep driving to the edge of town, where the paved road ends and the rocks mix with the dirt, and the dried dust lifts up and above the car's wheels.

"I sure hope we'll be able to get this out of our hair." Margot said looking at her image in the bathroom's mirror. She touched her sticky, colored hair, and shifted her eyes at Edith.

"Aren't you worried this will never go away and we'll have to cut our hair short or maybe even shaved it off?"

Edith reached for a towel and gently wiped her wet face. "I guess we'll find out soon."

She kissed Margot on a cheek and retired to her bedroom. Just in case, she placed a clean towel over the pillow case; if the wonderful colorful spray on her hairdo bled, at least it wouldn't stain Margot's luxurious cotton bedding. Edith thought that was funny; the girl still liked to use high quality cotton. She most likely bought the sheets in Seattle and dragged them over here, to the last frontier, at the end of the world, to a town on the tip of the peninsula. Lingit, a pretty place with nice people and incredible nature. A place, where she's soon going to meet with the one person, she thought she would never ever see again until the day she dies.

When Kurt came over to her house, wanting her to join him and Alfred at the mushroom fair, Charlotte had already prepared herself for the inevitable meeting that tied her to her past and for all these years caused her inner pain, and countless sleepless nights. Although she's always been haunted by nightmares at night, panting and sobbing quietly, always crying alone; after she started her new life in America, the mind torture slowly subsided, and when she got to the land of midnight sun with Jack by her side, they even disappeared for a couple of years. Shortly after her second son Albert suffered the fall from the stairs, that left him with a stutter and damaged his mind, Charlotte's nightmare returned and has been with her for nearly forty years.

On the day of the Forest Fair, Charlotte got up early, putting on a high rubber boots and long gardening gloves. She took the rose clippers with her and walked outside. The third part of September air brought on cooler temperatures, but by the midday the sun warmed up and humidity subsided and the early fall days brought on Indian summer. One of the most spectacular times to visit the nature, and to enjoy the outdoors. The short period right after the summer heat and before the long winter was Charlotte's the most favorite time and season.

Drops of various sizes covered the grass in the Groeneweg's garden. Morning dew lay on the leaves of her roses, decorating them like gemstones. She knelt down, and her right knee touched the wet grass, making a stain on her pants. She watched as a lady bug made its steps on the thick green stable and stopped at the water drop, drinking the clear liquid early in the morning. Charlotte smiled and carefully moved forward, avoiding her step on the black dotted, red-winged natural beauty.

She reached into her pocket and put on the gloves, and then she slid her hand into the other pocket and took out the metal clippers. With her back bend over the rose bushes, she reached in between the thickest part, and started clipping the green, solid and very healthy stems. She worked fast and with a rhythmic movement of her long, thin arms Charlotte made her way through a portion of the fragrant, deep red thorn field. Throwing the cut roses behind her back and onto the lawn, soon she could see and reached the soil in the very back by the side of the house's foundation. She looked like a creature, down on her knees, her elbows stained by the dirt, she encountered several cuts on the arms and shoulders even though she dressed in a long sleeve, but the thorns went through the layers on her arms and did the damage to her skin.

Charlotte didn't stop, didn't check her scrapes. She was on a mission on the early September morning. Giving up wasn't in her nature.

A few minutes later, she stood on the wide lawn, praying water through the garden hose over her gloves, and rubber boots. Thick pieces of soil separated from the boots and fell onto the green grass. She kicked the boots on the wooden porch and barefooted walked in the house, carrying the roses in her arms. The dining room table lit with the newly added colors and the wide, deep and heavy crystal vase, hand carved in central Europe shined with the sunbeams that reflected through the window and onto the dining table. The sweet, aromatic fragrance immediately entered the air an intensified as soon as the green stems of the flowers touched the water. Charlotte took of her clothes and checked on the several cuts on her skin. Her arms carried many old scrapes, short and long, all of them very thin, and healed naturally and all of them from the thorns from her own garden. The cuckoo on the living room wall came out of its house and loudly announced the time. At eight minutes after seven, Charlotte poured milk into her coffee and cut a slice out of the sachertorte she made herself a day ago. The brown, chocolate taste with a peach marmalade melted topped with a homemade chocolate icing melted on her tongue. Her husband had always wanted her to bake for the grocery store; he said she was the best skilled out of the scratch baker he's ever tasted. Charlotte's cherry pies or apple strudels and her favorite sacher were made out of her mother's recipe, a well treasured family secret that came from good old continent, and from her grandmother's side who lived in Vienna. Locals in Lingit tried to recreate Charlotte's recipes after Jack shared her tortas and pies without her permission in the store, and people demanded and wanted their own, Charlotte got very upset and even more shut herself down in front of the world. Jack never pushed her like that again, trying to understand his wife but was never being able to understand why or what secrets she brought with her from the war.

The combination of sweet chocolate and tart peaches was something she loved. She only shared this kind of love with her sons, but never telling Kurt the recipe, never allowing him to help or to be in the kitchen when she baked. And now, she was surrounded by the things that have made her company for all those years, she's lived in the seaside town. She took a sip of her coffee and the sound of the fork scraped the last pieces of sacher on the plate.

"It's time," she said out loud, but there were no listeners.

Edith didn't tell Margot when she found the handwritten note in her pocket. The small piece of paper had a printed header with the initials Ch. G., and the paper had a light, flowery scent. Her hand still trembled when she read the handwritten note. She found it in the pocket of her pants the night after the Fourth of July celebration. The handwriting was very nice and neat, the letters readable and without grammar mistakes. No words were crossed or written over. The few sentences were in perfect German language. Edith felt the goosebumps rise on her arms, and her stomach turned sour. She met so many people on that day. Downtown Lingit was so crowded, and people pushed and bumped at one another, and even though she went over the day many times in her mind, and tried to remember the faces she spoke to, there was no one who would fit the profile, no one who would be quite elderly, in his nineties, to who would be able to move through the crowd unnoticed. Even though Edith was seventy herself, she looked much younger, and she was in a great physical shape, didn't have to use a cane, dressed youthfully, and when she didn't speak, no one would guess she has a foreign accent. She looked very American and thought the person who slipped the note to her pocket had to look similar like her. She wanted to show it to Margot many times since the summer day, but decided to keep it a secret instead. The instructions said:

Meet me at 7.30 in the morning by the west end of the beach, by the Devil's cove on the first day of the fall. Come alone.

She wore a cotton shirt and a pair of jeans and slippers and reached for a dark blue jacket that she placed over her shoulders. Edith grabbed her silk scarf and placed it over her hair and crossed it on her collar bones and left the ends fall down over her shoulder blades. She made sure the silk scarf covers her neck well, checking her image in the mirror and placing the German written note into her jacket pocket. She quietly opened the large sliding door, and closed it, and stepped over the wooden patio and onto the sand. She turned around, but the private beach was empty, not even Leaf didn't surf the ocean on that morning. The wind blew strong and the water rushed to the shore, with whitecaps splashing up high and disappearing into the wet sand. The sun shined on the open skyline and the air smelled somewhat different. Perhaps that's how the autumn wanted to let everyone know, it has arrived.

She got all the way to the west end of the private beach. The color of the sand changed, and became more of grey and mixed with little rocks and sharp scattered broken shells. She looked at the tall cliff in front of her. As if the land suddenly broke apart, and chipped, to make space for the majestic ocean, she heard of the place before from Margot, but this was the first time she actually visited the Devil's Cove. She hesitated, placing her right hand over her stomach, she suddenly felt unwell. Margot had warned her, telling her the cove was a dangerous place to go to. The wide beach suddenly ends and the stripe of the sand narrows and the space between the salty waves and the cliff can become a human trap. When the tide comes in, all the sand buries under the weight of the water. The cliff's slow corrosion of the waves that wash over it has become unstable, and loose rocks fall down onto the beach. Margot had told her the first time she came upon the place, she wasn't aware of the danger. Kurt was the one she had met there that day and who told her, how the locals nicknamed the cliff. He said he goes there, when the tide is low with his dog, to get away from the public beach and other people. Kurt knew his way around. Was it possible Edith was actually meeting him there right now? She shook her head and said out loud, "No, that would be ridiculous."

She glanced at the ocean; the waves were higher that the day before, and she had no idea when the tide rushes in. She knew so little about tides, never really paying attention to the moon phases and low and high tides. She wasn't a fisherman, but she could do a better job for her own. After all, she reads the papers every morning, aware of the back cover page with the bold print and times of the tides.

If the tides come, then the devil and her both die on this morning, she thought. Edith placed her hand over her mouth when she realized she didn't even write a note to Margot where she was going. Edith tipped the top fingers of her right hand over her forehead, "Stupid, stupid, so stupid," she cursed at herself. Then she checked the time on her wrist. "Seven thirty three," Edith whispered, twisting her body, looking around one more time. She was surrounded by the cliff, sand and water. Edith felt, as if she is going to suffocate. She clenched her palms into fists and with firm steps Edith Altman walked into the Devil's Cove.

A person stood on the higher end of the narrow sand passage, facing back to Edith, and leaning her right shoulder onto the rocky cove. Dressed in a long dark coat, Edith could see only the ankles, and even those were covered in black, polished boots. The person's hands were tucked in the pockets, and there was a black hat, not leaving a strand of hair out of the highly raised collar. The person that has been waiting for her was about her height and weight. Edith realized she could not remember how tall the doctor in the Bavarian hospital was. How much did she actually could remember? She either saw him sitting down behind his desk, or leaning over her when she was delivering her baby or she was drugged and her mind and vision clouded by the powerful cocktail he injected into her arm when he came in that morning to deliver her the horrible, tragic news. Edith felt her heartbeat go up, and her breath shortened and her chest moved faster as she slowly approached the person dressed in black.

"You're late," the voice said in German.

"I'm sorry," Edith replied in her native language.

She touched the stone wall, and immediately felt the coldness from the wall enter through the fingertips all the way through and into her heart. Edith heard her own breath as she inhaled the salty air through her nostrils but let it out through her half-opened mouth. Inside, she was a nervous knot and she felt uneasy and scared, not because of the water on one side and a tall, rocky wall on the other, but because of the truth, for which she came to see this person.

"Hallo Edith," the person said, slowly turning on the side, with the head low to the chin and the large hat sat over the forehead. As much as Edith wanted to see the eyes, all she could see was a tip of a nose and red, full lips. Who was she?

CHAPTER 19

§

EDITH ALTMAN STARED AT THE woman in front of her.

"I'm Charlotte Groeneweg." Charlotte slowly removed her hat, keeping her eyes and chin low to the ground, before taking a deep breath and lifting her chin, she looked Edith directly into her eyes. A moment of silence thick as a fog entered the space between the two women. The Pacific Ocean rumbled in the background, with each wave that washed over the shore, spilling over the sand, bringing the past to the very moment after so many years of silence.

Edith studied her face, keeping very still, only her eyes shifted, mapping Charlotte's hair, neatly tied in the back, and into the high bun, her face saddened, but her eyes still very much alive, few permanent lines imprinted on her forehead and around her eyes. She had nice light skin, kept herself out of sun. Light green and purple thin veins protruded through the fair, thin skin light, on her temples. Her lips were stained with a lipstick, red like roses, and Edith smelled the flowery perfume, the same one, that was left on the paper handwritten note, she had found in her pocket in early July.

"We share something from the past..." Charlotte's words sliced the air between them and joined the whispers of the deep ocean. She rolled up her sleeve and raised her left arm in the air. A golden chain glittered in the morning sun, decorated by a gold, beautiful half-rose pendant.

Edith's lips parted as she let out a sigh, "Oh my God...." She placed her right hand over her heart, and then moved her palm over her mouth.

"Where...where did you get the pendant from?" she asked, but her voice sounded foreign to her. Tears filled up her eyes. Charlotte's nervousness showed on her, as her voice trembled, and her hands started shaking.

"Someone placed it on my baby, when I was in the hospital, a long time ago, in Bavaria," she said, never leaving her sight of Edith.

Edith started shaking. She couldn't believe she would ever see the other half of the pendant again. She'd waited 46 years for this moment. It felt so surreal to her. She had imagined and played a moment like this in her mind many times, trying to see what it feels like to be able to placed the two roses together and unit them again. Now, the time has come and Edith's legs felt wooden, she couldn't move, her tongue dry in her mouth and her hands shaking. She watched as Charlotte took of the golden chain from her wrist and extended her hand toward Edith.

"It belongs to you. It has always only belonged to you." Edith felt her arm lift, and open her palm, every movement felt mechanical to her, like a reflex. Charlotte placed the chain and the rose pendant into her palm and then touched her fingers and closed Edith's palm. Charlotte's hand was warm, and soft and calming. Edith didn't expect that at all.

Edith brought her hand close to her chest and paused for a brief moment before she opened her palm and stared at the golden rose and the tiny chain it was attached to. The pendant split in half, hasn't been completed in over four decades.

"Please, start from the beginning," Edith said with a coarse voice.

"I will tell you what I know and how I know it. I'll let you know everything you deserve to know." Charlotte said, and added with emphasis, "Let's take a walk on the beach."

Edith felt a sense of relieve to exit the narrow space that separated the ocean from the cliff. She turned and walked out of the Devil's Cove and instantly felt the sun on her skin and took a deep breath. Charlotte walked next to her; they had the entire place for themselves.

"The first time we met, was at the Bavarian hospital, I came in to deliver my baby, you did the same…"

"It was the early spring of 1944," Edith said breathlessly.

"Yes, and we shared the same hospital wing, and the floor, with the black and white checker's tile, and where the walls desperately needed to be repainted, but the world fought in the war, and the walls remained chipped and shabby and the hallway was always cold…"

Edith's mind wondered back in time, and she saw herself young again. She'd entered the hospital corridor, a small luggage in her hand, she placed her other palm over her very pregnant belly. She smiled at the nurse dressed in white, looking forward to her firstborn child.

"But because there was war going on, life didn't stop. People kept on moving forward, and while some lives ended, new ones were born. That's the circle of life." Edith heard Charlotte's voice, but now it became young again, and full of expectations and excitement. Edith relived the moment, when she gave birth to Rolf. And then Charlotte, in another room, at the same time gave her birth to Kurt.

"The first time I saw you were when we passed one another in the hallway," Charlotte continued, as young Edith walked alone, around the corner, and there, another woman, Charlotte passed her closely and smiled at her. Charlotte suddenly stopped and touched Edith's shoulder. This brought the older one back to the reality, on the sandy beach of Alaskan town Lingit. "Edith, we both delivered our babies on the same day and stayed in that damn Bavarian hospital for six weeks. I was twenty one years old…"

"And I was twenty four." Edith said firmly.

The women started walking slowly, side by side, Charlotte's black boots coming in and out of the grayish colored sand, as she lifted her feet. The breeze blew into her hair pulling loose strands off of her bun. Edith's silk scarf danced on her back and shoulders as they strolled down the empty beach.

"The doctor that delivered our babies had always listened to opera, often leaving his office door opened to the hallway, the sound of the chamber orchestra reaching my room…" Charlotte said, as she saw herself young, at barely twenty one years old, a fan of the opera, and big symphonies. "Sometimes I left my door open on purpose, so I could hear the music. This was the second time I saw you…You came upon my door, and watched me, when I had my baby in my arms. I knew you were standing there for a while, just watching the two of us, and the music came in with you and I noticed you moved to the rhythm of the of the instruments…That's something I do often, and I thought, perhaps, you could be my friend, and we could share the joy of our newborn babies together…"

Edith relived the moment again, and as Charlotte spoke, Edith was there with her, watching the stranger, cradle a baby, smile, and whisper to the bundle of new life.

"The two of you looked so peaceful," said Edith. "They brought me my boy Rolf, and I nursed him, but every time I was done feeding my son, a nurse entered the room and took him away from my arms, saying, 'The baby needs to rest now.' She left my door opened, and I heard the music, and got up and walked through the hospital's corridor, and that's how I ended up at your cracked door.

Charlotte stopped again, and with a profound sadness in her face, looked deeply into Edith's eyes.

"Oh Edith, I wish I knew. I wish I knew…." She repeated and shook her head. "But I didn't, I had no idea at that time!"

"You wish you knew *what*?"

Charlotte took a deep breath, "After you exited the door, I got up and shut it. I went back to bed and took my baby in my arms, and a golden chain with a half rose pendant slipped onto my chest from his white cotton wrapper."

Edith's face turned pale, and her head spun around, as her lungs gasped for oxygen, she couldn't move, and couldn't speak and stood like a statue in front of a woman, she knew nothing about.

"What did you say?" she heard herself say finally. Then she felt Charlotte's hand on her arm, as her own legs failed her she leaned onto the other woman and the blackness and complete silence took over her human mind and body.

Edith woke up and stared at the unfamiliar looking chandelier above her head. The crystals carried six individual bulbs, each decorated with a hand carved, sharp pointed pieces, in a shape of a tear. Then she tilted her head and mapped the room she laid in. There were smaller, and bigger, shorter and larger crystal vases, with various cuts, made to a precision, a European glass, that only a European or a big fan of crystal would have at their home. She lay in Charlotte's house, and then remembered, that she had fainted on the beach. The familiar sweet aromatic smell entered her nostrils, as she looked at the many red roses in those spectacular crystal vases. She brought her legs onto the floor and pushed herself from the bed. Just before she touched the door handle, music entered the air, beautiful melody of an aria, sung by a soprano singer. Edith looked at her hand, shaking slightly. She pressed her lips together, and firmly pushed the door handle down and opened the door, walking into the unknown, unfamiliar large living room.

She looked around and didn't see anyone. And then, in the corner of the room, the darkest spot, a cloud of smoke arose up and above an old, tall, fabric armchair. Edith walked slowly walked over and before she could see the person sitting there, a voice came from behind the armchair and said, "How are you feeling, Edith?"

"Please sit down. I'll get you a glass of water. Or would you prefer something stronger, maybe a cognac?"

Edith sat down, opposite Charlotte, looking at her she replied, "I don't need anything."

"Well then, perhaps I can finish my story now." Charlotte said and shut the cigarette in the ashtray on the side table next to her.

Edith rested her back against a large pillow and crossed her legs, folding her arms in her lap.

"I found the necklace. It had a rose pendant, but the rose's single bloom was cut in half, and I thought, how strange it is, how strange it looks like this, on its own. I called a nurse and when she came in; I showed her the necklace and asked her where it came from." Charlotte said, and tried to remain as calm as she could, while the music played in the background. When the signer sung the highest notes of the aria, she closed her eyes and slowly moved her head from side to side to the rhythm of the music.

"An inspiration can bring an enormous beauty into your heart," she said suddenly and added with emphasis, "Music and things that develop the sense of hearing connects to the element of space and space connects all things, singing and chanting and music are very important for our soul."

Edith remained seated and very still, she listened to the aria and listened to Charlotte, a woman she just met, yet they already saw one another over four decades ago. A stranger, yet someone she had a connection with. She just hasn't figured it out yet.

"I'd say that human default is that we're somewhat immature. If we truly connect to the heart," Charlotte placed her right palm over her chest, "Then it's often immature."

Edith couldn't keep silent anymore. Her stillness grew into nervousness and she finally said, "Charlotte, tell me what you know. I must hear it now."

The singer finished the aria and the gramophone became quiet. Charlotte took a deep breath. She spoke in a quiet, broken voice. "We're born alone, and we die alone. That's the simple truth. And your salvation is entirely up to you. The nurse told me, I'd have to ask the doctor about the necklace."

"Dr. Siegfried Muller…" Edith said breathlessly.

"Yes, precisely Dr. 'Sigi,' as all the nurses liked to call him."

"What did he say?"

"He told me that a young woman, a mother, placed it in the cotton wrapper there for my baby, for good luck, for all things good." Charlotte lowered her eyesight and stared at her hands folded in her lap. "He said, 'It's for the baby's sake. You've got to keep the necklace.'

"And I said, 'But the rose is split in half. It makes no sense, unless I get the other half. There must be another necklace, another pendant. I want to meet the woman. Is she still here?' Charlotte's words fill in the space between the women. "And the doctor replied," 'She wished to stay anonymous.'

"Anonymous. As if I never existed…" Edith said. "How long did you stay in the hospital?"

"Six weeks. How long did you stay?"

"Six weeks."

Edith nodded. "And now I know why. I had to stay there to feed your baby. For which I thought,…the entire time I thought, I was under the illusion that the baby the nurses brought me, was mine…" Edith's eyes filled with tears and the tears rolled down her cheeks, and onto her neck, and she felt them to go under her blouse and then she said, "I kept your baby alive. The doctor needed me, he used me to keep your infant alive!"

Charlotte got up from her armchair and moved forward, shifting her knees on the carpet, she knelt down in front of Edith, grabbed her hands and pleaded, "I'm so sorry Edith. I didn't know. I swear, I had no idea what the doctor did. You've got to believe me. Please." She had tears in her eyes when she stared into Edith's.

"I gave the necklace to my Rolf when he was born...," Edith said. "But the nurses insisted that it not be kept on the baby's neck. They said to wait at least a month, for the baby to grow a little. So I took it off and kept it safe, while I wore the second half of the rose on around my own neck. Edith unbuttoned her blouse. There, a golden chain with a half rose pendant came from upon the collar. Charlotte shrugged and moved back, but still stayed knelt down. "Oh my God," she whispered.

Edith took the necklace off and placed it in her lap. Then she slipped her right hand into her pocket and took out the other necklace, the one for the baby, with a small chain but an equally large half rose attached to it. And for the first time in more than 46 years, Edith Altman brought both pendants together, in her own hands, and connected the roses. A perfect fit, they slid one into another right in front of Charlotte's eyes. "What happened to my baby?"

Suddenly, from the corner and behind Charlotte's armchair, a figure stepped out and walked toward the women.

"Margot?!" Edith gasped. "What are you doing here?"

"She came here to resolve the puzzle, to put the last piece together – Margot did this for you, Edith," Charlotte replied and got up from and sat back into her armchair. Edith watched as Margot sat down next to her on the sofa, two women facing one.

Edith let go off the pendants and they separated in her lap and she placed her hands over them, as if to protect them, in front of the others, so no-one would take them away from her, ever again.

"The first time your secretiveness sparked my young, hungry and curious mind, was when I was a teenager," Margot said. "I must have been sixteen, when I noticed you staring at a photograph in your hand, whispering something in German. And then I saw a glitter of gold, you clutched in your fist. When you noticed me standing in the doorway, you changed, and got angry at me, and shut the door at my face."

Margot paused, and when Edith's face showed, she remembered that very moment from the past.

"You had a secret. And I wanted to know, what it was. I wanted to know so much, I went through your things, on a day after school, when you were still at work, and dad was at the newspaper office." Margot paused and glanced over at Charlotte.

"I'll go in the kitchen and prepare some coffee," Charlotte said then left the two women alone.

"I was down on my knees, looking under your and dad's bed, going through drawers, your cloths, pockets…and I couldn't find anything. It drove me crazy."

"I know it did," Edith said bluntly and Margot shrugged, not expecting Edith to say that.

"You did?"

"Yes, of course. I was sixteen once myself. I know how a young mind can be ambitious and curious. I thought about it for a while. What if…what if I want to go back, to visit the past, to face it again for a chance to know the truth? I was scared to do it on my own. But when I saw you, your eagerness, I gave it a try. And I made it easier for you."

"You left the photograph on the floor for me to find it?!" Margot gasped.

"Precisely." Edith replied and stared Margot in the eye.

"Mother...You knew what I was up to, what I was after?"

"Yes, my dear Margot, and I hoped from the bottom of my heart that whatever you'd find would bring a conclusion to my own past. And this entire time I had hoped, whatever you'd find, will not break you, or discourage you from putting the last piece of puzzle into its place."

"You are not mad at me?"

"No. Why would I be mad at you? I am glad you came into my life and made it so much better and richer, and I am grateful for Adam, your father, and for everything the life has brought to me here, on the new continent." Edith took Margot's hand into her own, "But everyone has a past and the past is a part of our life that we cannot erase. Each of us need to accept our own past, whether we like it or not." Edith paused, and then she said with emphasis, "It took me a long time to accept what happened to me."

Margot let go of Edith's hand and wrapped her arms around her and hugged her tightly.

Charlotte came back to the living room carrying a tray with a hand painted china coffee cups and saucer and small, silver spoons. A separate cup held sugar cubes with a silver thong placed across the beautiful china. She set the tray on the coffee table and went back to her armchair, facing the two women on her sofa.

"Thank you, Charlotte," Edith said in whisper and reached for the coffee, placing a sugar cube into the black liquid and watching it to slowly change from white to black and dissolve until it no longer existed. She didn't pour any milk and just brought the painted china cup to her lips and took a sip. Charlotte looked over at Margot and watched her as she poured a generous amount of cream into her coffee and placed two sugar cubes in it. When she stirred the liquid, the silver spoon touched the insides of the cup and made several high tones that reminded Charlotte of the musical instrument triangle.

"I thought I would be meeting with *Dr. Sigi*. I thought you found him alive, and when you told me to come and visit Alaska, I thought I would be coming over here facing this monster in the eye after 46 years. I guess I was wrong."

Charlotte and Margot looked surprised, and Charlotte spoke first. "Edith! Oh, I'm so sorry, you didn't know..."

"I didn't know what?"

"Dr. Siegfried Mueller died." Charlotte looked at Margot, and Margot finished the sentence. "I found out that Siegfried Mueller died ten years ago. He stayed in Germany where he lived after the war was over, until his death. I was able to find out through a librarian an old diary; he kept where he wrote down the names of the babies that died. He called his diary *"Sigi's Angels."*

Edith's hand started shaking as she placed the coffee back on the tray. At that moment, Edith wished to be a bird, to spread her wings and lift up to the sky and fly far away.

"Was Rolf's name there?"

"Yes. I am sorry, Edith. I am so sorry." Margot replied. She got up and kissed Edith lightly on a cheek. Then she passed Charlotte in the armchair and Charlotte raised her hand and softly touched Margot's palm and whispered, "Thank you." As Margot exited Charlotte's house and left the two women alone. Charlotte moved over and sat next to Edith, but Edith shied away and leaned on the other side, tears entering her eyes, she folded her hands between her tights.

"Rolf was one of the babies that the heartless doctor killed. Your son became a victim of *"Sigi's Angels."*

"I couldn't feed my son. I wasn't able to provide him with milk..." Charlotte said as her mind took her back to the Bavarian hospital.

Young Charlotte laid on the bed, a pillow pushed against the cold, iron bed rest, she leaned her back and moved the blanket over her legs. The nurse entered and brought her baby boy and gently placed him into Charlotte's arms. The nurse stayed and watched as Charlotte struggled to feed her boy. The desperate new mother had tears in her eyes, as the sharp, loud cries echoed through the room from the hungry infant.

The nurse's shadow crept over Charlotte as the woman abruptly picked up her baby and gave her a disappointed frown. Charlotte stretched her arms in the air for the nurse to return her baby boy, but eventually she was left alone in the hospital room. The sound of the crying baby faded into a distance until it was heard no more. A terrible silence accompanied Charlotte as she buttoned her top and brought the blanket to her chin and curled up on her side and wept quietly into her pillow.

In another room, on the same floor, at the very same moment, young Edith smiled at a beautiful face of her newborn son, Rolf. The babies' wide toothless grin and big eyes stared back at her, as she touched his little hand; the boy wrapped his tiny fingers around Edith's forefinger. She leaned down and kissed his chubby cheek. The newborn's soft skin and warmth stayed on Edith's lips and she wished to remember the feeling and the smell of her baby boy forever until the day she dies.

The same nurse that left Charlotte's room, now opened the door and entered into Edith's.

"It's time for the baby to rest," she said with her sharp voice as she took Rolf from Edith's arms and carried him away and out the door.

"That's the last time I saw my baby," Edith wiped the tears away from her eyes.

"How could I not notice it? How could I not see the next time they brought me the baby to feed, it wasn't my Rolf? What kind of mother am I that I didn't recognize the baby I fed wasn't my own?" She looked at Charlotte.

"Can you answer me? Can you answer that?" Edith pleaded desperately?

"You can't imagine what I went through, and how much I've struggled! Or what it feels like to lose a child!"

"Edith, with all respect, you didn't lose Rolf. The doctor deliberately killed him! And I had no idea, at that time they told me, there is a good Samaritan who offered to helped out and I believed it. I didn't question it. All I wanted for my boy was to not go hungry, to live. The evil took over; the devil itself orchestrated this and destroyed a healthy life in order for another to live. The world we lived in was cruel."

Out, the open window, the autumn breeze gently moved the sheer curtain then brought in a gust of fresh, cool air. Alfred stood in the front yard with his head tilted close to the house he listened to two different voices coming through the window; one familiar, who belonged to his mother, the other he didn't know. He wrapped the fingers of his left hand around the nozzle of the garden house and pressed them firmly. He dared to move, staring at his stained boots with the tips and heels sunk in the fresh soil that nurtured the many colorful roses alongside the bridge of the front of the house. The air carried Charlotte's trembling, coarse voice as Alfred's chest lifted more frequently up and down as he listened to his mother's words.

"I can never tell them. Alfred would not understand and Kurt would never forgive me!" said Charlotte.

Alfred tilted his head and shrugged when he heard the other woman's reply. Edith said quietly, and softly, "Charlotte, you couldn't have known what the doctor would do." Edith paused, and Alfred lifted his feet from the dirt and stood on his toes, stretching his back and neck his eyes peaked through the gap in the window and through the sheer curtain that moved in the breeze he watched, as Edith placed her hand onto Charlotte's shoulder and continued, "Neither did I know when the nurses brought over the baby boy to me and placed him into my arms... You wanted your child to live. The world we once lived in was wrong."

Charlotte's tears rolled down her cheeks as Edith looked at her, Charlotte knelt down in front of her, and Edith moved her hand from her shoulder to Charlotte's arm to let her know to get up. "I'm sorry, Edith. I am so sorry! I've always felt responsible."

"Charlotte, we've both have been victims of circumstances. Edith paused and then she looked deeply into the other woman's eyes and replied, *"I forgive you,"* Edith said and tightly hugged Charlotte. "I forgive you." She repeated holding the hug.

Alfred dropped the garden hose and ran away as fast as he could. He ran through the front gate and out onto the sidewalk and across the street. He continued through the evening traffic and jumped between the cars crossing the road, cars furiously and loudly honking behind him, until he got to his house, where he finally slammed the door behind him.

CHAPTER 20

Margot Sat In The Sand that the all-day sun had warmed. And even though the Indian Fall came with cooler temperatures over night and in the mornings, brining dew over the mountain grass and open fields above the Chetan Mountains, the sun still shined and the late September days were among the last to enjoy the sandy beaches in Lingit. Soon, the wind, fog and rain will come and fill most of the short autumn before snow falls and covers the nature's beauty in white blanket. Margot deliberately left the other two women alone. She didn't need to be there, she didn't want to be there when Edith hears the truth for the first time in forty six years. When Margot spoke to Charlotte, she realized how much this woman has suffered her own ordeal, and when Margot showed her the images from the doctor's book, the devil's book that the doctor kept, Charlotte broke down and her worst fears became reality. She told Margot she could never find piece after the day she and Kurt left the hospital. She felt that something was not right, but was too afraid to search for answers.

Margot soon realized how much these two German women had in common. Charlotte's hospitality came in a shape of sachertorte, so delicious, Margot knew of only one person that could bake it the same way. When she saw the old fashioned gramophone, she asked her to turn the black vinyl that was on the top on. When the opera entered the living room, Margot nearly felt nauseous, recognizing the aria that she heard many times at her home when she was growing up. She told Charlotte why she came over, and told her about Edith and Charlotte agreed to meet with her stepmother and for once and for all uncover the truth behind the day, when she witnessed the young mother's cries through the cracked open door in Bavarian hospital.

A happy, repeated bark came from the top of the beach and soon became louder as Holton cheerfully announced his presents. He bumped his furry mutt body into Margot's back, then quickly came around and pushed his wet nose from down under her arms that wrapped around her calves.

"If humans had tails, mine would wiggle a lot," Kurt said as he kissed the top of her head and sat down next to her. He threw a ball to his dog and Holton chased after it all the way to the white caps of the ocean waves.

"Are you okay? You're awfully quiet..."

Margot deliberately avoided her eye contact with him. She moved her knees closer to her chin and pressed her arms against her shin bones, until it hurt. She stared at the Pacific Ocean, letting the wind blow through her hair, and make her eyes watery.

"Do you want to talk?" Kurt asked.

"Kurt..." She looked at him for the first time. He saw a change in her eyes and in her face, but wanted her to talk, wanted her to tell him what's going on. "I don't even know how to say this..."

"Just try, whatever it is, whatever you have to say...I'll listen..."

She moved both of her hands to her face and for a brief moment her palms covered her eyes, and cheeks until the back of her right hand wiped over her mouth, Margot took a deep breath and looked at him.

"I know deep inside you've always questioned me and I know you've wondered whether me coming to Lingit was purely and only for the reason to make a study of photo documentation of the migrating birds."

"No, that's not completely true. I didn't question you, Margot..."

"The bird study gave me the opportunity to come here and not to raise an immediate suspicion of my trip."

"What suspicion? What are you talking about? I don't understand..."

"Your mother Charlotte and my stepmother Edith share something from the past."

"What do you mean?" Kurt looked deeply at Margot, and she shied away and turned her head and looked at the dog, playing like a puppy, and trying to catch every one cap that washed on the shore. The wet, dirty mutt stretched his front paw and tapped the white foam and bubbles that came over the sand. "Margot?!" Kurt said aloud and wrapped his right arm around her shoulders. "Talk to me."

"Charlotte and Edith first saw each other in the Bavarian hospital in the spring of 1944. They both came in to deliver their babies. Edith had a baby boy…so did Charlotte." Margot tilted her head and looked at Kurt. She read his confusion in his eyes and in his face lost its natural color and became pale and the cheerful light from Kurt's blue eyes faded as he stared in silence at Margot.

A flock of seagulls flew over their heads and with their loud screams interrupted the silence between them. The dog noticed the feathered visitors and lifted his head toward the open sky and barked at them as they flapped their wings and lowered their bodies and settled on the edge of the rocks in the distance. The white and grey eavesdroppers with yellow sharp pointed beaks mapped the ground in search for food. Some jumped from the rocks and into the wet sand, hopping between the salty waters of the Pacific Ocean.

Kurt took his arm off Margot's shoulder, and said quietly, "Go on."

"When I became older, I started seeing a trait in Edith's, my stepmom's behavior. She would never speak about her life when she was young; she said there's nothing to talk about. One day, when I came early from school, I must had been fifteen or sixteen, I saw Edith sitting on the floor of her bedroom, the door cracked, she leaned her back against the mattress, crying, clutching a golden chain in her fist. I stood there, staring, and I knew I was glimpsing her past." Margot paused and ran the fingers of her left hand in the sand, the gap that separated her hips from Kurt's. He shrugged slightly, and didn't say anything. "Now I know, she had to see me, because shortly after that day, I found a photograph lying on the floor in my parents' bedroom. Edith left it there for me to deliberately see it. She laid it there for me, in hopes to allure me to start the search and built the puzzle of her own past."

"Who was on the photograph?" Kurt asked curiously.

"It was an image of young Edith and a baby boy."

Kurt's nervousness showed in his body posture. He wiped the strands from his bangs away from his eyes, he let out a deep sigh, and biting his lower lip he blinked several times and stared at the sand between his knees.

"Years had passed before I started digging into her past. Eventually, I was able to go back and through the help of other people I found out, that Edith had a son in 1944 in Bavaria." She looked over at Kurt.

"Edith is *not* your mother?" Kurt gasped in disbelief.

Margot replied softly, "No. My birth mother died when I was five years old. My father remarried two years later, and Edith is the woman who brought me up and became my second mother; she's my stepmother. But I've always thought of her as my own mother."

"I had no idea."

"How could you, Kurt?"

"Who's the baby on the photograph with Edith? Was it... is it?" Kurt looked at her with the worst worry in his eyes.

"It's not you." She said and let the air carry the words for a moment, before she continued. "It's Edith's own son, Rolf."

"*Rolf?* What happened to *him?*"

"He died."

"He is *dead?* So, what does it have to do with me?"

"Everything," Margot said breathlessly.

"What do you mean? I don't like where this conversation's going."

"I'm sorry Kurt. I don't think I can be the one to tell you..."

"Tell me what?! If not you, who? Who can tell me?"

"Charlotte, your mother can tell you."

Margot got up and Kurt reached for her hand and grabbed it, but she pulled away from him and ran up the beach, and didn't look back.

Kurt yelled after her, "Margot, wait! Don't go! Talk to me!"

The seagulls that landed on the rocks in the distance abruptly flew up in the sky, flapping their grey wings, as they stretched their white necks and heads with sharp beaks against the sky, screaming aloud, heading to their next destination.

§

The living room windows covered by heavy dark drapes changed the room's atmosphere into a dimmed cloud with only two side lamps providing light, Kurt sat on the sofa, a photograph in his hand. In a complete silence he studied the face that looked at him from the black and white paper. Tall, and fit, with broad shoulders and long arms, the man could had been in his thirties. A head full of light colored hair, and gentle eyes, a strong chin and nicely shaped lips, Kurt got an intense feeling in his gut, as if he was looking at his own image. Except her knew, this is not him, it couldn't had been him, because the picture he stared at in his hands was taken a half century ago. The man on the photograph wore wide woolen pants with high waist and a thick, leather belt, a white shirt tucked behind the belt with the two top buttons carelessly open. His lips parted, but the man didn't smile. Yet he projected a feeling of warmth and gentleness.

Kurt wiped the corner of his eye; he didn't want his mother to see him cry. She sat next to him and softly touched his left forearm.

"His name was Klaus Groeneweg," she paused, before she quietly adding, "Klaus was your father."

Kurt shifted his left hand and took his mother's palm into his and pressed firmly.

"You've got his blue eyes, and lips and cheekbones. You've inherited your father's looks," Charlotte said looking at her late husband's picture.

"Klaus' family came from Holland and settled right across the border. His parents moved more in land, where the land was more suitable for farmers. They built the house Klaus lived in, and they farmed on the same land as us, until…" Charlotte pressed her lips together and Kurt lifted his eyes and looked at his mother, but didn't say a word.

"He was a good man with a strong head on his shoulders. Klaus was one of a kind. And you are a lot like him, Kurt. If he were alive, he would be so proud of you, who you become as an adult, as a person."

Kurt had a nauseous feeling in his stomach. "How could you keep this a secret from me for all these years? I was born in Germany? Mother? What about dad? What about Jack?"

"Jack knew my first husband died. When I came to America, you were sixteen months old. Jack took you as his own son, right from the beginning. He loved you, Kurt, as you were his own son!"

"What about Alfred? Are there any secrets, mother?"

"No. Alfred is you brother...your half-brother. Alfred was born here, in Lingit."

"I suppose, he doesn't know any of this," Kurt whispered.

"No, he doesn't know anything."

"Kurt, I wanted to protect you!"

"If Margot and Edith haven't come over, if they have never showed up here, would you have ever told me, who my real father was?"

Charlotte stared at the floor.

"Mother, answer me! Had not there been for Margot, would you keep your secret away from me, would you take it to your *grave?*"

"I...I don't know." She shook her head from side to side and shrugged her shoulders.

Kurt angrily got up and passed his mother, and ran out the door. She heard the slam and then the house became very still and silent.

A few hours later, he pushed the nearly empty bottle of whisky down, and the glass rolled on the hardwood floor, and across the wide, strong beams, a golden liquid twisting inside until the bottle hit the wall on the opposite side of Kurt's living room. He pushed himself up from the sofa and drunkenly stumbled out the door and into his Defender truck. The rumbling engine roared aloud, Kurt leaned over the steering wheel and switched the headlights on. He grinned when his eyes stared at the bright lights that reflected from the house's large windows. Kurt moved his hand and shuts the light.

"Much better," he muttered under his lips.

Four heavy, wide tires with deep tracks rolled into a dark night on the paved road, swaying to the sides, as Kurt wasn't able to keep his wheel straight on the road. He rolled down the window and the night cool air blew into his light colored strands and covered his eyes. He removed his bangs away and stepped on the gas, the truck crawled through the darkness like an angry lion chasing his prey. He parked the car sideways and stumbled his feet to the door, banging loudly until he felt the pain on the side of his fist.

"Open the door! Open the damn door!" he yelled out loud from his lungs. He leaned his drunken body onto the wood, his face sweating from the alcohol, his lungs breathing loudly and heavily. Footsteps came from the other side, and as Kurt pushed himself away from the door, as he heard a single lock and then the door opened to a dimmed room. Kurt's shrieked his face as he saw the person standing opposite to him. His vision blurred as he mumbled something under his liquored breath before his body leaned forward, weighting its entire body mass onto the small, thin shoulders in a shirtless cotton top.

Leaf's strong knees pushed Kurt's body away as he grabbed his arm and crossed it over his bare shoulder he dragged his friend's feet over the floor and onto the bed by the wall in the single room.

"Lies. All she's ever told me were all lies!"

Leaf placed a pillow under Kurt's head and then moved over to his feet and took off the drunk's boots. He spread a blanket over him and without a word turned off the lamp and crushed on the sofa.

The next morning, Kurt woke up with a pounding throbbing pain in his head. He sat down and the migraine expanded over his entire brain. He placed his head between his palms, when Leaf approached him with a mug of steaming hot liquid.

"Here. Drink this; it'll make you feel better." He handed him the dark colored, light-scented tea.

"What is it?"

"Chamomile, it helps with the headache. Ginger is the bitter taste, but it helps to settle your stomach. And I promise, there are no mushrooms there."

Kurt wetted his lips and grinned. "Uff, it's bitter."

Leaf lifted his arm and with his fingers he slightly pushed on the bottom of the mug, moving it back to Kurt's face. "Go on, drink."

Kurt obeyed and finished the cup of ginger chamomile tea. He coughed and his face showed few wrinkles on his forehead and around his eyes. Leaf took the empty mug and walked few steps to the kitchen sink where he sat it down. Kurt look around and saw that everything inside were made out of one, quite large room. The entrance, the living room, the bedroom with a single bed by the wall, where he slept, and a simple kitchen, handmade and a single sink without a dishwasher. Behind the kitchen stood a door frame, but no door attached to the wooden arch.

"That's the bathroom," Leaf said as he watched Kurt mapping his place.

The simple vegetarian food, Leaf had prepared for breakfast helped to settle Kurt's stomach and the bitter tea took away his splitting migraine.

"Thank you."

"For what?"

"I don't even remember how I got here. I'm sorry, Leaf."

"You drove here, Kurt. You shouldn't drive when you're drunk. Isn't it what you told me many years ago?"

Kurt's corners of his lips lifted into a slight smile. "Did I say anything last night?"

"Yeah, you did. You said something about 'Lies. All she's ever told me were all lies!'

Kurt lowered his head and paused, before he took on a deep breath and with shy eyes he looked at Leaf and said, "My mother kept a secret from me for 46 years." He went on and Leaf listened quietly, nodding here and there, tapping his fingers on the table, paying attention to Kurt, as the other confided in him.

The native Indian danced around Kurt in a circle, singing an unfamiliar song in his native language. Vapors of deferent strong, sweet smells entered the air, so did steam around Kurt's body. Leaf took him there, to do a soul cleanse. He said to him, "That's where you leave the past and forgive yourself and learn how to love yourself."

Leaf watched his friend and blessed his ritual with positive, good wishes. Leaf told him, "Kurt, you helped me, when no one else did. When I returned from Vietnam, and spent four years drinking and drowning myself in my sorrows, you were the only one who reached out and helped. And now, I can be here for you."

Kurt didn't expect the ritual to have such an emotional impact on him.

"It's okay to cry. You need to let it out. Forgive yourself, and learn to love yourself." Leaf paused and pointed at a nearby tree. "Let's go hug a tree."

"What? Why? No, I don't want to."

But Leaf already walked to the tree trunk and placed his arms around it and hugged it like a bear.

"All right, I can't believe I'm going to do this." Kurt joined him on the other side of the tree, and spread his arms around and leaned his chest onto the bark. He tilted his head and softly pressed his ear to the tree and shut his eyes. The words of his mother Charlotte came to his mind, she used to tell him when he was a little boy, "You can be child-like once you're an adult. You can be child-like, but not childish. There's a difference." At that time the little boy didn't understand the meaning of his mother's words. Now, he knew what she meat. Leaf was a child-like, and so was Kurt at that very moment and it felt wonderful.

"Wish for more but expect less. Everybody's different. You learn to give others more space. Trust is a peculiar thing. At the end it's up to you how you deal with things. You have a gift. There's something you project to others that's valuable, something that will last. Why some people have it and others don't? I don't know. It's just the way, life is," Leaf told Kurt.

"You can do it! Believe in yourself, Kurt."

Later, Leaf told Kurt to go and speak to Edith. After the Indian cleanse he felt, he's got the strength to do it and arranged a private meeting with her, asking Edith not to tell Margot. She agreed and the two of them met at the Wildlife rescue where his brother Alfred volunteered and where Leaf worked.

"Thank you for meeting me, Edith," Kurt said nervously.

Edith raised her hand and softly placed it onto Kurt's left shoulder. "Kurt, don't be nervous," she said quietly and looked him in the eyes. "You've got beautiful blue eyes. They're very kind."

Kurt smiled and felt more at ease. "Thank you. You're very kind." He took a deep breath and continued, "Edith, I...I don't know how to say this..." His voice quivered and Edith took his hand into hers and said, "It's all right. Everything is exactly the way it's supposed to be."

"Thank you."

Kurt hugged her and they held the hug for a moment surrounded by orphaned baby moose who sat in the middle of the grass, looking at them intently.

§

Alfred looked at every room in the house. He checked the bedroom first, then the living room, kitchen he entered the back yard and the front and her ran upstairs and opened the doors of every room, "K...Kurt?"

When he didn't find his older brother, he grabbed the keys from the wall's hook and exited the house, glancing over the rose bushes, that grew too long and to the sides, he brushed his checkered flannel sleeve over the green, thorn stems as he walked out the gate and across the yard. He unlocked the back door leading to the Groeneweg's grocery store and one more time called loudly,

"Kurt, are y...you here?" The empty store stared back at Alfred, as he finally proceeded to the front door, unlocking the entrance and switching the open neon sign on. The mutt barked several times, greeting him, as he forgot to shut the back door, Holton charged in, full of energy, dancing with his four, large furry paws on the concrete floor, his bushy tail swinging from side to side, hitting the bags of potato chips and sending them on the floor.

"No! G...go outside!" Alfred ordered the happy mongrel, who ran outside the back door and into the yard. Alfred bent over and picked up the bags of chips when the entrance door bell announced the day's first customer.

"Alfred, how are you?"

"Not, not good. Things are n..not good, Margot!"

Margot lifted her arm and slightly touched Albert's flannel sleeve. He shrugged and took a step back. "You're shirt is torn," she said gently.

Alfred tilted his head and looked at his left arm. He covered the hole with his right palm and stared at Margot.

"Is Kurt here?" she stretched her neck and lifted her heels from the ground, standing on her toes for a brief moment, looking behind Alfred and to the other end of the store. "Can I speak to him, please?" she added with emphasis, lowering her heels back on the concrete grocery floor.

"He's not here."

"Where is he, then? Alfred, tell me..."

"Don't know."

"You don't know where your brother is?" Margot asked with a concerned.

"He left last n...night."

"Left? Where'd he go?"

"I don't know. I don't know!" Alfred cried out loud. Margot wrapped her arms around him and slightly rocked him to the side. "Shh, everything's going to be all right."

"You made him leave!" Alfred said upsettingly and Margot let go off the hug and looked at him deeply and with concern.

"I'm sorry, Alfred. I'm sorry for causing you pain," she said and left the store.

Margot walked through the beach, but didn't see him anywhere. She even visited the Devil's Cove in hopes to find Kurt there, but the place was empty, grey and profoundly sad. Her fears turned to reality and for the first time in her life, Margot Smith felt she'd hurt the ones that she cared the most about. Overlooking the Pacific Ocean, she let her tears roll down her cheeks as distant screams of seagulls mixed with the whispering waves that crashed hard on the shore under the force of a windy morning. She shivered as cold feeling washed over her. Margot wiped off her cheeks and returned to her jeep. She drove up to the Wahya Lagoon, a camera bouncing on the passenger seat as the truck rolled over the uneven dusty surface of rocks and potholes. The sun warmed up the top of the hill and the air felt much better as she hiked over to the sweet water lagoon. Scattered patches of bare fireweed stalks with their light purple color stood firmly against the Alaskan wide open skyline, stripped of their pretty blossoms, Margot heard the local's folklore about the summer being over and the winter's coming when the tops of these wildflower plants shed their last flowers.

Clutching the camera in her hand, Margot moved over the path and across the meadow, closer to the Wahya Lagoon when she noticed the place being unusually still and very quiet.

The usually happy chirping in the air no longer existed, as majority of the birds headed south for the many months of winter. She zoomed through her lens onto the lonely Canadian goose, careful not to disturb the bird, while it swam toward the island in the center of the lagoon.

She took pictures and watched as the feathered beauty emerged from water and walked onto the rocky shore that curbed the natural island. Margot wondered why there was only one Canadian, knowing these birds are always in pairs or in flocks. She turned around, in hopes to see more, but there were only occasional screams of magpies and mallards that still cruised the clear water in the Chetan Mountain range. Margot pointed her camera again toward the big bird, zooming slowly and watching it walk through the little rocks, into the grassy patch and there it disappeared in the long, green grass. Perhaps there is another one, hiding and the pair is just getting ready for their migration, she thought. Margot sat down and deeply inhaled the autumn air that smelled like Indian summer, with sweet and alluring with blends of wildflowers in their fullest blooms and all the newly grown pine branches and bumblebees still bussing from one petal to another. She brushed her fingers through her hair and raised her chin against the blue sky and shut her eyes and let the warm rays soak into her skin. A light breeze gently moved her red strands around her face and some went across and tickled the bridge of her nose. The wild birds have been gathering into their flocks on the Wahya Lagoon to get ready for their winter migration. Margot associated their departure with a farewell. She was never good at saying goodbyes. A melancholic feeling washed over her body. She wondered how this lagoon will look after all the birds are gone.

"I'll be back to check on you," she whispered to the air around her.

As she drove down the rocky road, Margot looked around for Kurt, or his dog Holton, but she didn't see any signs of the man or the dog nowhere near the Wahya Lagoon.

"Where'd you go, damnit?!"

As she looked away to the side, she lifted her foot off the brake and let the wheels roll faster down the dusty road, Margot turned her head and there, in front of her headlights, a black furry fear stood in the middle of the road, on his hind legs, his nose sniffing the air, staring at her fast rolling Jeep.

"Jesus Christ!" she let out, and her foot quickly stomped on the brake, swaying the car to the side and lifting a huge cloud of dust in the back and front of her vehicle. The Jeep came to stop and she stared through the windshield to a grey cloud for a moment, before the air cleared a little and the view of the road opened. There was no bear anymore. "Oh, shit," she cursed, fearing the worst that she hit the poor animal and it got scared and ran injured into the woods.

Margot opened the glove box and took out a bear spray. She hesitantly opened the driver's door and stepped out, slowly moving to the front of her vehicle. She looked down and didn't see any splatters of blood; lowering her back she leaned and looked under the car. There, she saw four, black furry paws firmly standing on the dirt road in the back of her trunk. She quickly brought her chest up and rushed to the car, slamming the door behind her. Margot looked at the central console mirror and saw the bear walking casually, uninjured, away from the Jeep and into the grass, eventually disappearing from her view and into the spruce forest. She let out a loud relief sigh as she started the car and headed back to Lingit.

CHAPTER 21

Kurt Has Not Talked or seen Margot for nearly a month. After his mother Charlotte told him about Klaus Groeneweg, he returned back to his mother's house seeking more answers, demanding to know more about his heritage, his family legacy and hoping to see more photographs of his biological father Klaus. Charlotte told him everything she remembered about her first husband, how they met, who Klaus was as a person, and how happy he made her. She told Kurt what kind of life they lived on a farm close to Dutch's border and how the war and the circumstances interrupted and forever changed their lives. Kurt listened carefully, taking in every word his mother told him, and for the first time in his life, he felt a sense of relief, and understanding, who he is as a person, as a human being, and why he could never see a certain little things in Jack, whom he thought was his real father for all these 46 years. Now, his ears and his mind took in that just like him, Klaus never liked red meat, always eating chicken or going hungry, or why he would place his left thumb over his right, when he folded his hands in the lap, even though he was right handed. He liked the story his mother told him how much Klaus liked dogs, and all animals, and that he wouldn't hurt a fly. Kurt saw a close resemblance, not only a visual looking at many photographs in black and white his mother kept hidden away from him for nearly half a century, but he felt the closeness to the man, whom he never met, through the stories of his mother, and he felt in piece, perhaps for the first time in his life. The mother and her oldest son spent hours each day talking about the past, and suddenly these times became their present and the people on the black and white, rough ridged thick paper photograph came to life and existed again, even though for the moment when Charlotte talked about them and Kurt listened and wished he could hug his father Klaus and hear his voice. Alfred joined them and his fingers touched the past as he stared at various faces, quietly and somewhat shyly batting his eyelashes, and through the speech of his mother, joining the stories of the past she used to experience and lived through herself. All three sat on the living room sofa until Kurt shifted to the floor and brought his knees to his chin as Alfred handed him pictures, and Kurt noticed his mother's smile and her face changed when she revisited her past life in Europe, and talked about Klaus Groeneweg and relatives and family she used to know. Charlotte's face softened, and her eyes glittered with a special warm light in them, her smile expanding and her cheeks growing rosier, Kurt's mother's voice softened and quieted, and calmed down, before it gained colors and got more dramatic and louder. Her hands told the stories together with her voice and her heart beat fast as she talked about the happy times and the worst times of her life in war Germany. Alfred reacted to his mother's tears first, because he was sitting right next to her, he grabbed her with both of his arms and gave her a tight bear hug. Charlotte disappeared into her younger son's arms and Kurt got up from the floor and sat on the other side and hugged both. In the background, the fragrant red roses decorated the living room, the blooms proudly crowning their green thorn stems in many hand carved crystal vases on the side tables and alongside the windows and in the corners of the two curious, that held more china and crystal, and next to the old fashioned vintage gramophone, and its shiny large brass tube, through which their mother loved listening to her operas, and many various arias of beautiful solo voices. Next to the widest, deepest and heaviest crystal vase that held the most of the roses, lay a photograph of a young, handsome man, looking back at Kurt.

※

Edith stared at the midday sky decorated with clouds that looked like giant jelly fish with a long veil, and through the longest white skirt a light shined yellow in the middle and red on the sides a rainbow, but upside down, like a human smile. Edith's never seen it like this before. As if someone's lips were on the sky, she was drawn to the warm colors of the rainbow's smile and imagined it descend from the clouds down and kiss her lips. She was witnessing something spectacular; water waves like harmonica came across the upside down rainbow and the breeze picked up and birds started chirping through the air. She knew she's seeing a message of peace and beauty. Her entire heart filled with immense joy, and her mind felt in piece and kindness shined trough her entire body. Edith shut her eyes and her face broke into a wonderful, soft smile. She knew that everything in life is as it supposed to be.

Edith stayed in Lingit after the huge revelation that connected the two German women together. She called her husband Adam on the East Coast and spoke to him for a long time. He listened and told her to take as much time as she needs, he'll be waiting for her in Fenwick once she decides to get back. His last words on the phone echoed in Edith's ears. Adam said to her, "You need to bring humor to your life; otherwise life is not worth living. Life without humor is only half way lived."

And then he told her jokes, and she laughed out loud, using her stomach muscles that rested for many months, and her belly hurt from all the laughter, but her heart felt happy and Edith was grateful for all the people in her life and the life itself she's lived.

When Charlotte returned the half rose pendant to her, Edith made a clutch and a warm feeling washed over her and calming, angelic voice whispered to her, Edith Altman was finally at piece. She simply let things come to her and heal her soul through acceptance and forgiveness.

There was more than just the past that these two women had in common. Just like Edith, Charlotte liked listening to classical music and invited Edith for an afternoon coffee and cake. This was their own private time, just the two of them, the vintage gramophone, and Edith baked her strudel and Charlotte told her, she's never eaten a better piece than this, and Edith told her, her sacher reminds her of the old world, of her youth and brings all the nice memories she cherished when she was a little girl and her mother would bake sacher on Sundays. This torte represented home and closeness of the loved ones to her. Edith told Charlotte she'd tried many times to bake it, but never was able to master it to taste like her mother's. This meant a lot to the other woman, as they sat on the porch, enjoying the last warm rays of the autumn sun, listening to somber violin music.

"Do you want to know why I like listening to classical music?" Charlotte asked, and when Edith quietly nodded without saying a word. "Because when we're listening to music, our emotions *are not calculated.* People get caught up in different emotions, happy or sad, high and low, just like the ocean waves, and often forget the depth of our feeling, the one that comes from the heart. And it's so simple, when I hear the music, when I feel the music I become the music."

"That's beautiful, Charlotte. You and I have more in common than I would have ever imagined," Edith replied as she watched Charlotte move over and switch the vinyl on the vintage gramophone. Solo piano music entered the air, and Edith made a slight smile. "I thought what if one day I no longer am. I don't exist anymore. The world will go on uninterrupted with or without me. Just like it kept on going without my Rolf. And it was music that helped me to overcome my deepest, darkest sorrows. All the somber music and upbeat, happy jazz music and soft or solemn music had helped me heal my soul and helped me to forget for a moment and I made these moments last and eventually made it through. And my life has changed with Adam, and Margot and music." Edith took a deep breath. "The war took everything and everyone I had ever loved. I lost my parents, my baby, and I asked myself what else is there to live for? Later, I found out that music offered me peace and was always there for me when I needed to sooth my soul. Music put smile on my face or let me cry. I told myself, what else this evil can do to me? Rob me of my hearing? I have my memory and will always keep music in my heart and if my heart fails then I'll be dead and everything will be over. But music will stay and help other people overcome their struggles and tragedies or accompany them on their happiest days of their lives. And that's why I will never get bored and I will forever long for the music as long as I live." Edith looked directly at Charlotte who listened to her and her face softened and her eyes showed gentle, warm emotion. Silence, stillness solitude and peace filled in the room where the women sat.

"Charlotte, I see you're a lot like me." Edith reached over and Charlotte extended her arm across the vintage gramophone and their hands met in the middle and Charlotte felt the warmth of Edith's soft palm that pressed onto hers until it let go and Charlotte folded her red nail polished nails into her lap and whispered, "Thank you."

Margot sent off her latest report to John Ford to the Natural Bird magazine with attached pictures of yellow eyed loons. She felt restless, tapping her fingers on the wooden desk, typing imaginary words. She couldn't get her mind off of the afternoon the last time she saw Kurt on the beach and wasn't able to tell him herself the reasons why she came to Lingit. It's been over a month and she still hasn't seen him or spoke to him.

Every time she went over to the Groeneweg's grocery store, he would walk out the back door, leaving Albert to check out her purchases at the register. Every time her stepmother visited Charlotte, Margot would ask her whether Kurt was at the house. The answer remained the same, Edith hasn't seen him.

The outside weather changed quickly and nights became damped and cold. She was grateful Edith stayed with her in the log house and happy to see that at least the women found a common language and they didn't hold anything against her for putting the last piece of puzzle of her stepmother's life. But Kurt held a grudge and she knew it, and she felt responsible for interrupting his life and uncovering his past via his mother's without letting him know in advance. Margot didn't know whether she can live with that thought and the horrible feeling she's had for over a month.

John Ford pressured her to return back to Seattle, telling her she could lose her job, that there's nothing why she would still stay in Alaska, and that all the migratory birds had left some time ago. But Margot couldn't just pack and leave. She had to speak to Kurt, longed to communicate to him, and every time she tried, he disappeared through the door in front of her.

She placed more fire logs in and rubbed her cold hands, staring at the yellow flames, listening to the sound of cracking birch wood. Margot reached for her glass of white wine. The wind outside strengthened and beat onto the large, glass sliding door. Earlier that day her and Edith removed the patio furniture and placed it into the garage for the upcoming winter. The waves on the Pacific Ocean roared with nostalgic cries and the beach remained empty and distant. Tourists had left the coastal

Alaskan town, and only the locals remained. Kids returned to school and adults lost their summer tan and everything around became quieter and the colors of the nature subsided and became pale and grey just like the open sky above.

After the women removed the summer furniture away, Margot needed to clear her mind, in hopes if she goes for a hike, her thoughts will calm. She drove her Jeep to Wahya Lagoon and walked over to the very quiet, almost serene surface of water. She was surprised to see the Canadian goose still there. Margot grew concerned and looked to see if the bird is accompanied, like she thought it had been three weeks ago, when she saw it swimming across to the mid centered island.

On that morning, Margot woke up to see the top peaks of the Chetan Mountains covered in white powder. She knew the snow would slowly descend to lower portions of the rocky ranges, and that the Wahya Lagoon sooner or later will freeze over, pushing the Canadian goose out of water and into the frozen grounds. The bird would have no chance of surviving the winter in Alaska. Margot watched the goose as it noticed her presence and walked closer to her, curiously stretching her neck and moving his beak from side to side. The goose wasn't hissing at Margot, and its wings were perfectly folded by her sides, none hung loose in a sign of an injury. Who knew why the migratory bird chose to stay? Margot had read about the Canadians staying very loyal to their partner, making them wonderful companion pairs. But if one was injured or died, the other usually stayed near, mourning and perhaps waiting for a miracle to come. Could it be the reason why this one was still here? Margot took photos of her. The grass around turned to yellow, making it unsuitable for nutrition, and the edges of the Wahya lagoon already created a thin frozen crust of ice. The lake would close from the outside edges to the middle until it held a thick layer of white, smooth substance, where the local kids come and ice-skate over the coldest winter months.

Margot didn't have much time to act. She lifted her knees from the ground and clapped her hands in the air, deliberately scaring the bird that came too close to beg for food. The Canadian goose got startled and spread her wings to the sides, and ran away from her only human companion and into the water. Margot quickly focused her camera and took as many photos as she could in that short moment, before the bird entered the icy edges of the lagoon and swam away.

Later that evening, Margot went over the pictures and no longer asked the reasons why the bird stayed behind its flock and never lifted into the sky for the winter overlay stay in warmer parts of Canada or United States. She checked the clock on the kitchen wall; ten after eight and grabbed her coat and entered the dark driveway before she shined her headlights onto the white garage door and drove off to town. Margot rang the bell, and waited. No one came to answer the door. Margot took few steps back and lifted her head looking at the windows of the three-story house ahead of her. The lights were on only on the highest floor, where two windows lit into the dark night. She took a few steps forward and banged her fist onto the door, and again and again, until she felt a sharp pain in her hand. Angry for him not to answer the door, she ran back to the front and yelled out of her lungs.

"Open the damn door; I know you're in there!"

As soon as she shut her mouth, the front door opened and Kurt lifted his arm and leaned it onto the frames of the doorway. She didn't move, she stayed in a distance and said upsettingly,

"I need your help."

"You need *my* help?"

"Yes."

Kurt paused and looked at her. A part of him wanted to run to her and hug her and kiss her, while the other wanted to shut the door and go back to his house.

"I'm still mad at you."

"I know."

"You do? Are you sure? Because I don't think you have an idea what you did to me!"

"I'm sorry." Margot didn't look at him, she kept her head low, and her eyes staring at the little natural rocks that lined up to Kurt's front door.

"Kurt, I didn't mean to hurt you. You've got to believe me, please." This was the first time she looked at him.

"How…how do you expect me to believe you, how can I trust you, Margot? Tell me… I don't know, I honestly don't know…"

Margot kept quiet and again, she lowered her chin to her chest, and placed her arms into her coat. She shivered.

"How can I trust *you*? You lied to me. You said you've never left Lingit. That you've never traveled anywhere outside of Alaska! You lied; you said you didn't finish high school."

Kurt bit his lower lip, and stared at her surprised and in silence.

"You graduated a year ahead of your classmates and were accepted to Atlantic University." She stared him in the eye.

Kurt looked down at the ground and finally spoke, he said quietly, "Yes. That's all true. After the university I worked in New York city for about six years. And I didn't like it. I didn't like for about the person I became. I missed the small town, I missed the ocean, I missed the weather, and the trees, and the freedom...I missed the old myself. Maybe the world out there isn't for me. Maybe I don't fit in such world. Maybe the only place, where I can be, is right here in the middle of nowhere... So I left the cosmopolitan life and returned here, and opened a small grocery store, and you know what? I could care less about the expensive cars, huge jobs and salaries. I have enough, I can live on, and every day I wake up, I'm happy, who I am now. It took me years, but I am finally at peace with myself."

"Don't you miss your friends? You had friends in New York–"

"Let me tell you something about those 'friends.' The people like that, who think they own the world, they control other people, and direct their lives. I didn't even leave the room yet, and I heard them talking bad about me. And just a minute ago, they smiled in my face, and said pretty words, and I thought, they are my *friends*. I know better now." Kurt spread his arms to the side and with a desperation in his voice said, "You came here on a mission. You came to my town and turned my life and the life of my brother and my mother upside down...You broke my heart!"

Margot felt her tears come down her cheeks as she bit her lower lip, she heard the door slam. She looked up and stared at the closed entrance door. Kurt no longer stood there. Margot whispered, bringing her right hand from her coat and wiping her tears away from her eyes and cheeks. "I'm sorry. I'm sorry Kurt, I never meant to hurt you."

Then she took out her left hand and walked quietly to the front door. She lowered her back and placed several photographs on the wooden porch.

After Kurt heard her Jeep leave his driveway, he opened the door and noticed the pictures there. He picked them up and saw a Canadian goose in run, her left wing stretched to the side, with perfect uninterrupted, undisturbed feathers, while her right wing opened only partially, from her torso out, but the last part never extended to the side, and rather stayed crippled and folded.

"*I need your help.*" Margot's words echoed in his mind.

Margot could see her own breath, as she spread the cracked on the sides of the Wahya Lagoon's shore. The Canadian goose slid across the patches of ice, starved, cold and weakened. Margot cautiously went to the side as Kurt approach with a wide round net attached to a long, wooden pole. He waited for the goose to nibble on the cracked corn, and when she did, she lowered her feathers and brought her wings down, covering her cold feet, and eating while lying down on the frozen ground. Margot took few pictures, with very slow movement, not to disturb the bird. And then Kurt lifted his net and slowly and gently placed it over the poor, injured bird. The hunger prevailed, because the goose didn't mind to be covered with netting. Kurt walked over and lifted the bird, holding it under its ribcage.

He placed it in a large dog crate, where Margot had previously laid a blanket. The Canadian goose twitched for a moment and Margot noticed the bottom of her feathers on her lower chest had frozen crust of ice. There in the crate the goose placed its beak into a plastic dish and fed herself with more pieces of corn, dried and crushed, suitable for her digestion.

"Thank you," Margot said and looked at him, while they drove down the hill and away from the lagoon.

"You saved her life," Kurt said suddenly, never leaving his eyes off the road.

"I wouldn't be able to do it without you," she replied, still looking at him. Kurt's hair moved loosely around his forehead, as the heater in his Defender poured warm air inside the truck. He tilted his head and his blue eyes looked into hers. The corners of her lips lifted and curled into a wide smile. Kurt moved his hand from the steering wheel and reached over to her. She clutched it all the way down the hill and to the small airport. The sound of rolling wheels over the uneven natural surface and rocks flying to the side of the curbs were their companion, so was the clipping beak in the back of the Defender.

The familiar looking plane awaited them, and the Beaver pilot Frederick "Fritz" Martinson that took Margot and Kurt on the glacier trip in the summer shook her hand again.

"That's one lucky goose!" the pilot said as Kurt uploaded the crate with the bird into the Beaver plane.

"Thanks, Fritz!" Kurt briefly hugged his friend pilot.

And the pilot shouted, "Off to Seattle. Got a special, precious delivery here!" the bearded Fritz jumped into his plane and started the engine. He placed his headset on, and waived through the window to Margot and Kurt.

Margot called John Ford and told him to expect the bird in a couple of hours and thanked him for making the call to the local wildlife bird rescue, who accepted the Canadian goose. Seattle's milder winter will allow the bird to stay there, on open water in a natural preserve, where it can live its life uninterrupted. The X-rays from the local Lingit's vet's office showed, the bird was most likely grabbed by an eagle, and was able to get out of the snatch, permanently injuring the last part of its right wing.

"It will never be able to fly again," the vet said. "But it can live a normal life someplace else, where the water doesn't freeze over the winter."

Alfred watched his brother as he leaned over and whispered something to Margot's ear. Whatever he said made her laugh. Alfred smiled and called for the dog to come to his feet. Holton sat next to him, and Alfred finished carving the rose in his hand. Margot walked over to him, holding Kurt's hand and both sat on each side of Alfred.

Margot asked, "It has no thorns."

Alfred lifted his head and smiled, "No. No m…more thorns."

"Oh my God! There's mouse in the house!" Edith screamed and pushed herself from the floor where she was enjoying the fireplace, and rushed onto the sofa, lifting her legs up, looking across the wooden beams of the living room floor. Margot picked her head from the kitchen's doorway.

"What?"

"We've got a mouse on the loose here," Edith said and pointed her finger over the corner of the room. "I think it's under the radiator."

Margot walked over and leaned down, and there she saw the tip of the pointed nose sniffing the air, long whiskers moving to the sides, and a long, brown tail that stuck out form the heater.

"No. It's just a vole," she said and smiled at Edith.

"A what?"

"A vole. It's not a mouse," she said amusingly.

"I don't care what it is. Get it out of here!" Edith said and nervously laughed, pressing both of her knees close to her chest and away from the floor.

"But it's cold outside." Margot joked as the vole kept on hiding under the radiator.

"They're pushing themselves inside. They're survivors."

"It's time to go back." Edith said firmly.

Later, the night set in and everything became very quiet in the house. Margot loved the serenity of these Alaskan nights. During a day, the town would get noisy, with people walking and talking and cars rushing through the Main streets of Lingit. But at night, the streets would silence, and that's what she appreciated. Although, her rented log house on the hill was far away from downtown, she knew if she lived more locally, she would like the quiet nights. With that thought she drifted into a deep sleep.

A knock on the window, and then another woke her up. The little rocks bouncing off the glass became more frequent. She turned the lamp on and looked at her watch. Then she got up and walked to the window, opening it, and instantly feeling the cold air on her bare shoulders.

"Kurt, what are you doing here? Did something happen?" she asked sheepishly.

"No," he replied casually staring at her.

"But it's 2:30 in the morning."

"I know. Come with me. There's something I want to show you." He whispered into the dark night.

He drove her up the Chetan Mountain, Holton sitting on the back seat, a happy mutt alert and fully awake, just like Kurt. When the Defender stopped, he reached for a blanket and brought it over onto a patch of frozen grass.

"Sit down." He waited for her, and then he lowered his body and sat close next to Margot. Holton followed and tried to push himself between the adults, and when he didn't succeed he laid down next to Margot's hips.

"Look up."

Margot lifted her eyes and looked at the three o'clock morning sky. "Wow," she gasped, watching the beautiful colors on the open, unobstructed skyline.

"Aurora Borealis," Kurt whispered. They watched in silence, the three of them on the top of the mountain, a memory they would keep forever. The northern lights made a spectacular appearance in the darkening skies of late autumn on that early morning above the Chetan Mountains, and Pacific Ocean and the small, peninsula town of Lingit. This was the first time

Margot witnessed this auroral activity live and with her own eyes. She was grateful, she could share this experience with Kurt.

The next day, Margot finished writing her last article and looked over the pictures from the Canadian goose's rescue. She whispered aloud the last words she wrote, *"I long for the nature; and out of these moments, I realize, I am forever mesmerized by birds."*

To be continued…

Epilogue

Germany, 1991

The Open Countryside Offered nice views of hills and valleys, with forests on one side and open farmer's fields on the other. Kurt and Margot drove on the road next to a private apple orchard, and young and old apple pickers, harvesting the fall produce. They traveled through villages and admired the many houses, kept in neat conditions, with gardens and flowers and landscaped front yards, they heard loud roosters herding their hens and laughed at little piglets, when they stopped the car in front of a house, that had a stand, offering fresh eggs and vegetables.

They continued through the country heading west. They would stop and enjoy wiener schnitzel and potatoes and draft beer, but Margot sensed the closer they got to the Dutch border, the more restless Kurt became. This was a trip he wanted to do, and she encouraged him and supported his decision, knowing how important it is for him and how much seeing the place, his mother Charlotte and her first husband Klaus, Kurt's real father came from.

He had asked his mother to join them, but she declined. Before they flew to Europe, Charlotte told him everything about the town where she and Klaus were born, and where they spent the first twenty one years of their lives together. She told him about the tragedy, the Hollandaise soldiers they kept in hiding on their farm, because Klaus wanted to help them, because of his legacy and roots he had through his parents in Holland, he felt it was his duty to help these soldiers and so Charlotte agreed and they kept them in their house, until someone from the village told on them, and then the German troops came in, and took Klaus and the four Dutch soldiers and Klaus rode his horses up the road and into the woods, where they all lost their lives under the firing squad.

Kurt drove up slowly to the house at the upper end of the small and charming village. He stopped the car and turned off the ignition. Through the opened window, he stared at the bricked house, painted with clean white color and decorated with dark brown wooden poles, that went vertically one across another on the front of the house and under the sharp V-pointed roof with a deep balcony, that had another hand-carved decorated dark stained wood in the shapes of hollow hearts on each end of the railing and in the middle of the balcony. The front gate to the long, deep yard was carelessly wide opened, and made of equally detailed and beautiful hand carved details on the top portion of the two-sided wooden gate.

The grass leading to the yard was green and kept short and had no weeds. The windows on the house were dressed in sheer curtains on the inside and two of them were open, and the curtains moved lightly to the breeze. The house had been fixed and reconstructed under a new facade, but with a modesty to preserve its old feeling and the year, it was built.

Margot reached over and across the hand shift stick and touched the top of Kurt's right hand. He tilted his head toward her and kissed her. The cheer and laughter of three children disturbed them and made Kurt shriek. He looked out the window and saw two boys chasing a girl through the yard. The girl screamed loudly when one of the boys finally grabbed her around her waist and wouldn't let her go. They all could be around ten to twelve years old. Then one of the boys noticed the car parked in front of their house and two people sitting in it. He walked over to Kurt's car and the other two, the boy and the girl followed him.

"Can I help you, sir?" the freckled boy asked in German. Kurt stared at him, and when he didn't say anything, the freckled boy asked again, "Are you lost?"

"No. I'm not lost. I know someone who used to live here." He pointed at the house.

"Now, I live here," the boy replied proudly.

"Are these your siblings?"

"No, they're my cousins." All the kids curiously stared at Kurt and Margot. She waved at them and said hello, and told the girl, she's got very pretty hair, braided into two ponytails, the girl smiled and politely thanked her.

"You talk funny," Johann told Margot.

"Yeah, you sound funny!" Hans joined him. Kurt turned to Margot and his face broke into a wide smile. She shrugged her shoulders and smiled at all of them.

An adult female voice came from the distance calling, "Johann, Lotte...Hans?" Then a woman appeared on the threshold of the house, shielding her palm over her forehead from the bright midday sun.

"Johann?!" she called again. "Who is it?"

Lotte and Hans ran back through the yard and Johann rolled his eyes at Kurt and said, "That's my mother." Kurt waived smiled and waved at him and the boy followed his cousins back to his house.

"It's nice to be here and now. It's nice to see this place had found new lives and that life goes on…" He let out a sigh before he started the engine as they drove off.

"I found it!" Margot shouted and her voice carried with an echo through the spruce forest. Soon, Kurt stood right next to her as they looked at the thickest three trunk and a simple grave with five hand-carved names into a wooden cross that was nailed to the tall, wide spruce tree.

Kurt whispered reading the name off the cross.

Casper 'Cas' Janssen
Kristoffer Bakker
Gerhard Hoitink
Joos Van Dijk
Klaus Groeneweg

He knelt and with the palm of his right hand he touched the cross, then he brushed his fingers across his father's name. He shut his eyes and heard the distant shots of firearms coming closer and louder to him, as he tilted his head back, and opened his eyes and stared at the blue sky through the crowns of the spruce trees. A bird flew above, and the overwhelming shots echoed through the air. He felt the pain in his heart and tears came out of his blue eyes. Margot came closer and leaned her back down and wrapped her arms around Kurt. The gunshots quieted and as Kurt opened his eyes, he heard birds chirping around. A feeling of piece and calmness washed over him as he placed his right hand over his heart. Margot placed a bouquet of flowers on the moss that grew around the thick tree trunk and expanded onto the lower portion of the majestic spruce.

Several days later, Kurt clutched Margot's hand feeling the warmth of her soft palm pressing against his. They stood in front of a large building, with a new white façade and red shingled roof. There were many people passing them around, young, and old, children and adults all of them speaking German rushing to the building or walking out and hurrying to be someplace else. Margot turned and looked into Kurt's eyes, and then she leaned over and kissed him.

"Are you okay?"

He nodded. "Yes, I am now." He placed his arms around her and they held their hug for moment, before holding hands, and walking away from the hospital where he was born. This time, Kurt held a smile on his face and whispered something into Margot's ear. The evening came fast, and the outside light dimmed with the dark, heavy rain clouds that spread over the sun. The light rain drizzled over the town as they walked over to their car.

The music blasting out load from the stereo, Kurt leaned back in his seat, and put his foot down, looking at the open road ahead of them. With the windows down, Margot's hair blew to the wind, the air smelled fresh, just after the rain, but the night sky cleared out now, and the stars and moon shined up high above. Margot tiled her head out of the window and looked at the endless open skyline. She had butterflies in her stomach.

Once, he told her, "The way you know if somebody loves you is the way they make you feel." She looked at Kurt and smiled, thinking, *This is the life I choose, this is the life I want to live. It's my life.*

THE END

www.ingramcontent.com/pod-product-compliance
Lightning Source LLC
Chambersburg PA
CBHW061630040426
42446CB00010B/1340